The European Union and the End of Politics

The European Union and the End of Politics

James Heartfield

Winchester, UK
Washington, USA

341.2422
HEA

First published by Zero Books, 2013
Zero Books is an imprint of John Hunt Publishing Ltd., Laurel House, Station Approach,
Alresford, Hants, SO24 9JH, UK
office1@jhpbooks.net
www.johnhuntpublishing.com
www.zero-books.net

For distributor details and how to order please visit the 'Ordering' section on our website.

Design: Stuart Davies

Printed and bound by CPI Group (UK) Ltd, Croydon, CRO 4YY

CONTENTS

Introduction: The Soft Coup d'État

Winter 2011/12. The Greek parliament is besieged from without by angry protestors. They riot burning down banks and government buildings. The Italian government, too, faces mass opposition – a general strike in protest at €450 billion government spending cuts. In Ireland, Spain and many other European countries there are angry protests. But the Greek and Italian governments are not only under pressure from the public. They are answerable to other masters than the electorate.

Greek Prime Minister Lucas Papademos took office on 11 November 2011, though he stood in no election. Before becoming Prime Minister Papademos had been a senior official at the European Central Bank, and an advisor to the outgoing PM George Papandreou. Italian Prime Minister Mario Monti was appointed on 12 November 2011, having been made a life senator three days earlier by President Giorgio Napolitano. Before becoming Prime Minister Mario Monti had been an economics professor and a member of the European Commission. On the face of things, both Papademos and Monti draw their authority from their own parliaments – but everyone knows that is not so. Both of these unelected experts came to power in a 'Soft Coup'; both deals were brokered by the European Union, in the middle of a harsh public debt crisis.

In the case of Greece, the European Union had been dealing with Prime Minister George Papandreou, leader of the largest, and best-polling political party in the last democratic elections, PASOK, twisting his arm to agree spending cuts. (Papandreou was under pressure because he owned up to what governments before had hidden – that Goldman Sachs had helped the country disguise its debts through creative accounting – his reward for such transparency, to be put out of office.) Talks were held between the Greek government, and the 'Troika' of the

International Monetary Fund, the European Central Bank and the European Commission. Having agreed one round of cuts after another, Papandreou baulked at just how unpopular these were, and in October said that he would let the people vote on more cuts in a referendum. The European Union was outraged at the idea that the voters should be asked.

'The announcement has surprised the whole of Europe,' said French President Nicolas Sarkozy. 'Giving the people a way to express themselves is always legitimate, but the solidarity of all the euro-zone countries cannot be exercised unless everyone agrees to make the necessary efforts.'[1] In a parliamentary session in The Hague, Dutch Prime Minister Mark Rutte called the threatened vote a 'very unfortunate development' and said 'we have to do everything to prevent it.' After crisis talks Papandreou agreed to cancel the public vote and to suspend normal party politics in favour of a government of 'national unity', and to stand down as Prime Minister in favour of Papademos. Robbed of a voice Greek people were more willing to protest and even to riot. German Finance Minister Wolfgang Schäuble wants the Greeks to cancel future elections and have a government without any politicians, only 'experts'.

Around the same time another European leader – of the right in this case – was forced to stand down. Silvio Berlusconi had often been attacked by the European Commission, charged with corruption. But each time the question was put to the polls the wily Berlusconi won over voters. In November 2011, though, the debt crisis gave the Commission the lever it needed to prize Berlusconi out, and he resigned. European Council President Herman van Rompuy told Italians on 11 November 2011 that 'the country needs reforms, not elections.' Mario Monti was appointed Prime Minister and, in turn, appointed a 'Professors' Cabinet', or 'technocratic government'. Monti's first reforms were to cut spending and to attack trade unions.

Greeks protest against austerity measures

In a single week the elected governments of two of Europe's democracies had been swept aside. At the very moment that Italian and Greek people needed to deal with the problems they faced, they were robbed of the chance. Before they could see their own political representatives argue out the best outcome on party lines, with the parliamentary contest mirroring the contest for votes. The party political system was a lever for ordinary people to push their goals right into the centre of government. But without it, public administration stopped being democratic, or even political. It was called 'technocratic' – government as technique, not as a negotiation; mechanical, not through dialogue. Instead of leaders there were experts. Instead of a contest 'national unity' was imposed (though many outside did not feel they were a part of it).

The events of November 2011 were called a 'Soft Coup', or a 'coup without tanks'. But what Junta was taking over? Even the angriest protestors were not sure who to blame. If there were no tanks, where was the confrontation?

It would be hard to avoid the role that private financiers played appearing at every corner to warn against any backsliding on cuts. The 'technocrats' were not experts in juggling or medicine, but in finance. Mario Monti has been an advisor to Goldman Sachs, Coca Cola and the listing agency Moody's as well as European Commissioner responsible for the Internal Market, Financial Services and Financial Integration, Customs, and Taxation. Massachusetts Institute of Technology graduate Papademos taught economics at Columbia University and even served as senior economist for the Federal Reserve Bank of Boston in 1980, before taking up positions at the National Bank of Greece and the ECB. Not surprisingly the anti-cuts protestors have been outraged to learn that Monti is a member of the secretive Bilderberg Group – all of which adds to the sense that government has been subverted by a secret coup led by high finance. Still, pointing the finger of blame at 'capitalism' or finance seems too vague. Down with capitalism, for sure, but does that really tell us any more about the forces arraigned against democracy?

Greek protestors have seen a German hand behind the changes, and they are not wrong. Chancellor Angela Merkel has called loudly for tighter rules on government spending, and for wayward governments to be reined in. In Athens the protestors have even burned the German flag (and alongside it the Swastika flag to heap on the insults) while the newspaper *Demokratia* reports the new austerity agreement with a parody of the sign over the gates at the Auschwitz Concentration Camp 'Memorandum macht frei'. Greeks talk more often of the wartime occupation when the German Wehrmacht starved the country. Pointing the finger at Germany seems to make sense, except that Angela Merkel is not alone in her demands for Greek probity. Nicolas Sarkozy (whose country was also occupied by Germany in the Second World War) is so close to Merkel that the press have coined a collective noun *Merkozy*. Just before he was bundled out of office, Silvio Berlusconi, too was lecturing the Greeks on the need to stick to their promises. Greek protestors wish that their enemy was just Germany's leaders.

The Coup d'État against democracy in Greece and Italy does have a shape, however soft it looks. Its shape is the European Union. The pressure brought to bear on both countries came through the European Union. The 'Troika' of the European Central Bank, the European Commission and the International Monetary Fund brought pressure to bear on the Greek government to change its policies and make-up. Though an ad hoc body, the Troika is

The 'Troika'

reported to be renting an office in Athens to keep an eye on spending there.

The Troika does not just oversee Greek spending. There is a Troika looking at Portugal's budget, too. Jürgen Kröger, Head of EC mission, Rasmus Rüffer for the ECB and Poul Thomsen of the IMF visited in May 2011, returning in February 2012 to spend two weeks looking at the budget there before deciding whether to release the latest batch of Portugal's €78 billion rescue loan.

In January 2012 all but two of the 27 heads of state at the European Summit agreed to German Chancellor Angela Merkel's new *fiskalpakt* with binding limits on budget deficits and quasi-automatic sanctions on countries that breach deficit and debt limits enforced by the European Court of Justice. 'The debt brakes will be binding and valid forever,' said Merkel: 'Never will you be able to change them through a parliamentary majority.' Later that year Merkel's finance minister Wolfgang Schäuble went further, saying: 'I would be for the further development of the European Commission into a government.' Schäuble explained that a long-term response to the current eurozone crisis, which many have said has been exacerbated by the fact that the EU lacked the tools - such as a central transfer system - to effectively deal with it. [2] From the European Union viewpoint Merkel's goal of putting questions of government beyond democratic control is a great success. Binding limits, with automatic sanctions, policed by unelected officials is what they want. 'Parliamentary majorities' overriding the expert officials is what they hate.

Trade unionists march against austerity in Spain

In the summer of 2012 Miners led protests and riots against the EU-imposed austerity package in Spain. 'There's plenty of money for the banks, but none for us,' said Jorge Rodriguez, a 36-year old miner: 'We're under occupation by the EU, there's no other way of putting it' he said, 'We no longer have control over our own country.'[3]

The European Union, though, is not only jealous of political rivals on the left: it targets right-wing populists, too. In the same month that the European Council was cooking up the fiscal compact, the European Commission wrote three separate letters of warning to Hungarian President Orban charging him with bringing in 'undemocratic' laws. By 'undemocratic' they meant that the new constitution put the Central Bank under the control of the democratically elected government, instead of leaving it in the hands of the expert technocrats, while threatening, too, that judges and information commissioners would be subject to the rule of parliament. Step through the looking glass into the EU-world where the rule of the people is dictatorial, but the rule of unelected experts is democracy.

Ex-sixties radical Daniel Cohn-Bendit stood up in the European Parliament to demand that Orban's constitution be investigated for breaching the EU's Lisbon Treaty. The man once known as Danny the Red ranted on that the Hungarian leader was striving to be Europe's equivalent of Hugo Chávez or Fidel Castro.[4]

Cohn-Bendit as a student radical wrote

The emergence of bureaucratic tendencies on a world scale, the continuous concentration of capital, and the increasing intervention of the State in economic and social matters, have produced a new managerial class whose fate is no longer bound up with that of the private ownership of the means of production.[5]

It was far-sighted indeed to spot the very trend towards bureau-cratic-managerial rule for which Cohn-Bendit himself would become a spokesman. The only thing he did not foresee was that the bureaucracy that was emerging would be transnational, not just national.

In this current moment some of those who are standing up to the EU's austerity packages have shouted about the attack on democracy. They think that the EU is attacking democracy so that it can push through its spending cuts. So it is. But much more so it is using the debt crisis to push through the abolition of national sovereignty.

Two and a half years ago a very prescient sociology professor Ulrich Beck wrote 'The crisis cries out to be transformed into a long overdue new founding of the EU'. Beck went on: 'until now there has been no joint financial policy, no joint industrial policy, no joint social policy - which, through the sovereignty of the EU, could be pooled into an effective response to the crisis'. The only real barrier, thought Beck, was 'the national self-delusion of its intellectual elites' who 'bewail the faceless European bureau-cracy'.[6]

December 2011's Brussels summit, drawing its moral imper-ative from the sovereign debt crisis, ended with a commitment to create a much-greater coordination of economic and financial policy. Under the agreement national governments must submit balanced budgets, and face 'automatic penalties' if they do not. The thesis behind the agreement is that the southern European countries' spending and indebtedness has undermined confi-dence in them and because of that in the Euro.

Shifting the blame onto Greece, Spain and Italy for the Euro crisis twists the truth. Throughout the buoyant years of the noughties the success of the European periphery was cited proof that the European Union was working. More, exporting countries, including Germany, were glad that easy credit boosted Greek and Spanish buying of their goods.

Apart from the economics, though, the important shift is towards 'stronger economic union'. When the crisis began Greece's troubles suggested to many that the European Union would 'fall apart'. Professor Beck's intuition that the crisis would drive the greater integration of economic policy proved to be as insightful as the fears that the whole thing would fall apart. Where he misleads us is in portraying this movement as a greater democratisation of Europe. On the contrary, the trajectory is towards a much-diminished role for democratic oversight, and a much enhanced role for unelected officials dictating terms to elected governments. 'Automatic penalties' is European code for 'not subject to political negotiation'.

The reason for the 'automatic penalties' is that as national elites European governments do not have the authority to see through tough measures. For many years now, governments have leant on the European Union as an extra-national source of authority. Governments that are not willing to make the case for tighter budgets honestly in their own terms, have hid behind the claim that they must make adjustments to meet the external restraints imposed by Europe. That is what Italian Minister Guido Cali meant when he said that 'the European Union represented an alternative path for the solution of problems which we were not managing to handle through the normal channels of government and parliament'.

Not just Italy or Greece, but Britain and Germany sought again and again to 'tie' or 'bind' themselves into European Union rules that would limit the political temptations of excessive spending. Quite why sovereign states should choose to bind themselves and their successors in obligations that they cannot change or renegotiate is a conundrum for students of international relations. The answer to the puzzle is that these elites no longer derive the same authority that they used to from national electorates or constituent assemblies that once they did. Instead it is in the international summits, most notably the European summits that leaders feel secure, bound together in their mutual fear of the unruly electorates.

Fear of economic crisis is driving the integration of European policy, and it is not being consolidated as a democracy, but as a technocracy, where officials follow procedures, rather than make policies. Six years ago the voters of France and Holland voted down the centralisation of Europe under its then proposed constitution – which was abandoned soon after. Now, using fear of economic collapse, European elites have talked themselves into submitting to a more onerous set of impersonal and bureaucratic rules.

Robbers of the world, having by their universal plunder exhausted the land, they rifle the deep. If the enemy be rich, they are rapacious; if he be poor, they lust for dominion; neither the east nor the west has been able to satisfy them. Alone among men they covet with equal eagerness poverty and riches. To robbery, slaughter, plunder, they give the lying name of empire; they make a desert and call it peace. (Calgacus of the Caledonian Tribe, according to Tacitus)

German chancellor, Angela Merkel, announced that the EU faces

perhaps the toughest hour since the second world war. If the euro fails, then Europe fails, and we want to prevent and we will prevent this. This is what we are working for, because it is such a huge historic project.[7]

In Germany, Chancellor Merkel's popularity has risen during the crisis. Ordinary German sentiment is that the country cannot afford to 'subsidise' wasteful southern European governments. Hans Werner-Sinn, Director of the Center for Economic Studies at the University of Munich complains that 'It is unfair for critics to ask Germany to bear even more risk.'[8] Even in Germany, though, there were fears that the country's decisions over the European Stability Mechanism – the rescue fund that is – are being taken behind closed doors, sidestepping the democratic process. In the event the German Constitutional Court ruled that the bailout fund was a matter for the European officials, not Germany's parliament. It was, Merkel told the Bundestag 'a good day for Europe'[9] – which is true, if 'Europe' means unelected officials sidestepping national governments.

The habit of dictating terms to elected governments comes easily to the European Commissioners. They learned that habit when they were pushing around the 'accession countries' – those countries that joined the Union after it was first set up. The countries making up each new wave of countries joining the European Union (in 1973, the 1980s, 1995, 2004 and 2007) have found that they must adopt the existing body of European law, the *acquis communautaire*. The acquis is voted into national laws as a whole, as a condition of membership. There can be no substantial negotiation about its content, which reflects the interests of the core of the Union. Member states are made to perform a degrading ritual of submission, voting on thousands of laws without consideration. To gain admission, accession states have found that they are set special tasks, conditions upon membership that they must adopt to prove their European-ness. The Czechs must alter their community relations towards Gypsies. The Hungarians must become more liberal towards homosexuals. Turks – though they are still denied membership – must get hunting licenses. In each case, no doubt, there is a very good case to be made for the change in the law. But the way that the reforms are imposed from outside, as conditions, militates against a national debate, and makes these reforms into perfor-mative acts, undertaken not for their own sake, but to gain access to markets. The appearance of the reforms is egalitarian, but the content of the changes is that accession states are subordinated to an external authority. The ritual of accession, and the habit of setting external conditions on recalcitrant states that the Commission got into with the East European states, sets the mood for its relations with the budget-constrained states in the current crisis. The language is about bail-outs, fiscal responsi-bility and a return to growth. But the real meaning is that national governments must get used to doing what the European Union tells them, and stop listening to their own electorates.

Many commentators saw the fiscal and social crisis that broke out in 2011 as a sign that the European Union – or at least the Eurozone – was on the point of breaking up. For some states it still seems possible that the crisis will lead to a departure, forced or voluntary, from the Union. On the whole, though, the crisis has led to more, not less power for the European Union over its member states. In the following I will argue that the dynamic towards European integration is driven by the decline of nation states and in particular the decline of the political life of popular democracy in those nation states. Just as European officials were taking decision-making power out of the hands of elected officials in Greece, Italy and Portugal, British citizens were being polled on the conduct of their own politicians. Just 24 per cent of respondents believe MPs are capable of 'debating issues of public concern in a sensible and considered way', and most think that the political system is 'fundamentally flawed'. Alarmingly 38 per cent thought that it would be a good idea if the European union sent technocrats to run the British administration, too.[10] The bureaucratic institutions of the European Union are growing to fill the vacuum left by the shrinking political spheres of the nation states. The Union's ascendance is caused by the decline of democratic politics in those nation states.

Some theoreticians, like Alain Badiou, have seen in the recent public protests the return of the political. Before Badiou, Frank Furedi saw healthy signs of the return of a populist moment in the protest movements that de-railed the proposed European constitution in 2005.[11] Popular opposition to the technocratic elites that have suborned democracy are indeed to be welcomed. The protests in Europe against EU-imposed austerity programmes are a healthy sign that the governing elite has failed to win support. However, new shoots of popular political contestation, while striking, have as yet failed to put down strong roots. The No Campaigns that challenged the proposed EU constitution are coalitions that while broad, have little in common beyond opposition to the change. The rise of the radical-left SYRIZA coalition in Greece is no doubt an important development, as are the many grassroots anti-austerity campaigns in that country and elsewhere. Yet SYRIZA leader Alex Tsipras' programme of renegotiating Greece's Eurozone membership lacked credibility in the eyes of voters who could see that Europe's political leaders were not reciprocating. The anti-cuts campaigns, like so many radical movements of the post-Cold War era have blown up great squalls of protest, but these have not been sustained challenges, and have failed to build up enduring organisations to keep them going.

As much as we might hope that new popular political movements are emerging, to understand the way that the European Union has developed we need to look at the opposite and more enduring trend, the decline in the mass organisations and political parties over the last twenty years. So far, at least, the challenge to the European Union's imposed austerity-drive has failed to de-rail it. Rather, the powers-that-be in Brussels and at the European Central Bank have weathered the storm. Their strategy has largely been to sit tight, and wait out the storm, and it has worked. When decision-making takes place outside of the country protest movement have no clear target for their protests. High politics has gone off-shore, or perhaps floating above the nation states like Swift's Island of Laputa, where it cannot be reached. Most pointedly, national assemblies, national elites, and indeed nationally-based opposition movements have failed to come up with an answer to the crisis in Europe. Unless the opposition movement substantially alters the political culture in Europe, the outcome of the events of 2011-12 will move further in the direction of an apolitical European administration, governing the continent's peoples technocratically and at an ever greater distance from popular accountability.

In the following we look first at the decline of the idea of national sovereignty as an ideal, and the growing preference for transnational governance. Then in the second chapter Demobilising the Nation State, we consider what lies behind the decline of sovereignty, the decline in the political life of nation states, in particular the decline in the mass movements of left and right that gave sovereignty its vitality and meaning. In chapter three we look at the historical emergence of the European Union and its relationship to a decline in national political life. The fourth chapter looks at some of the domestic allies of European integration, using the examples of the Italian left, the German Greens, the Scottish National Party, the British TUC and – most importantly – the role of business leaders in promoting European integration. In chapter five we consider the development of trans-European administrative powers from the growth of the European Commission under Delors, to the re-stated importance of the European Council and Heads of State, but emphasizing the trend towards apolitical administration and technocratic measures like 'benchmarking'. Chapter six deals with the elusive problem of European identity, arguing that for the most part it is a negative identification, against outsiders, whether in the developing world, the East or in America, but most of all the Union is defined in opposition to the peoples of Europe, because of its transnational and elite character.

The last two chapters deal with theoretical accounts of European integration. In chapter seven we consider first the integrationist and functionalist theories of David Mitrany, Ernst Haas and Karl Deutsch, and query their technocratic indifference to political contestation. Then we look at the realist and intergovernmentalist outlook, in the works of the British Committee, Alan Milward, Stanley Hoffmann and Andrew Moravcsik, their insistence on the priority of nation states, and the challenges that poses in creating an account of European integration. In chapter eight we look at the critical theorists' account of the social construction of Europe, its insights into the end of national sovereignty and its curious inability to grasp the meaning of democratic will formation.

The research for this book was undertaken at the Centre for the Study of Democracy at the University of Westminster, with the Sovereignty and its Discontents Workgroup and on projects at Plan in London. I am grateful to Ian Aitchison, Chris Bickerton,

Fanny Cabanne, Phil Cunliffe, Frank Furedi, Tariq Goddard, Alex Gourevitch, Richard Green, Solomon Hughes, Mick Hume, Lee Jones, Tara McCormack, Frances Lynch, Kevin McCullagh, Brendan O'Neill, Julia Svetlichnaja, Lizzie Terry, Bruno Waterfield, James Woudhuysen, Jan Zielonka and most of all David Chandler, for encouraging the development of the ideas here in different ways.

CHAPTER ONE

Pathological Nationalism?

In the following we look first at the critique of sovereignty to understand what is at stake. We will argue that the contemporary case for the European Union is bound up with the idea that nationalism in Europe is a pathological condition that needs the European Union to contain it – even though the actual historical record indicates a different origin. We will argue that the anti-national claims of the European Union are more contemporary and correspond instead to the ideology of globalisation. And we will take issue with the critique of sovereignty, aiming to show that its real meaning is a retreat from subjectivity.

In the many accounts of the case for the European Union and its predecessors the European Community and the European Economic Community, it is implied that nationalism is a pathological development. The Union exists to constrain pathological nationalism

According to Till Geiger

Many politicians attributed the outbreak of the Second World War to an aggressive political and economic nationalism of the interwar period. Following this logic, the creation of a united Europe would eradicate the root cause of international antagonism by replacing the existing nation states.

Simon Bulmer claims that 'Europe's founding fathers 'sought to avoid the excesses of nationalism and of the nation-state system that had been demonstrated by the Nazi regime'.[3] Gerald Hackett also sees the European Community's motivation coming from a retreat from the war-like nation-state

There was in this period [immediately after the Second World War], a general if ill-defined rejection of nationalism and a belief that organizations standing above the nation-state were essential for peace. ... seeking a different approach to the European political system which had produced two world wars in 25 years.[3]

According to Derek Urwin (who attributes these views to federalists like Altiero Spinelli):

nationalism and nationalist rivalries, by culminating in a war had discredited and bankrupted the independent state as the foundation of political organization and international order, and that a replacement for the state had to be found in a comprehensive continental community.[4]

Certainly it was the case that the 'architect of the European Economic Community' Jean Monnet, looking back in 1978, saw the shortcomings of international organisation before the Second World War as arising out of a failure to constrain the nation-state: 'At the root of them all [international crises] was national sovereignty', wrote Monnet of the failure of the League of Nations, which he put down to the 'inability to go beyond national self-interest'.[5] It is a judgement echoed by Monnet's biographer François Duchêne: 'of all the international bodies invented to correct the weakness that led to war, none addressed the fragmentation of authority in the hands of numerous states, which arguably had been one of the greatest flaws.'[6]

Jean Monnet putting the European plan in motion

Simon Bromley underscores the failure of the nation state in the period before the founding of

17

the European Economic Community, even in its most basic promise of security:

> As far as the domestic authority of Western European states was concerned, it is important to recall that most of them (including all the original members of the Union) had failed in their primary task: to guarantee the security of their populations.[7]

Historians Alan Milward and Tony Judt take issue with the argument that the European Economic Community was created to overcome the war-like nation-state on grounds of historical inaccuracy.[8] Milward, and following him Judt argue that far from being a means to overcome the nation-state, the European Economic Community was one of a number of intergovernmental organisations whose great purpose and achievement was to 'rescue the nation state', after the disaster of the Second World War. Milward agrees with Simon Bromley's argument that most European nation states had indeed failed their citizens during the war. And for just that reason, he argues, international cooperation in Europe was the condition for the reconstruction of the nation state.

The post-war years saw an unprecedented extension of the state into domestic life, through the extension of welfare benefits, health services, pension, social services, economic planning, nationalised industries, all of which were widely embraced as the foundations of a new *national* identity. As Alan Milward rightly says

> After 1945 the European nation state rescued itself from collapse, created a new political consensus as the basis of its legitimacy, and through changes in its response to its citizens which meant a sweeping extension of its functions and ambitions reasserted itself as the fundamental unit of political

organisation.[9]

The argument that the European Economic Community was created to constrain war-like nation-states after the learning experience of the Second World War, then, is hard to justify, not least because it is a consideration that was by no means important at the time. Rather, the argument that the Community was a reaction against World War is at best a retrospective judgement, or even a *post festum* construction, an origin myth for the Union today.

Globalisation and the end of the nation

If it is difficult to account for the origins of the European Union as a reaction to the war, there is a more contemporary explanation of what drives it, and that is *globalisation* – the argument that the Union is necessary to meet the challenges of the more open and competitive world market, and of other global trends that are today rendering the nation-state impotent. In the words of the European Commission President José Manuel Barroso 'No nation state can meet the challenges of climate change, mass migration, global competition and terrorism on its own.'[10]

In the first instance the 'globalisation' discussion appears to be about the economy. So even a radical welfare socialist like Oskar Lafontaine argues that 'the instruments of national policy are no longer adequate to deal with the demands of a globalized economy'.[11] Radical economist Kavaljit Singh makes the point that 'the growing globalization of finance has led to the rapid decline in the degree of control and manoeuvrability of national governments which find it increasingly difficult to intervene to reduce the volatility and establish stability in the financial markets.' What is more 'The state and its agencies are no longer the most important actors in the global economic system; they have been replaced by the TNCs [Trans National Corporations].'[12]

Anthony Giddens paraphrases the business guru Keniche Ohmae, 'we live now in a borderless world, in which the nation state has become a "fiction" and where politicians have lost all effective power.'[13] In a Speech to the German Business Federation (Bundesverband der Deutschen Industrie) in Bonn, on 18 June 1996 the British Labour Party leader Tony Blair drew out the link between global competition and the limits of the nation state: 'good government' is 'minimal government' and it is important to recognise that 'choices are constrained'.[14] Those sentiments found their way into the Blair government's White Paper on Competitiveness and the building of the knowledge economy (drafted by Charles Leadbeater): 'In the increasingly global economy of today, we cannot compete in the old way.'[15]

Linguistics professor Norman Fairclough comments on this passage that the movements of the global economy are 'represented as actions, but without any responsible agents.' Further, Fairclough parses the argument: ' "We" are confronted with change as effects without agency, rather than being participants in change able to affect its direction.'[16] Anthony Giddens, an advisor to Blair, argues that 'Globalization "pulls away" from the nation-state in the sense that some powers nations used to possess, including those that underlay Keynesian economic management, have been weakened.'[17] Giddens sees globalisation as not just a matter of impersonal market forces, but the impact of much better informed and less traditionally-minded citizens, who are not shy about taking their custom elsewhere. As he puts it 'Liberal democracy, based on an electoral party system, operating at the level of the nation-state, is not well equipped to meet the demands of a reflexive citizenry in a globalizing world.'[18]

In Germany, the sociologist Ulrich Beck paints what he sees as the limitations of the nation-state:

Territorial states originate in exclusive powers over

geographical space. This is the basis for their monopoly of violence, their legislative autonomy, cultural identity and moral autonomy ...

By contrast 'Globalisation threatens national sovereignty'.[19] As we can see, Beck combines the association of the nation state with violence and the argument that globalisation renders the state useless. 'The road to the nation-state is paved with oppression,' he says. 'Its law reads: Either-or.' But 'Owing to global mobility ... the possibilities of a national Either-Or are disappearing...'[20] Globalisation renders the logic of national sovereignty redundant, and makes the case for post-national institutions like the European Union.

The thesis that globalisation has rendered the nation-state superfluous, or just limited, has its critics. Paul Hirst and Graham Thompson have argued that 'globalisation' is not a real world phenomenon, so much as a subjective retreat from responsibility, in particular the responsibility to construct national policy. The way they tell it, globalisation is an alibi for inactivity, the wish being father to the thought: 'One key effect of the concept of globalization has been to paralyse radical reforming national strategies, to see them as unfeasible in the face of the judgement and sanction of international markets,' argue Hirst and Thompson: 'A truly global economy is claimed to have emerged, or to be in the process of emerging, in which distinct national economies and therefore domestic strategies of national economic management are increasingly irrelevant.'[21] As they detail in their book, the claim that the world market is qualitatively more integrated than it was at the turn of the last century is not justified by the statistics.

Like Hirst and Thompson, Colin Hay thinks that globalisation is something of a myth, at least in so far as it becomes an excuse for a retreat from policy. 'Globalization is seen as the enemy of political deliberation in the sense that it is seen to dictate policy choices while itself being beyond the capacity of domestic political actors to control,' he says. The policy choices that global-isation dictates are in a certain direction, which is to say towards market liberalisation: 'globalization is held to necessitate a certain privatisation and depoliticisation of public policy, rendering it less politically accountable', says Hay. He adds 'Here it is the distinctly public character of political deliberation that is challenged by globalisation.' Hay explains the mechanism by which globalisation is supposed to limit national policy:

> To reduce the risks of co-ordinated speculative dynamics being unleashed against one's currency by global financial markets, for instance, it is argued that monetary policy must be removed from political control and rendered both predictable and rules-bounded rather than discretionary.[22]

As we shall, see, this argument is drawn from the European experience, in particular of French and Italian submission to the economic criteria for membership of the European Monetary System. Usefully for the argument we will explore later, Hay explains 'Here globalisation is cast as a powerful agent of *depoliti-cisation.*'[23]

Very few people doubt that there has indeed been an increase in cross-border trade since the 1970s (on the long trend) and again since the 1990s (on the shorter trend). Nor do they doubt that technologies favour broader and deeper communications across national boundaries. From the perspective of 2009, though, one might ask whether it was the global financial markets that had proved to be the historically transient mode of social organ-isation, and the nation-state the enduring one. It might have seemed clear to Keniche Ohmae in 1995 that the state was a fiction, but in 2008 it became clear that it was trillions of dollars invested in over-valued financial assets that was fictitious. Under the United States' Troubled Asset Relief Program (2008) government spent $700 billion buying major shareholdings in Goldman Sachs Group Inc., Morgan Stanley, J.P. Morgan Chase & Co., Bank of America Corp. (including Merrill Lynch), as did the British government in Royal Bank of Scotland and Northern Rock to prevent their collapse. Further the US government took over General Motors, the German government bought Opel and the Heidelberg print company as the British did British Rail.[24]

Hay, Hirst and Thompson, then, all point to an important part of the debate: The concept 'globalisation' is working too hard in these arguments. The suspicion is that the cart has been put before the horse. The theory of globalisation has been written after the event to justify something that was already happening – a delimitation of the political authority of elected governments over wider society.

Looking at the discussion of globalisation with an eye to the European Union, there is now a second argument on top of the first, that we need the Union to contain nationalist aggression. Not only are states too belligerent, now they are toothless, as well.

The default position in these discussions seems to come back to the same point, that the state is pathologically ill-suited to our times. Over and again we hear an orchestra of arguments against the nation state. Given that the European Union is often represented as a limit or moderating influence upon the nation state, the perception that the state is problematic plainly has a bearing on the argument. Indeed, we will argue that the main driver of the European Union today is a retreat from national sovereignty, and a demobilisation of the nation state.

The critique of sovereignty

The most strident polemics against nationalism and the state today are made to the background of demands for humanitarian intervention against dictatorships in the less developed world (in which there are fewer constraints on forceful expression). In particular, the concept of *sovereignty* exercises the humanitarian interventionists – because it is the concept that stands in the way of military action in other people's countries.

Queen's Council Geoffrey Robertson, head of the Doughty Street chambers in London, has been a passionate advocate of human rights acting for Tasmanian Aborigines in their case against the British Museum, and as a UN Judge in the war crimes tribunal in Sierra Leone. His book *Crimes Against Humanity* is a popular rehearsal of the argument over human rights and sovereignty. In fact he says bluntly the 'movement for global justice has been a struggle against sovereignty': 'The great play of sovereignty, with all its pomp and panoply, can now be seen for what it hides: a posturing troupe of human actors, who when off-stage are sometimes prone to rape the chorus'.[25] It was a point made also by Kenneth Roth, executive director of Human Rights Watch: 'sovereignty cannot be used as an excuse to avoid human rights commitments'.[26] The non-governmental organisation *Medicins Sans Frontières* 'from the outset, chose to step away from the classical Red Cross approach of a "silent neutrality" and sought to put the interest of victims ahead of sovereignty considerations'.[27] Sovereignty, to its humanitarian critics, is just a 'show', a 'prejudice', a 'convention', a 'legal fiction', behind which, grubby and degraded politicians pursue their own selfish and individual interests. In the Ireland the one-time leaders of physical force nationalism, Sinn Fein the Workers Party repented their excesses and decided to 'stand up against the tom-tom drums' of nationalism – saying 'freedom's just a flag' in their election broadcasts.[28]

Surprisingly, perhaps, even movements for state reform consider the concept of sovereignty to be faulty. Neal Ascherson titled his 1994 lecture for the organisation Charter 88 'Local Government and the Myth of Sovereignty', and dismissed without argument 'the British doctrine of parliamentary sovereignty, which I have already suggested to be obsolete and pernicious' (25 February). The Charter 88 supporter and now British

Member of Parliament Tony Wright vigorously denounced the concept of the sovereignty of parliament, which he imagined to be dictatorial, in his book *Citizens and Subjects*.[29]

The growing clamour against the concept of sovereignty focused on its origins in the Treaty of Westphalia, a polemical gambit that rendered sovereignty at once historically transient, and also archaic.[30] Perhaps it is to be expected that a catholic scholar would take issue with the Peace of Westphalia, so when J. Bryan Hehir writes that 'the Westphalian concept of a modern sovereign state...does not exist in a geopolitical vacuum and "must share the stage of history today with other actors"' it is not that surprising. Hehir goes on to argue that 'Economic interdependence, human rights claims and other factors all work to "limit national sovereignty."'[31] The British democratic reformer Anthony Barnett joined the argument, welcoming the decline of 'Westphalia': 'We are indeed witnessing the decline of the "Westphalian" nation state, with its absolute domestic sovereignty and rejection of external influence over its "internal affairs."'.[32] After the US intervention in Iraq, Norman A. Bailey of the Potomac Foundation and Criton M. Zoakos President of Leto Research thought that 'The 350-year reign of the nation-state system is over' and 'diplomatic niceties aside, the United States of America is the cause of the breakdown of the Westphalian nation-state system'.[33]

Substantially, though, it was in Europe, site of the original treaty of Westphalia, that the 'end of the Westphalian system' is most often seen. According to the British European Commissioner Lord Cockfield, the arguments seemed to be unassailable: 'The gradual limitation of national sovereignty is part of a slow and painful forward march of humanity'.[34]

Nations as subjects

There is of course, something very strange about talking about nations as if they were persons, which is what we are doing when we use the concept of sovereignty. The oddness of it is drawn out by the economic libertarian Nicholas Dykes in a review of Thomas Paterson's book *On Every Front: The Making and Unmaking of the Cold War* (1992). Dykes protests that

> Dr Paterson also talks continuously as if "nations" had a living identity of their own, viz: "the nation's competitiveness"; [p.28] "Nations do not simply react.... They also act purposefully..."; [p.97] "Nations seek to fulfil their ideological preferences and to realise their economic-strategic needs". [p.108][35]

Dykes' libertarianism takes for granted the sovereign individual as the agent of market exchange, but is immediately sceptical about the 'collective subject' of the nation. From a rather different perspective, international relations professor Justin Rosenberg takes issue with E.H. Carr's realism, saying 'Carr's is from the outset a discourse of *raison d'état*: as a prescription it is committed to the idea of state as subject.'[36] Intriguingly, Rosenberg does not feel the need to spell out what is wrong with the 'idea of state as subject' as if it was obviously doubtful.

The Gestalt psychologist Fritz Heider noticed that 'Nations are in some ways like persons, and it is common to apply to them the person-concept which we have developed in the commerce with individuals.'[37] Philippine sociologist F.V. Aguilar, Jr. calls this the 'serialization of nations-as-persons' whereby human qualities are projected onto the nation 'such that the nation could be concomitantly fetishized as though it were like you and me.'[38]

In his critique of Westphalian sovereignty, *The Myth of 1648*, Benno Teschke attempts to draw the distinction between absolutist sovereignty and modern sovereignty in terms of the peculiar, dynastic qualities of sovereignty invested in the person of the sovereign on the one hand, with the modern and more rational 'notion of sovereignty ... predicated on an abstract impersonal state, existing apart from the subjective will of its executive'.[39] Teschke thinks that it is particularly funny to see '"states" marrying "states"'.[40] That international relations should be managed through dynastic unions exemplifies for him the pre-modern character of absolutist sovereignty. He is struck by the strangeness of marriage between states, but fails to notice that the personification of states persists to this day, a truly mysterious thing that Teschke takes for granted. States *recognise* states, states *divorce* from states, states *admonish* states, states *make reparations* to states right up to the present day, and yet Teschke is amazed that states marry states. What he fails to understand is that the modern sovereign state, which is to say territory, which we credit with the characteristics of personality, is the thing that needs to be explained, and its mysteries are not dismissed by relegating this one archaic facet of the personification of the state to the past.

Substantially the question at issue is the one of sovereignty. Both in fact, and in the theoretical analysis, the question is sovereignty. The issue is sovereignty for European national leaders, like Jacques Chirac for example, for whom 'the sovereignty of each state must be defended',[41] or for such as the German Constitutional Court, which ruled in 1994 that Germany's basic law takes precedence over EU law.[42] Theoretically, the question is whether the European Union is an extension (as neorealists claim) or a moderation of national sovereignty (as argued by functionalists and social theorists of international politics).

Sovereignty is a complicated subject. Steven Krasner who has thought very hard about it breaks it down into four sub-categories: domestic sovereignty, the 'organisation of public authority in a state'; interdependence sovereignty, the control of borders; international legal sovereignty, the mutual recognition of states; and Westphalian sovereignty, the 'exclusion of external actors from domestic authority configurations'.[43] This diremption of the concept seems to help, but it also loses something of the inner vitality of sovereignty, rather like the coroner who unveils the dissected corpse with the phrase, 'behold, your husband'.[44] But then Krasner does warn us of his lack of sympathy for the concept of sovereignty with the subtitle of his book, *Sovereignty: Organised Hypocrisy.*

What the analytical approach loses is the life of the concept, sovereignty, which is something like subjectivity, man's dominion in the world. Specifically, sovereignty is the subjectivity of the sovereign, or lord, and is for that reason bound up with the idea of territoriality, since lordship is in essence dominion over territory. For us today, the rights of the individual appear to be primary, and the 'rights' of the 'nation' a derivative, or extrapolation. Historically, subjectivity in the individual is preceded by subjectivity in the sovereign prince. The first human individuals to adopt the social form of subjective agents are the renaissance princes, like Lorenzo De Medici, who Machiavelli addressed, or Henry VIII.[45] States were the original actors, and their subjectivity resided in the personality of their sovereign rulers.

Against expectations, perhaps, the *subject* appears in international relations before he does in social science. Pashukanis says that the doctrine of the legal subject in modern law owes more to the Roman *jus gentium* than to the *jus civile*, because the law of nations implies a mutual recognition that is not to be found in the domestic realm.[46] The rights accorded the stranger in the ancient world are closer to the rights accorded neighbours in the modern, than to those accorded kinsmen. Says Pashukanis, the legal subject, like exchange, first occurs on the margins, between societies, only later penetrating societies (like trade), embracing the towns, and then eventually generalised in the rights of the people, which finally displace the rights of the sovereign prince with those of the sovereign people. 'The rights of the untrammelled individual was in fact the democratisation of the baroque concept of the despotic prince', sneers Lewis Mumford, though he should say, 'renaissance concept of the despotic prince'.[47]

Amongst intellectuals today, scepticism towards popular sovereignty is high.[48] But the enduring appeal of the slogan Power to
the People is something that they ignore at their peril.

'Princely sovereignty' was conceived of long before the 'rights of man'

Machiavelli *The Prince* 1513
Grotius *Rights of War* 1625
Hobbes *Leviathan* 1651
Locke *Two Treatises of Government* 1688
Rousseau *Social Contract* 1762

Sovereign states are subjects, just as corporations can be subjects.
This is not a psychological mis-recognition, or a legal fiction. The
logical structure of sovereignty is essentially similar between the
person as subject and the state as subject. In the *Philosophy of
Right* Hegel derives the concept of the state, starting from the
concept of the Will, so that 'the State is the will which manifests
itself'.[49] The middle term[50] is the 'general will', of Rousseau.[51] In
a less developed form, this is the basis of Hobbes idea of the state
as a leviathan, or 'Artificiall Man'.[52]

Patrick Jackson argues that the personification of the state is
under-theorised, though it stands as a common assumption in
the ordinary understanding of international relations.[53] The
personification of the state argued in Hegel provokes a sceptical
reaction not just from libertarians, but also from deconstructionists who are equally doubtful about the 'collective will'
embodied in the state. In the end, though, this is not a theoretical
question, but one of belief in the democratic process itself.
Whether the state is a plausible collective subject rests on our
confidence in the process by which the general will is formed. As
we shall see, a declining identification with democratic processes
damages the authority of the state as collective actor.

Sovereignty, the subjective agency of states, is curiously out of favour today. The reasons, as we shall explore are to do with a generalized downgrading of agency as a mode of human organization, of which doubts over sovereignty are only the manifestation in the realm of international relations.

In the end it was neither the Second World War, nor indeed the global market, that created the need for the European Union. Rather it is the *perceived* decline in state sovereignty that creates the need for a set of trans-national and pan-European institutions that supervene over national sovereignty. As we shall see, the member states of the European Union, as represented in the European Council, continue to be the source of its authority. Still the curious need for those European states to slough off responsibility for monetary and trade policy, environmental and technical regulation and a whole host of other government competences drives the Union forward.

In the following chapter we look at the domestic political processes that have led to the decline of national sovereignty, namely, the depoliticisation of European nation states and the decline in public participation in national will formation.

CHAPTER TWO

Demobilising the European State

'If you have no real confidence in the political system or political leaders of your own country', wrote the former British Prime Minister Margaret Thatcher, 'you are bound to be more tolerant of foreigners of manifest intelligence, ability and integrity like M. Delors telling you how to run your affairs.' 'To put it more bluntly', she added 'if I were an Italian, I might prefer rule from Brussels, too.'[1]

The main driver of European integration since 1983 has been a process of *depoliticisation* that has lessened the power of legislative assemblies.[2] The trend leaves national political elites more reliant on their European counterparts for support and legitimation, as they are less so on the mandate of their domestic electorates and political parties. This is a trend that is Europe-wide (worldwide, in fact) but rooted in domestic political processes, and so has many national variations and some exceptions. It is a trend that has an international dimension, the end of the 'cold war' division of Europe between the Communist east and free market West, but substantially mirrors trends taking place in each of the major home countries of what we now call the European Union.

Political disengagement

The crisis of political disengagement since the 1980s has led to a rapid decline in popular support for political parties and mass civil society organisations. In the 1980s the era of consensus politics established after the Second World War in much of north western Europe began to break down. This consensus was corporatist – based on the partnership of business, the state and organised labour. Its political manifestation was the party system that divided legislative assemblies between parties of left and right, the former usually allied to trade unions, the latter more closely allied to business.

The loss of influence of the party system was in evidence first on the Communist left and was connected, perhaps unsurprisingly, to the collapse of the Soviet Union and its satellites in Eastern Europe. Mass Communist parties across Europe haemorrhaged supporters more than during the invasion of Hungary in 1956, or even at the height of the Hitler-Stalin pact. In many cases these parties were important, if awkward, elements of the polity. The Italian, French, Greek and Portuguese Communist Parties were either involved in or supporting ruling coalitions in the 1980s. In the 1990s, they had become relics, either trying to mask their difficulties by name changes (as in Italy[3]) or doggedly persisting with the old slogans in the face of ridicule (as in France).

Figure 1: Membership of Communist Parties in France, Italy and Spain[4]

	1978	1980	1981	1987	1989	1991	1998
PCF France	632 000			604 285			210 000
PCI Italy		1 753 323			1 417 182		621 670 (DS)
PCE Spain			160 000			44 775	

The more moderate Socialist Parties seemed well placed to gain from the eclipse of the Communists, and in electoral terms, some of them did. Niels Finn Christiansen tells of the Danish Socialists' 'high optimism that the breakdown of the Communist regimes in Eastern Europe would lead to a spread of social democracy in the region', but that 'it came as a painful surprise to realise that "socialism" was so compromised in Eastern Europe that even moderate social-democratic solutions were out of the question'.[5] Not only was statist socialism out of the question in Eastern Europe, it was compromised in the west, too. The membership of many of the Socialist Parties also suffered sharp losses.

Figure 2: Membership of Socialist Parties in Germany, France, UK and Austria[6]

	1978	1980	1987	1988	1989	1990	1998	1999	2000	2003	2005
SPD Germany		986,872		921,430			755,244			660,000[a]	
SFIO France	632,000		604,285				210,000				
Labour Party UK	675,905[b]			265,927[b]						200,000[c]	
SPÖ Austria		719,881			620,141			400,000			

The Irish Labour Party, coming from behind, did enjoy some success in the 1980s and 1990s but failed to achieve the breakthrough that was often promised, despite a merger with the Democratic Left in 1999.

The damage to Socialist Party membership showed that the problem was not just a reaction to events in the Soviet Union. Commentators thought that perhaps this reflected a broader collapse of the left (like Eric Hobsbawm). Both Communist and Socialist Parties had an intimate relationship to trades unions, and pointedly, these too showed signs of decline.

Figure 3: Trade Union Density (% of workforce), 1975-1995[7]

Country	1975	1985	1990	1995
Austria	59	61	56	52
France	23	17	15	9
Germany	37	36	35	32
Greece		17	15	11
Ireland	60	61	57	53
Italy	49	42	39	38
Netherlands	37	28	26	26
Spain	19	14	17	17
UK	52	49	38	32

The European Values Survey also registered a decline in trade union membership in most west European countries

Figure 4: Respondents belonging to a trade union (%)[8]

	1981	1990	2000	Change
France	10	5	4	-6
East Germany		55	8	-47
West Germany	16	15	7	-9
Ireland	14	9	10	-4
Italy	8	6	6	-2
Portugal		5	2	-3
Spain	6	3	4	-2
UK	21	14	8	-13

There were exceptions, like Belgium, which saw a small rise of three per cent of respondents. Sweden, which joined the European Community in 1995, and is one of the most unionised of all developed nations,[9] which saw a rise in membership of twenty per cent of the respondents between 1981 and 2000, though the trade union share of the workforce has fallen since 1995.[10]

Some commentators related the decline of organised labour to a shift from manual to clerical labour.[11] And trade unions were certainly important supporters of Socialist Parties, both in terms of funding and campaigning. As such, their decline hurt the traditional base of socialist support. However, it would be closer to the mark to say that trade union membership tended to fall where trade union activism declined, as indicated in the fall in days lost through strike action.

Figure 5: Days lost in strike action, Germany, peak years[12]

1971	1978	1984	1992	2000
4 484 000	4 281 000	5 618 000	1 545 000	200 000

Figure 6: Days lost through strike action, UK (000s)[13]

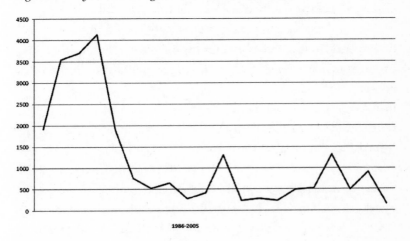

In France strike notices in 2000 were at their lowest for 15 years, at 850.[14] (There are of course speculative investigations of a return to militancy from time to time.[15] While it is not excluded that new conditions, like economic slump might change things that has not happened yet.)

The radical philosopher Slavoj Žižek saw a trend towards depoliticisation as the leftist movement had been de-railed: 'the ultimate cause of this moralistic depoliticisation is the retreat of the Marxist historico-political project,' he wrote.[16] On the other hand, the era of liberal-capitalist triumphalism as announced in Francis Fukuyama's (1992) essay, 'The End of History?', was short lived. Not long after the socialist left fell into disarray, many of the parties of the pro-market right found themselves in comparable difficulties. The French UDF shrank from 145 000 members in 1978 to half that in 1999, while its Gaullist counterpart was reduced from 760 347 to just 80 424; Britain's Conservative Party lost one million members between 1973 and 1994, leaving it at just 500 000 strong; the German Christian Democrat Union's decline was more modest, losing just a tenth of its 600 000 members between 1980 and 1998. The social constituencies that the right depended upon as a counterweight to the city-based socialist votes, like farmers' lobbies, were de-mobilised, as organised labour had been before them.

The fact that conservative parties, too, were subject to the downward trend in membership suggested that this was a wider problem of party identification in which political elites had lost contact with the public. According to Colin Hay, 'party membership has fallen precipitously throughout the OECD countries'.[18] Now it was not the decline of the left that people were talking about, but the end of both left and right. A prescient – or perhaps just defensive – Italian Communist leader Achille Occhetto said 'we are at the end of an epoch, the epoch of opposed systems'.[19] The parties of the right were in a sense defined by, even dependent upon, the threat of socialism to mobilise their support – once that threat diminished, so too did their appeal.

An historical comparison: legitimacy crises in the 1970s and 1990s

One way to understand the crisis of legitimacy of the 1990s is to contrast it with a previous era where the problems facing governing elites were quite different. The 1970s were also characterised by a crisis of legitimation.[20] The difference was that this crisis did not arise because of popular disaffection or demobilisation, but rather from its opposite – what the *Financial Times* called 'a revolt of rising expectations'.[21] The revolt of rising expectations found the state struggling to cope with the sheer extent of popular identification with the state, and with expectations of advantageous social reform.

The mass parties that grew up in Europe in the twentieth century were like a pyramid with their tip in the constituent assembly and a broad base in the population. One should not romanticise the rule of the party machines[22] – they were often rigidly bureaucratic and deeply conservative. Still, their existence allowed questions of economic and social policy to be routinely debated not by experts alone, but by thousands, sometimes tens of thousands, of ordinary people in halls and clubs across Europe.

The historian David Starkey recalled his Oldham childhood on Saturday Live, radio 4, 10-11 am, 17 May 2008. It was a world of trade unions, friendly societies, choirs, Sunday schools and night schools that was thoroughly communal. Today it is completely gone. He watched the great cotton mills close down, and saw that world pass away.

When I hear Handel's Messiah I am reminded of the Mary Wakefield festival in Kendal, where I was born in the old St George's Hall that has now burnt down, I am reminded of the world my parents came from. They came from Oldham and Rochdale the great cotton towns where life was so heavily communally structured with trade unions, friendly societies, night schools, Sunday schools and with choirs, and bands and orchestras that went with them, and it is a world that we have lost utterly and totally. I still remember going back to Oldham and the disintegration of the great cotton mills as they closed down one by one.

The corporatism that Starkey was describing was a mainstay of social order in the mid-twentieth century. In Britain the Conservative Party had two million members at its height, the Labour Party half a million ordinary members, with most of the 17 million trade union members affiliate members, even the Communist Party of Great Britain had 250 000 members in the years immediately after the war. Out of a population of 55 million, one in twenty were members of mainstream parties, and as many as a third were members of affiliated organisations. That was a powerful transmission belt between the ordinary public and their parliamentary representatives. But by the 1970s, it was breaking down. There were just too many calls on the state, or so it seemed to establishment figures. Clause Offe paraphrases the conservative theory of 'ungovernability' that arose at that time warning of 'an "overstretching" of claims to welfare-state services and democratic participation – an inappropriate politicisation of themes and conflicts, whereby expression is given to "the unbridled and mindless covetousness of the citizens"'. Back then Offe explained that the elite perception of a crisis of governability consolidated into the view that it was no longer possible to go on in the old ways: 'The limits of growth and of the welfare state, the world economic, financial and environmental crisis – including the crisis of legitimation or "the crisis of the authority of the state" – have become standard topics, presented in every conservative or liberal newspaper'. 'No individual thesis was more influential in the public dramatization of the crisis than the overload thesis', concurs Colin Hay.[23]

'A crisis of rising expectations' - school children join the strike wave in 1972. TUC library collections

Ruling strategy in the early 1980s was largely an attempt to *contain* popular expectations. In the first instance, this meant a struggle to contain wage demands and state spending on interest groups. Friedrich Hayek recalled that, having persuaded Labour chancellor Denis Healey that he could not spend his way out of a crisis, there were still 'onslaughts of popular forms of Keynesianism' to be faced.[24] Through a series of set-piece confrontations – the renegotiation of the *scala mobile* in Italy in 1984, the reversal of France's Socialist economic plan in 1982, the steel and miners' strikes in Britain in 1980 and 1984 – the advance of organised labour was halted and, then, reversed. Following Margaret Thatcher's lead, European governments embraced neo-liberal economics and set about 'dismantling socialism'. What they succeeded in doing was disaggregating social collectivities that were not only the basis of the left's appeal, but also of the post-war social consensus. In policy, Public Choice Theory, suggested that welfare provision should be removed from political contestation and subsumed to the criteria of rational choice theory.

The 'end of the cold war' was an international event, prepared by the *glasnost* and *perestroika* policies pursued by Soviet leader Mikhail Gorbachov, and marked by the popular breach of the Berlin Wall. The great symbolism of that event, though, had great resonance throughout western Europe not only because of what it meant for the international arms race, but also because it confirmed a view that was already well grounded, that the left-wing alternative to capitalism, both in its Moscow-allied Communist variant, but also in its state-socialist social democratic one, was programmatically exhausted. According to the historian Keith Middlemas, the collapse of the Soviet Union, the fall of the Berlin Wall and German reunification were the 'three events that conditioned everything that happened in Europe thereafter'. 'In the years 1989-93,' says Middlemas 'many of the vestiges of the post-war settlement in welfare programmes, industrial relations and state benefits also died'.[26] And in truth, most of the west European parties of the left were already in decline by the time the Berlin Wall was opened.

As indicated above, the crisis of the mass parties of the left, was quickly followed by a mirroring crisis of parties of the right. 'The collapse of Christian Democracy in Italy and the undermining of the political right in Britain can be traced to the same origin' of the end of the cold war says Middlemas.[27] In Denmark, Poul Schlüter's popular right-wing coalition fell apart in 1993.[28] That year the British Conservative politician Douglas Hurd gave a series of speeches, responding to the decline in active participation in the Conservative Party, where he argued that the right's problems were a response to the left's.[29] Psephologist Paul Whiteley and his colleagues, situated the decline of the Conservative Party in 'a long term decline in party identification' among the British electorate.[30]

In short, the 1990s were the working out of social processes set in train in the 1970s and 1980s. Gopal Balakrishnan has talked about 'low-level legitimation' crisis in the West:

> One of the central, little-theorized sociological transformations in Western societies over the past twenty-five years has been the decline of the masses. The low-level legitimation crisis of the democracy in this period is the harvest of this decline: not over- but, rather, depoliticization; not the multidimensional expansion of public power but, rather, its constriction and immobilization.[31]

Unlike past political and economic crises, such as in the 1970s when 'critics discerned a crisis of governability' argues Charles Maier, today 'citizens do not so much confront their states with demands as they back away in disillusion'.[32] Whiteley and his colleagues thought that the trend to party decline 'clearly serves to undermine the party system on which pluralist democracy is built'.[33]

In 1994, the British Labour politician (later Foreign Secretary) David Miliband summed up the anxieties of the political establishment:

> Politics in the advanced capitalist world has rarely been held in lower esteem. Whether measured by opinion polls or by the rise of protest parties, the formal institutions of politics, and the politicians who populate them, are held in low regard. At best, they are seen as impotent in the face of economic complexity and social change; at worst, they are part of a conspiracy to defraud the general public.[34]

A survey conducted on behalf of the World Economic Forum in 2002 found that more citizens of European Union countries had little or no trust in their national parliaments to act in society's interest than had some or a lot of trust.[35]

Furthermore, survey evidence suggested that Europeans were becoming more individualistic in outlook and associations, participating in fewer public bodies and organisations (though more cultural ones[36]). In Britain in 1994, *Social Trends* reported that the National Federation of Women's Institutes, The Mothers Union and the National Union of Townswomen's Guilds all saw their memberships fall by nearly half since 1971. The Red Cross Society, the British Legion, the RSPCA, the Guides and the Boy Scouts all suffered major falls in membership over the preceding 20 years. In fact, almost all major public institutions from the National Farmers Union to the Green Party were affected by the decline in popular participation.[37] Across northern Europe, single person households are on the rise adding to fears of social atomisation and declining social capital.[38]

Elites, in turn were putting more distance between themselves and their electorates. Keith Middlemas describes the process whereby nations moved away from the old welfarist consensus, through neo-liberalism to a much-diminished role for government: 'Each country described its own parabola of declension: the new thought, first enunciated by the new right in Britain and the United States, passed through a sort of contagion, causing questioning, then fiscal and moral panics, and finally a scaling down of promises and expectations'.[39] Middlemas is describing the way that elites began to see national aspirations as something to be damped down, or avoided.

Scandals

One consequence of the growing distrust of the political class has been the growth in public scandals as electorates, journalists and magistrates have become much less willing to turn a blind eye to questionable practices, and much more willing to believe the worst of politicians.[40] In their book *Sleaze: The Corruption of Parliament*, David Leigh and Ed Vulliamy, architects of the campaign to oust the Tory MP Neil Hamilton conclude 'corruption has really been the political norm' at Westminster.[41] According to Justin O'Brien, the Moriarty Tribunal in Ireland did not only show up former Taoiseach Charles Haughey's 'symbiotic relationship' with his financial backers, it also 'served to increase the antipathy towards the entire political class'.[42]

It was in Italy, though, that the crisis of legitimacy was most intense, leading to the disintegration of the political class and the suspension of parliamentary democracy. Corruption scandals saw leading politicians accused of constructing a city of bribes, *tangentopoli*. First the Socialist Party leader Bettino Craxi fled to Tunisia. Then the former Prime Minister Giulio Andreotti was jailed pending investigation under the Milan magistrates 'clean hands' campaign (in and out of prison for years, he was eventually cleared of all charges in 2003). Andreotti's party imploded as more and more politicians were jailed. Special powers granted magistrates in the pursuit of the Red Brigades in the 1970s were turned on the political elite[43] and the Carabinieri were sent to arrest representatives as they sat in the Chamber of Deputies. Crucially, the public supported the magistrates until, exhausted by the campaign, they turned to the charismatic figure of Silvio Berlusconi and his Forza Italia party to bring an end to the uncertainty. The Christian Democrats had for years succeeded in avoiding criticism of their links with business and in some cases organised crime, by pointing to the greater threat of a mass Communist movement. As that danger subsided, the established right's ability to mobilise middle class supporters collapsed, and the voters recoiled from the party's seedier connections.

A crisis of legitimacy

Italy, April 1992: Magistrates launched 'Tangentopoli' investigations, bringing
corruption charges against leaders Craxi and, Andreotti.

Denmark, January 1993: Paul Schlüter's government resigns over
illegal restraints on immigration

Britain, July 1994–May 1997: 'Cash for questions' scandal.

Ireland: Beef scandal rocked Haughey's successor Albert
Reynolds.

France, 1998: Ministerial flats scandal damaged Jacques Chirac.

Belgium, 1998: Ministerial cover-up in child torture case shook
Jean-Luc Dehaene's government.

Switzerland, 1998–2000: Sustained campaign over Jewish bank
deposits.

Germany, 2000: CDU funding scandal.

Italy, 2005: renewed corruption investigations into Premier
Berlusconi.

Britain, 2006: 'loans for peerages' allegations.

France, 2006: Prime Minister de Villepin accused of smearing his
rival Sarkozy in the Clearstream scandal.

Greece, 2008: Siemens' bribery of government exposed.

Britain, 2009: MPs second-home expenses.

The European Union's own 'Eurobarometer' polling of citizens' attitudes towards their national democratic institutions demonstrates the crisis of legitimacy that lay behind the proliferation of scandals, in particular, the ascendance of *dissatisfaction* over *satisfaction*.

How about the way democracy works in your country?

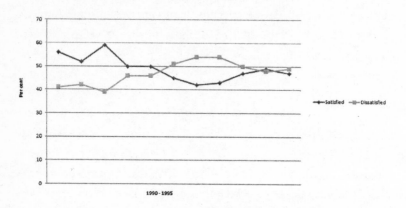

1990 - 1995

The end of left and right and the trend towards apolitical governance

The declining social base of the major parties of both the left and the right naturally has had a marked influence on the rhetorical appeals of governing elites as it has on less conventional actors. In 1994, in his book *Beyond Left and Right*, Anthony Giddens, wrote 'the terms right and left no longer have the meaning they once did, and each political perspective is in its own way exhausted'.[44] One early expression of the transcendence of left-right political appeals was made in 1986, when the French Socialist Party campaigned under the slogan *'Avec le President'* – an appeal to keep the assembly in socialist hands, in line with the presidency.[45] It was a curiously apolitical appeal, but that was perhaps not so surprising since the preceding period of socialist rule had seen the party abandon many of its left-wing commitments. What was there left but a 'feelgood' appeal to stick with the party of the still-popular leader Mitterrand?

In the introduction to his pamphlet Prime Minister Blair describes a 'Third Way' in politics that is neither left nor right:

My vision for the 21st century is of a popular politics reconciling themes which in the past have wrongly been regarded as antagonistic - patriotism and internationalism; rights and responsibilities; the promotion of enterprise and the attack on poverty and discrimination.[46]

In 1994, Gordon Brown, later to become Blair's Chancellor and then British Prime Minister, could say that 'markets and the state should no longer be seen as counterposed' adding 'The old battle of public and private has been superseded'.[47] Brown's assessment contains the essential component of the latterly elaborated Third Way. Where the left organised around the state and the right around the market, the contrast between those two aspects of social organisation was politicised. With the massed ranks of the labour movement lobbying for the extension of the welfare state and the middle classes railing against taxation, then the differences seemed to be absolute. But as the hostilities ebbed, the intellectual room for a Third Way opened up.

The Third Way has become the topic of international seminars of left wing political party leaderships as far afield as South Africa and Brazil. Prime Minister Blair has written his own pamphlet explaining what it means, and Anthony Giddens has written two books on the Third Way. But despite this extensive exercise in clarification, most people are still bemused about what the Third Way means. Linguistics expert Norman Fairclough analysed the new language of New Labour – as the party had started to call itself. Fairclough says that one judgement of the Third Way is that 'it allows the party to have it both ways'.[48] The binary counter-positions put together here are, mostly, those of left and right. Norman Fairclough accurately describes the way that 'the phrase "not only ... but also" pervades the political discourse of New Labour in a variety of expressions (e.g. "enterprise *yet also* fairness", enterprise *as well as* fairness", "enterprise *with* fairness", "enterprise *and* fairness"), which both draws attention to assumed incompatibilities and denies them'.[49] A marked influence on the Blair-Brown programme was the election of the US Democratic candidate Bill Clinton in 1992. Rather like the slogan 'Avec le President', Clinton campaigned in 1996 on the slogan 'building a bridge to the 21st Century' ('you were going there anyway', quipped the satirist Rory Bremner).

The apolitical character of contemporary politics is not restricted to the Anglosphere. In Italy, media tycoon Sivlio Berlusconi built a new party, seemingly overnight, with an appeal to sweep away the old parties, under the football slogan 'Forza Italia' ('go for it, Italy'). The 'Third Way' popularised by the British Labour Party leadership was anticipated by Gro Harlem Bruntland's modernisation of *Det Norske Arbeiderparti*, the Norwegian Labour Party, in 1986,[50] and of the Danish Social Democratic Party under Poul Rasmussen after 1992.[51] In Germany, the election of the Red-Green coalition in 1998 might have been expected to push Germany to the left, but as it turned out, the Social Democrat leader Gerhard Schröder was convinced that traditional ties would have to be broken: 'A Social Democracy that spent its time reminiscing about the past would be at best a glorious memory', he warned his critics on the left, 'at worst it would become a reactionary force'.[52] Schröder had support from his junior Green partners, who were dismissive of past policies: 'Our present programme is like an attic, a place where ends up that one used to cherish but has no longer any use for', read one manifesto, which continued in 'Third Way' vein: 'Market forces and the needs of society must be brought into accord with each other'.[53] Wanting to get away from ideological debates could be seen in Ségolène Royal's 2007 unsuccesful presidential campaign – the 'listening campaign', 'media savvy, youth-flattering, policy lite' according to Julian Barnes;[54] but opponent Nicholas Sarkozy also attempted to present his government as above party politics, with the inclusion of some pointedly left-of-centre ministers like socialist Bernard Kouchner. Struggling with a reputation for mean-spiritedness, British Conservative leader David Cameron, too, has promised to abandon many of the 'Nasty' policies that marked the party in the 1980s – and since coming to power in 2010 has had to share power with the Liberal Democrats in a markedly pragmatic and non-ideological partnership.

The trend towards apolitical rhetoric is both a symptom of – and like a feedback loop also becomes a cause of – popular disaffection with politics. Though it would surely not be possible for leaders to ignore the change in popular expectations and carry on making the traditional appeals to constituencies that were already in disarray, it is also true that the coalescence of policies around the centre ground has not engaged electorates with the passion that the old contested politics did.

Though political 'rethinking' did help the parties of the left in western Europe in the 1990s – winning power in Britain (1997) France (the assembly, but not the presidency, 1997) and Germany (1998) not least because their rightist opponents were politically exhausted and mired in political scandals, in the long run their influence continued to decline. The *Guardian's* Martin Kettle used the recent European elections to illustrate the left's difficulties:

> Most of the major social democratic parties in Europe have been sliding into decline for years. The reverses of June 4 did not come out of the blue. But they offer a strikingly similar picture. Labour's 16 per cent share of the poll in Britain was matched by the Parti Socialiste's 16 per cent in France, the SPD's 21 per cent in Germany, the Polish Socialists' and Dutch Labour's 12 per cent and the Swedish and Austrian social

democrats' 24 per cent. Italy's Democrats managed 26 per cent and Spain's socialists a dizzying 38 per cent, but both of these parties, like their colleagues, were well beaten by the centre-right. The reckoning for the left is Europe-wide.[55]

As the declining social base of the mass parties of left and right had an impact on the political fortunes of governments, so too did it lead to the emergence of a distinctive kind of political movement, less rooted and more ad hoc that the traditional organisations, which we go on to look at next.

'New politics'

Alongside the disaffection with the mainstream, votes increasingly came to be cast for 'third parties' or protest candidates. In Britain the Social Democratic Party (1981-1988) and in Ireland the Progressive Democrats (1985-2009) and on the left, the Workers Party (from 1982) emerged in the 1980s to challenge the mainstream parties. In 1989, the Green Parties won eight per cent of European votes. In June 1991, the Austrian Freedom Party made its decisive electoral breakthrough. On 26 January 1994 Forza Italia was formed, following the success of the Northern League, to win the elections in March of that year. In 1995 Jean Marie Le Pen won 15 per cent of the presidential vote (his highest ever, following 14 per cent in 1988, but just 11 per cent in the shock defeat of the Socialists for second place in the first round of the 2002 elections). Regional parties like the Lega Nord, the Scottish Nationalist Party and Herri Batasuna have also done well. In the 2002 elections the anti-immigrant Pim Fortuyn List in Holland won 26 seats, and in the 2009 European elections the tiny United Kingdom Independence Party came second, beating the ruling Labour Party into third place. Protest candidates of the far left also did well, like France's Arlette Laguiller, and Britain's George Galloway. In 2005 even the Communists made a comeback playing key roles in a new protest party, Die Linke in

Germany. For the most part, these advances were a reflection of the troubles of the establishment parties.

Though the traditional mass mobilisations of the labour movement and of rival conservative supporters were in abeyance, the depletion of the party system seemed to create a need for more random demonstrations and collective gatherings. These were fleeting in character and left few institutional structures, although they were often very large in number. The 1990s saw millions march against child abuse in Belgium, and thousands in Portsmouth, England; tens of thousands mourned the unexpected deaths of Princess Diana, Pim Fortuyn and Swedish Foreign Minister Anna Lindh; unofficial and alternative music festivals were popular in Britain and Germany; farmers protested in favour of fox-hunting in Britain in 2001; anti-racists rallied to the cause of immigrants *sans papiers* taking refuge in a Paris Church in 1996; between 1999 and 2001 anti-capitalists protested in London, Cologne, Bologna, Prague and Nice. Culminating on 15 February 2003, European capitals were once again site to mass protests, this time against the war in Iraq. In 2005 a coalition of the revived left organisations pulled together in a successful campaign for a vote against the proposed European Union constitution. No doubt there is much that is interesting or positive about many of these developments, but they are for the most part less rooted movements than before, and were, considered as a whole, a reflection of the declining authority of the old party system.[56]

The case is often made that the new politics and the new social movements are a replacement, and a superior one, to the old. Offe explains:

The process by which multitudes of individuals become collective actors is highly informal, ad hoc, discontinuous ... they have at best rudimentary membership roles, programs platforms, representatives, officials, staffs, and membership dues. The new social movements consist of participants, campaigns, spokespersons, networks, voluntary helpers and donations. Typically, in contrast to traditional forms of political organisations, they do not employ the organisational principle of differentiation in either horizontal (insider versus outsider) or the vertical (leader versus rank-and-file members) dimension.'[57]

The organisational ambiguity of the new social movements is presented here as an advantage over the old organisations. But is it? With officers elected by members, the rights of the members to challenge policy or leaders are clear. In an informal network, decisions cannot be tested, nor members held accountable for their actions. As journalist Andy Beckett reported on the anti-globalisation movement, 'people who are prepared to take risks, or possess useful skills, can come to dominate, or even have contempt for, the more cautious and amateurish participants'.[58] This is closer to what Max Weber called 'charismatic leadership'.[59] American labour researcher Stephanie Ross argues that the 'uncompromising ideological rejection of leadership tout court, results in leadership unbound by structures of accountability'.[60]

Melucci explains that the new politics leads to *'the selection of new elites'*:

In many Western countries during the 1970s, for example, collective action produced certain changes in left-wing or progressive political organisations (such as political parties and trade unions) and, above all, resulted in the emergence of a new generation of skilled personnel in the key communications media, advertising and marketing sectors of the "information society".[61]

Offe says that the new social movements 'are rooted in major sections of the new middle class'.[62] In Germany, a 1994 poll showed Green Voters were the most well off of any party.[63] According to the British Social Attitudes Survey, 'those in the professional and managerial class and those with O-level or equivalent qualifications or above, are much more likely than working class people or those with lower qualifications to have engaged in some form of activism'. Furthermore, they added, 'we find that young people are less likely than older ones to undertake direct action, which is somewhat surprising'.[64]

There is little doubt that the old party system was very regimented and doctrinaire in the way that it maintained ideological discipline. But one way that it is clearly very different from the new politics is that it embraced a much larger proportion of the population. Through party membership, trade unions, allied clubs and voluntary groups the old parties at the height of their influence took in a significant portion of the electorate. By contrast the circle of civil society is drawn more narrowly today. If it is stylistically more open, it is statistically more restricted. The new social movements are no doubt an interesting and vigorous development, but they are also symptomatic of a narrower circle of public participation in civic life.

Radical journalist George Monbiot faces the problem:

So this is the great question of our age: where is everyone? The monster social movements of the 19th century and first 80 years of the 20th have gone, and nothing has replaced them. Those of us who still contest unwarranted power find our footsteps echoing through cavernous halls once thronged by multitudes.[65]

If the new politics does not replace mass political participation, the question remains whether there is any need to do so. For some, it seems that the depoliticisation of key public and governmental arms is a positive development. There is no reason necessarily to characterise depoliticisation as a *decline,* except in the obvious sense of a decline in politicisation.

A positive case made for depoliticisation

Alongside the declining popular support for mainstream party politics, administrators in west European countries actively seek the removal of governing functions from control by elected officials. According to Colin Hay 'in marked contrast to almost all of the existing academic literature on the topic, the practitioners' discourse of depoliticisation presents it in a very positive light'.[66]

The London based European Policy Forum says that 'the depoliticisation of many government decisions' is 'one of the most promising developments since the last war'.[67] In March 2003, the solicitor Graham Mather of the European Policy Forum, submitted written evidence to the Select Committee on the Constitution of the House of Lords, arguing

In recent years Britain has experienced a very significant shift of power to a group of new decision makers in society commonly described as regulators [who] now exercise many decisions which 20 years ago would have been for Ministers to take.

Britain is likely to be better governed because of the arrival of the new decision makers. They have the potential to be better educated and trained, equipped with deeper skills and specialised knowledge, and operating in a more rational framework than the politicians whose decision they have taken over.

They are free from the vote-and rent-seeking behaviour inseparable from the political process.[68]

Mather is a former MEP and sat on the European Parliament's Economic & Monetary Affairs Committee, before which he was head of the Policy Unit of the Institute of Directors. It seems that in many respects, the British government is in agreement with Mather and the European Policy Forum. Constitutional Minister Lord Falconer set out the received wisdom on 'depoliticisation' motivating an independent Appointments Commission to select members of the reformed House of Lords, Britain's second chamber:

> What governs our approach is a clear desire to place power where it should be: increasingly not with politicians but with those best fitted in different ways to deploy it. Interest rates are not set by politicians in the Treasury, but by the Bank of England. Minimum wages are not determined by the Department of Trade and Industry, but by the Low Pay Commission. Membership of the House of Lords will be determined not in Downing Street but in an independent Appointments Commission. This depoliticisation of key decision-making is a vital element in bringing power closer to the people.[69]

Journalist Simon Jenkins explained how Britain's 'quangocracy' had grown to fill the role left when elected authorities were robbed of their powers by the state, with local authorities' spending was shunted off to Urban Development Corporations, for example.[70] British quangos account for 21 per cent of all government spending, or £123 billion a year.[71] Mike Power noted the 'auditing explosion', and its creation of special auditing institutions: 'the General Accounting Office in the United States, the National Audit Office in the U.K., the Bundes- and Landesrechnungshofe in Germany, and the Australian Audit Office' and 'Inspectorates General' that 'can be found in France and elsewhere'. Power argued that the preoccupation with auditing in the public sector arose out of a fundamental loss of confidence in the authorities, and more that the auditing culture would reinforce that loss of confidence, even as it was supposed to resolve it.[72]

The 'Red Togas' – magistrates who took over the Italian government

In Italy, examining magistrates played a key role in curbing the power of politicians during the 'Clean Hands' investigations. Milan Magistrate Francesco Borrelli, led the 'Clean Hands' investigation into elected politicians that saw hundreds investigated. 'Ours is a wise and legal revolution which has lasted a little more than a year' said Borrelli, adding 'Remember that the French Revolution began in 1789 and was completed in 1794'.[73] In May 1992 Borrelli boasted of the way that a pick-axe 'has been taken to the party system';[74] the following year Borrelli dismissed the democratic assembly: 'Parliament, as everybody knows, is what it is. It has not changed and is the expression of the old party logic'.[75] The magistrates' challenge to parliamentary rule is lauded by the International Institute for Democratic and Electoral Assistance research team who say 'the magistracy has contributed greatly to the modernisation of the country', and welcome the fact that 'the "judge's revolution" contributed to the collapse of the first Republic and the disappearance of the traditional parties'.[76] As Levi and Nelken explain the politics of corruption can be an 'attempt to relegitimate the rulers and/or specific political actors or criminal justice agencies'.[77]

German political leaders have long been familiar with the derogation of political power to officials at the central bank, the Bundesbank. Wilhelm Vocke, first president of what was then known as the Bank Deutscher Länder set out the case in 1948: 'The independence of the Bank and its leadership is an absolute necessity' he said. 'Only when independence is guaranteed on all sides will the central bank be able to earn that asset which is more important than popularity and applause ... trust at home and abroad'.[78] Arguably, the German central bank had unique questions of trust to deal with, namely the debauching of the German currency both under Weimar and then again during the Second World War. By contrast many other European central banks operated more as an arm of government economic policy, particularly in the boosting of the money supply in counter-cyclical economic policy. In the negotiations leading to the formation of the European Central Bank, preparatory to the introduction of the single currency, however, the German model of the independent central bank came to be the accepted norm to which other European central banks had to conform, to become part of the European System of Central Banks (precursor to the European Central Bank). Financial journalist Matt Marshall explained that under the agreement 'The EU's member states would have to change their banking laws to resemble those of Germany, to ensure their banks were independent before the currency was introduced in 1999' and 'the ECB would not be allowed to bail out any government with loans'.[79] Britain's new chancellor Gordon Brown claimed the credit for making the Bank independent as the first act of the incoming Labour government of 1997, and his letter announcing the change is proudly displayed at the Bank of England Museum. Ireland had to change her constitution – which had contained a clause tasking the bank with promoting growth – to meet the European System of Central Bank conditions. The removal of monetary policy from political control is a change that was made uniform through the European Union's creation of the European Central Bank, but it was all the same a change that many governments welcomed, and in which direction many were already moving.

Andrew Moravcsik makes the argument that the removal of functions from democratic control in the European Union is not a flaw, but an ordinary feature of modern governing institutions

> The apparently 'counter-majoritarian' tendency of EU political institutions insulated from direct democratic contestation arises out of factors that themselves have normative integrity, notably efforts to compensate for the ignorance and non-participation of citizens, to make credible commitments to rights enforcement, and to offset the power of special interests. These institutional adaptations are normal in the 'second best' world of advanced industrial democracies.[80]

More recently, Moravcsik underscored the point: 'more democracy does not mean more legitimacy: data shows that citizens do not, as a rule, dislike "opaque" courts and bureaucracies, and that they loathe parliaments and elected politicians.'[81]

A new style of social administration has been developed to match the removal of decision-making from political contestation. Policies must be 'evidence-based', and tested against 'outcomes'. This jargon has the effect of removing the political choices that always lie behind social administration and render them as intuitively given. The actual choices involved are masked, as if they were self-evident, leaving only the technical question of effectiveness open to question. The doctrine of social administration that lies behind much of the new public administration is Public Choice Theory, based on Kenneth Arrow's thesis that political contestation is a barrier to successful outcomes, encouraging the creation of constituencies of dependency and rent-seeking behaviour.[82]

As we have seen, mass public participation in making policy choices has declined with the decline of the mass parties of left and right. Governing elites have adapted to the new conditions by developing a political approach that eschews ideological argument in favour of technocratic decision-making. Protest movements and parties have emerged in the space left by mass movements, albeit with less roots and organisation coherence. Public authority has also become de-politicised, with many more government functions derogated to non-majoritarian institutions. These are the domestic political conditions in the member states where the European Union has flourished. In the next chapter we look at the ways that depoliticisation has shaped the formation of national interests and influenced the course of the European Union. We will look at the common dynamic of declining domestic political contestation and enhanced European Union competence, as domestic political leaders sought to slough off responsibility for their own choices onto the European Union itself.

CHAPTER THREE

The Decline of Nationalism and the Rise of the European Union

If depoliticisation is the major trend affecting social adminis-tration, how does it bear upon the European Union? A short answer would be that the European Union's institutions are themselves instances of social administration removed from direct democratic control. As the authority of regulators, magis-trates, the Central Bank and other unelected officials has grown, so too has the authority of the European Union. The Union's competencies expand to fill the space left by the diminished authority of the national assemblies, just as on a more local level do those other authorities.

To look at the process more closely, we look first at the way that the more contested and politicised environment of West Europe in the 1970s tended to work against integration, giving rise to a period of 'Euro-sclerosis'. Then we look at the way that the fall in political activism and expectations in the 1980s tended to leave political leaders greater room to compromise with their European allies, and also has made for many, a greater motive for the handing over of powers to the European Union. Here we look particularly at the end of national Keynesianism, and the way that left socialist governments looking towards Europe as a way out of their impasse. We consider, too, the way that governments, particularly in Italy, lacking the political authority to make the changes they needed, have tended to shift blame and responsi-bility onto Europe. We also consider some exceptions to the rule – at the debate with the British Conservative party of the 1980s between leader Margaret Thatcher, and those who wanted preferring the more bloodless style of European administration to her confrontational approach; and we look at the way that

Germany had already anticipated many of the styles of apolitical administration that were adopted in the European Union, and so had less distance to travel in meeting the norms of European governance.

Finally, we look at the way that national self-projection has been re-directed into a more performative exercise, a kind of 'grandstanding' on the world stage, and more specifically, within the European Council.

Notwithstanding the exceptions, we can see how the declining authority of the nation state, its mandated power as representation of the popular voice depleted, has created that vacuum into which the European Union has expanded.

Mobilising the popular nation was a barrier to European integration

In the later 1960s and 1970s the European project stalled, a phenomenon called 'Euro-sclerosis'. Van Appeldoorn argues that this 'Euro-sclerosis' is an ideological construct, coined by the neo-classical economist and president of the Mont Pelerin Society (1986-88) Herbert Giersch to mean rigidities in the 'economy caused in particular by interventionist governments, trade unions and excessive welfare states'.[1] But if we might want to differ from Giersch's argument against welfarism, Euro-sclerosis is still a fair characterisation of the deceleration of European integration in the 1970s, justifying the characterisation of 'a period of "Euro-pessimism" that lasted from the first enlargement to 1985'.[2] Around that time Commission President François-Xavier Ortoli, struggling with disputes over currency alignment, energy prices and agricultural policy worried that the Community had lost its vision and that its institutions were close to collapse.[3]

The period of Euro-sclerosis – 1968 to 1983 – was a period of heightened social conflict in west European societies, and one of greater political contestation. It was the period that the 'ungovernability' theorists characterised as 'overloaded'. Political leaders were obliged by the force of the demands upon them to pay more attention to national electorates. And in the face of social division, they wove a thick blanket of national unity. Playing to a domestic audience, political leaders were not in a position to make many overtures towards their European counterparts, but on the contrary, were often compelled to strike antagonistic postures that would play well at home.

Martin Marcussen and his colleagues, looking at the question of French national identity were drawn to the intense social conflict that engulfed the country over its conflict with the Algerian liberation movement at the end of the 1950s. 'The war in Algeria and the ongoing crisis of the French Republic only added to the crisis of French nation state identity' but 'Charles de Gaulle, reconstructed French nation state identity and managed to reunite a deeply divided nation around a common vision of France's role in the world.'[4]

Historian Alistair Horne agrees: 'With the passing of each successive day of the crisis [the army-pied noir revolt], it became evident that public opinion - from Left to Right - was setting solidly behind de Gaulle, solidly against the Algiers insurgents and their dissident allies in the army.'[5] De Gaulle's Bonapartist elevation above left and right to national leader was a response to the struggle over Algeria, consolidated in his return to power and in the 1958 referendum agreeing independence. In 1965, de Gaulle was facing an ambush at the European Council over the creation of a discrete fund of the European Economic Community's 'own reserves' at the hands of German Commission president Walter Hallstein and Dutch Commissioner Sicco Mansholt. De Gaulle's response was to refuse to take his seat on the Council, which, since it then operated a policy of unanimity, *nem. con.* meant that no decisions could be taken in his absence and the Council was paralysed, much to the dismay of the Commission, and the irritation of the other heads of state. De

Gaulle painted his opposition in stridently national, and democratic terms, calling the Commission 'a mostly foreign technocracy destined to trample on democracy in France' – a pointed appeal since he was on the verge of the first round vote for re-election to the Presidency. Jean Monnet announced 'On December 5, I shall not vote for General de Gaulle' adding that his policy 'is leading us down the outdated path of nationalism' and that he would vote instead for the Socialist candidate François Mitterrand[6] (at that time Mitterrand's policy was 'a Europe built by the process already begun in technical and economic fields' i.e. integrationist). De Gaulle was re-elected with 54.5 per cent of the votes.

Britain's policy towards Europe in the 1970s presents a very different reaction to social contestation. Like France in the 1960s, Britain's rulers were confronted with a fierce challenge to public order in the 1970s, with extensive labour disputes, protests as well as a small war in the six counties of Northern Ireland. 'Who governs', parliament or trade union militants was an issue that the Conservative Heath government fought the 1974 general election on – and lost. In 1973, Edward Heath took Britain into the European Economic Community, but the incoming Labour administration under Harold Wilson was committed to a referendum on membership, which was held on 5 June 1975. Claiming to have renegotiated more favourable terms, Wilson supported continued European Economic Community membership. The government's stance in favour of continued membership was arguably for geo-political as much as for domestic reasons. Echoing de Gaulle's view, the leader of the 'No' campaign Richard Body claimed that 'the Trojan horse argument appealed especially to Kennedy and Kissinger and the Americans thought that by having the Britons in, Europe would be more sympathetic to the Atlanticist point of view'.[7]

On the left, though, there was a pointedly patriotic identification with British democracy. On a visit to Brussels in 1974,

Tony Benn felt like 'a slave going to Rome' and that the Commission 'would be the decapitation of British democracy'. Benn found that the No campaign struck a chord amongst activists, addressing mass meetings of up to two thousand.[8] On the other side, the young Conservative (and future party leader) Iain Duncan Smith explained 'the Conservatives' support for Europe came about because they were all convinced that the argument against socialism had been lost in Britain, and that they could only hope to stop its advance in Europe' – in other words, they hoped that Europe would act as a limit on popular leftism.[9] Indicative of the establishment view, the Yes campaign had clandestine support from the Foreign Office's Information Research Department and the US Central Intelligence Agency – but in the event the less voluble part of the British electorate were anyway largely in favour of continued membership by 69 per cent to 29.[10]

Though the tempestuous events of the seventies favoured British membership of the European Economic Community that did not really help European integration, since the British were jealously independent members from the start. According to the former President of the European Parliament, Simone Veil 'once Europe expanded to include countries that are less European and more American (I am thinking of the entry in 1973 of Britain and Denmark) there were more supporters of an intergovernmental rather than a federal Europe'.[11] British commitments to Keynesian national economic management – a strategy vital to securing popular support for government – militated against European cooperation. Later, when the political conflict swung the other way, and a newly elected Conservative government set about 'dismantling socialism', Europe began to look like a barrier to its own version of populist nationalism. Iain Duncan Smith recalled 'So it was that when Mrs Thatcher showed them that they could win the popular vote in Britain, they came to look more critically at the European Union'.[12]

In the 1970s, national recovery plans frustrated economic cooperation in the European Economic Community. Even the Community-minded German government of Helmut Schmidt introduced capital controls. These national recovery plans were driven by a fear of social disorder, and showed European leaders putting the needs of their domestic electorates first. The demobilisation of the soldiers and munitions workers after the Second World War was the condition of the unprecedented degree of European unity in the fifties and early sixties; the re-emergence of the social conflict in the later sixties and seventies saw ruling elites retreat into nationalism to appear to rise above the class conflict, thus jeopardising their relations with one another. The return to class peace in the later 1980s again brought European unity back into view.

The end of the national recovery plans and the re-launch of Europe

In 1981, François Mitterrand led a coalition of socialists and communists to victory in France, in 'a campaign that widely ignored European policy, to concentrate on domestic issues'.[13] It would be hard to understate the expectations that the new government carried. The coalition of the left had fought closely contested elections for more than a decade, and lost. Mitterrand's socialist 'experiment' was an ambitious reflationary command economy that took 90 per cent of the Banking Sector, one third of industry and thirteen of the top twenty companies into public ownership, with big rises in family benefits (40 per cent), pensions (17.5 per cent), housing benefits (50 per cent) and the minimum wage (15 per cent), as well as introducing a 35-hour week.[14]

In the same year Andreas Papandreou's Pan-Hellenic Socialist Movement (PASOK) took power in Greece. Under Papandreou, PASOK was heavily influenced by radical economic thinkers of the 'underdevelopment' school, and committed to 'self-supporting national development', as well as withdrawal from the North Atlantic Treaty Organisation and the European Economic Community.[15] Papandreou boycotted the official celebrations of Greece's accession to the European Economic Community on 28 May 1979. In government, those promises of withdrawal were not kept, though the government did embark on a vigorous national recovery programme of price controls and nationalisation.

These economic plans for national expansion in France and in Greece proved to be the last of their kind. Thanks in part to European Economic Community rules limiting import controls, the effects of additional government spending could not be kept within the national economy. 'Extra purchasing power in the French economy tended to be spent on imports rather than home produced goods, unsettling the balance of trade and weakening the currency';[16] Greeks' extra earning power, too, 'was not translated into overall increases in domestic production, but rather into increased imports'.[17] British economist Will Hutton drew the lesson that 'the old instruments of dirigisme and state direction were plainly outmoded'.[18]

Faced with collapsing currencies, both Mitterrand and Papandreou made major political U-turns. In France, the change in policy towards austerity and spending cuts, as well as market liberalisation measures, was marked by the replacement of Prime Minister Pierre Mauroy by Laurent Fabius and led to a Communist withdrawal from government (that was followed by its decline as a mass organisation). As much as the economic and organisational difficulties challenged Mitterrand's socialist government, it was the ideological realignment that had the greatest impact. 'Conditions have emerged permitting a class armistice and class peace' Mitterrand announced;[19] though in fact his modernisation policy would punish his own working class supporters, Mitterrand was accurate in that the change marked a precipitate decline in trade union membership. The technocratic goal of 'modernisation' replaced 'socialism'. From a national recovery plan, Mitterrand redirected the party's orientation towards international competition: 'henceforth French grandeur must consist of our successfully competing on foreign economic and commercial battlefields'.[20] The French Finance Minister Jacques Delors, on the social catholic wing of the Socialist Party, was instrumental in persuading the hardliners to accept that the policy could not be defended in the face of the international economic pressures. Delors, who would go on to become the European Commission's most dynamic president, reflected on the limitations of the national solution in October 1983: 'Our only choice is between a United Europe and decline'.[21] Other Socialist leaders, like Poul Rasmussen in Denmark,[22] Sweden's Ingvar Karlsson and Tony Blair in Britain all drew similar lessons about the need to reorient their parties away from national Keynesian solutions, and towards European cooperation.

As well as a market for French exports, the United Europe became an ideological arena for the expression of French grandeur. Mitterrand redirected social aspirations from the nation outwards to the status of leading player in Europe. Pointedly, the experience of reinventing the French socialist government's appeal as one with a European orientation changed Delors and Mitterrand, too. Withdrawing from the negative experience of national recovery, they became two of the most dynamic agents of European integration, Delors as President of the Commission, Mitterrand as broker of the deal with Helmut Kohl to create a single currency.[23] Key figures in the re-launching of the European project after the period of Euro-sceirosis, they were both thrust onto a steep learning curve about the limitations of the national political contest. 'A high degree of supra-nationality is essential', Delors told John Ardagh, 'national sovereignty no longer means very much, or has much scope in the modern world economy'.[24] It was a lesson he had learned the hard way.

The end of the Keynesian road to national recovery was an historical moment that inspired the European Commission to push harder for integration (in particular the single market). The closure of the one road led to the opening of the other. Thereafter, it became more common for political leaders to deflect responsibility for their own national failures, and push problems up into Europe.

Blaming 'Europe' – the retreat from responsibility

'Brussels' is too easily blamed by Member States for difficult decisions that they themselves have agreed or even requested. (European Commission)[25]

Many commentators have noted the tendency for national governments to avoid responsibility for unpopular acts, by claiming that these were imposed upon them by their obligations to the European Union. Andrew Moravcsik argues that politicians can "reduce the political costs of unpopular policies by 'scapegoating' international institutions".[26] Blaming Europe for unpopular but 'necessary' changes is a common manoeuvre.

For the most part, these evasions are taken as signs of the – comical – irresponsibility of elected political leaders. Largely, they are seen as only episodic acts of hypocrisy. But in fact the trend to shift responsibility is an important indicator and cause of the shift in power between member states and the European Union. The Union accrues authority to the extent that national actors eschew it.

Quite why it is that governments *want* to avoid responsibility seems to be a question that is not asked, as if it was obvious that politicians are shifty crooks and liars. But that is to adopt the mood of our times too uncritically. The retreat from responsibility is not an intrinsic quality of political leadership, but it is decidedly one of our present era of depoliticisation, where publics hold politicians in low esteem. Removing political decisions from scrutiny, passing them off as bureaucratic rule-given obligations, taking them out of public contestation – these are all features of the contemporary apolitical administration, and by no means restricted only to relations between national governments and the European Union. Luxemburg's Prime Minister Jean-Claude Juncker voiced a common prejudice among Europe's leaders that electorates were a barrier to the right course of action, when he said 'we all know what to do, we just don't know how to get re-elected after we've done it'.[27] As Lord Falconer explained, the depoliticisation of appointments to the House of Lords, the setting of the minimum wage and of interest rates are just some of the decisions handed over to regulators in the UK. If we look at the instances of 'blaming Europe' it is more than clear that they are closely tied up with the trend towards depoliticisation, and of the alienation of populations from governments.

In Italy, Giuliano Amato's caretaker government, already paralyzed by the emerging corruption scandal, succeeded, where previous governments had failed, to persuade Bruno Trentin of the CGIL union to agree to end the costly inflation indexing of wages, the *scala mobile* on 31 July 1992. Amato did not confront labor directly, as Andreotti had when reforming the agreement in 1984, but by reference to the 'external constraint' of the European Monetary System. According to Minister Guido Carli, writing in 1993, 'the European Union represented an alternative path for the solution of problems which we were not managing to handle through the normal channels of government and parliament'.[28]

Reform of the *scala mobile* was recognised all round as a pressing need for Italy's political leaders, but none were willing to risk the responsibility of enforcing it. (In fact the *scala mobile* itself was an emergency measure to remove the wage round from national consideration, since it had become a flash-point for rolling strikes in the period of inflation.) Still in earlier times, political leaders would have had more confidence to face the problem. By the 1990s, when Italy's already weak state was in meltdown, the best way to effect the change was to appeal to European exigencies.

Telecommunications minister Maurizio Pagani was asked about his centralization plan in December 1992: 'Mr Minister, this is not the first time that somebody is blocking the reform. What will you do this time?' He answered: 'We have to. We have no alternative. How could we otherwise meet European competition?'[29]

On these grounds, Franco Morganti chairman of Logica CGM Italy, head of an independent commission appointed by President Spadolini to study the telecomms market, argued that 'the recent history of Italian liberalization originated entirely in Brussels'.

Policy innovation at European level is framed in terms of avoiding nationally-based ambitions. So elites often speak of 'locking-in' reforms, as in 'Germany's desire to "lock in" a guarantee of low inflation by creating an autonomous ECB'; or the French government 'locking in austerity' by subordinating spending to the European Monetary System. Raymond Barre's government committed France to 'microeconomic austerity and macroeconomic discipline'. The European Monetary System was a means to 'institutionalise disinflation'.[30]

British chancellor Nigel Lawson justified subordinating exchange rates to the European system as an economic policy based on rules rather than discretion. Lawson explained to Geoffrey Howe that an 'externally imposed exchange rate discipline' would help avoid the 'political pressures for relaxation ... as the election approaches'.[31] It is hard to justify binding future parliaments from the perspective of national sovereignty, but increasingly European leaders found themselves less willing to submit to the judgements of national electorates, and correspondingly more comfortable with European agreements and obligations.

Intriguingly, Margaret Thatcher clashed with both her chancellors, Geoffrey Howe and Nigel Lawson over the clandestine policy of 'shadowing the deutschmark', that is of submitting the British economy to the heightened monetary discipline of parity with the German currency. Andrew Moravcsik explains how Thatcher, though in agreement with the liberalizing bent of European Union policy, was still out of step with its technocratic application: 'in overt opposition to many of her advisors', she 'preferred to disinflate by confronting and conquering rather than circumventing domestic opposition'.[32] As great as their debt to her was, the European leaders that followed preferred to take the politics out of the struggle to restrict spending, by relocating it in Brussels. Thatcher, by contrast, was committed to winning the argument for market discipline, and was correspondingly committed to the national arena in which that argument was had out. Her government's explicit and self-confident struggle to 'roll back socialism' meant that she was out of step with those other political leaders in Europe, who saw fiscal discipline as a matter best sorted out under the European Central Bank's convergence criteria. That was why Britain continued to be the 'awkward partner' all through the 1980s and into the 1990s. But while she jealously defended *British* sovereignty, Mrs Thatcher thought it was a good thing that the rest of Europe be subordinated to European Rules on deregulation. European Commissioner Leon Brittan contrasted the 'anti-European rhetoric of Margaret Thatcher today to her pro-European actions in government':

the fact is that she, and indeed virtually the whole of the Conservative Party, both in parliament and in the country, viewed the Single European Act as a great step forward in forcing British-style liberalisation further and faster across Continental Europe.[33]

In 2005, British chancellor Gordon Brown's defence of his economic policy was reported to run 'don't blame me, it's the bank' – meaning the Bank of England, that he made independent in line with Europe's guidelines for the creation of a System of European Central Banks, was to blame for slow growth rather than his high taxes.[34]

The paradox of the EU and democracy

Andrew Lilico Director of the think-tank European Economics is remarkably candid about the meaning of the European Union

> a central function of the European Union has always been understood as delivering policies that domestic political systems would be unable to deliver for themselves. Trade barriers were removed, competition was introduced, subsidies for businesses were reduced, regulations were liberalised via the EU in ways that would never have been voted for had they been proposed domestically.

In other words, the Union is there to do the things that elected governments dare not. Lillico asks rhetorically

> Is it plausible, perhaps, that the spur of European Union duty/solidarity, plus the pressure to provide governments (and hence policies) approved by central European Union authorities, might be sufficient to deliver austerity programmes that would not be delivered if domestically dependent?[35]

One of the more remarkable things about the academic discussion on the European Union is that the question of where the right to decide lies is still up for dispute, between inter-governmentalists and integrationists. A question so fundamental ought to have been decided by now. In fact, the ambiguity is not just a matter of different points of view about the European Union, but an ambiguity within the relationship between the Union and its member states. Governments themselves create ambiguity about where the power to make decisions lies. And in creating that ambiguity, it becomes a reality. Investing authority in the European Union is a self-fulfilling policy. The alienation of political power into an institution that stands over and above the states creates that power. Therein lies the truth and the limits of the constructivist perspective on the European Union. It is not the inter-subjective relations between states, but their retreat from their subjectivity that calls the Union into being. Realists are right to see the relations between governments as the driving force behind the Union, but they fail to see that those governments are acting less and less like power-maximisers, more and more like power-shirkers.

One nation that did not have to change so much to get used to the new European politics was Germany – because it had been used to negotiating its sovereign interests with its neighbours throughout the preceding cold war era.

From German question to German answer

In 1990, the British Cabinet retired to Chequers for a weekend conference on the impending reunification of Germany. The discussion was not a happy one. On another occasion, Mrs Thatcher grabbed the (Communist dictator in Poland) General Jaruzelski 'by the buttons of my jacket and said to me very urgently, "We cannot allow German reunification! You have to protest against it very loudly!"' According to Thatcher, reunification presented 'a new and different kind of "German Question".'[36]

The British Cabinet was drawing on a theory of history that characterised a distinctively 'German Problem'. 'Internationally, a united Germany is often said to have been too big and and dynamic for any stable European state system' summarises

Calleo: 'Inevitably such a Germany threatened the political independence and economic well-being of its neighbours.'[37] The view that Germany, with its late development and lack of colonies, was a potentially disruptive force were held by British and European statesmen since the unification of the German principalities in 1871. Before the Second World War, the German Problem was characterised by E.H. Carr as a version of the challenge of the 'have-not' or 'dissatisfied Powers'.[38] During the war, understandably, the view that Germany was a pathologically dangerous nation featured heavily in allied propaganda. Carr's moderate version of the argument ran like this:

> If we are to solve the German problem, we must at least understand the state of mind, not of a few Nazi fanatics, but of nearly all intelligent Germans who concern themselves with international politics; and instead of being content to attribute this state of mind to the innate perversity of the German character, we must trace it back to the historical conditions out of which it has grown.[39]

After the Second World War, the allied administration oversaw German reconstruction on the basis that popular sovereignty was a potential danger, and helped create political institutions in the West that introduced many of what American constitutional theorists called 'checks and balances' to limit the 'tyranny of democracy'. 'Germany was explicitly created as a wherhafte Demokratie (defensive democracy), one with structures designed to "protect the Germans from themselves".'[40] The important structures were the German Constitutional Court, the Presidency, The Bundestag, the Länder and the Bundesbank. The Constitutional Court is part of the judiciary and stands above any elected institution with powers to strike down legislation passed by the Bundestag. Unlike France and the UK 'the German Constitutional Court does serve as a formidable check on governmental action'.[41]

It was the Constitutional Court that outlawed the Communist Party in Germany (1956), and sanctioned laws against radical civil servants (the Anti-Radical Decree of 1972). As discussed, the Bundesbank (as it is now called) is also independent. And regional political power is devolved among the Länder. The Presidency is apolitical. These structures were drawn up under allied leadership, but they were not without support from the populace. Peter Pulzer recounts that 'the experience of National Socialism had merely heightened disgust with all politics' and 'Hitler, many Germans thought, was not so much the antithesis of democracy as the product of its excesses'. According to Pulzer 'what Germans longed for was a return to privacy, family, inner peace and public morality'.[42] Throughout the 1950s and into the 1960s, German national aspirations were sublimated into economic success.

As well as limits upon popular sovereignty at home, West Germany was limited in its rights of sovereignty abroad. The clearest demonstration of that was the continued presence of the Four Power military command in Berlin and the division of the country. Beyond that West Germany was slowly allowed to make agreements worldwide that implied recognition from Israel, other west European countries, then east Europe. West Germany rejected non-alignment as a way of negotiating the Cold War, but chose instead multilateralism – 'a reflexive support for an exaggerated multilateralism' according to Jeffery Anderson.[43] In chancellor Helmut Schmidt's 1977 comment 'Germany did not want to be in the front row' in international policy initiatives. As Keith Middlemas explains, Germany's federal constitution worked against independent action, and the Chancelry could only be induced to act under the initiative of either the European Community, or, as was often the case, France: 'The principal weakness of this complicated, decentralised policy-making was that it disguised Germany's latent strength' – which was, Middlemas adds in parenthesis, 'paradoxically, German politicians' intention'.[44]

The Basic Law forbade Germany from sending troops beyond its borders (until it was changed on 16 October 1998).[45] A prejudice against military power definitely became a part of the German outlook.[46] Among the NATO powers Germany was again seen as somehow deficient, only now it was Germany's reluctance to fight that was seen as the problem. Mrs Thatcher even managed to connect the previous German problem, with an 'always present tendency to German neutralism' in the face of the perceived Soviet threat.[47]

The special characteristics of the German state were at times seen as a barrier. In the Historians' debate over German national identity in the 1980s some right wing historians, like Joachim Fest argued that the country's exaggerated pacifism was an unwarranted reaction to a past that it should not be so apologetic about, and in its own way left the country still prisoner of the Nazi experience.[48] Germany was an economic giant but a political midget. But as it turned out Fest misjudged the German mood. Germans did not see Germany's distinctive institutions as problematic, but positive.

What is more, those distinctive German institutions were a model for Europe. Following Thomas Mann's dictum, German political leaders after the war looked forward less to a German Europe than a European Germany. 'Our Basic Law obligated us to serve world peace in a unified Europe; we were therefore committed to the politics of responsibility, rather than to power politics'.[49] Rejecting power politics, successive German Foreign Ministers have rejected German unilateralism, too. When Germany's opposition to American policy in Iraq raised the question was this a new 'German Way' Joschka Fischer was quick to disabuse reporters of any misunderstanding:

No. That's nothing. Forget about it. Forget about a German way.[50]

More remarkably, perhaps, Germany's Chancellor Kohl made an agreement with President Mitterrand to accept a single currency (ahead of economic policy coordination that the Bundesbank had demanded) in exchange for France's support for reunification. This was widely understood as a policy of tying the newly independent Germany into the European Union. Peter Katzenstein posed the question that troubles scholars, especially of the realist school when looking at Germany: 'Why does Germany, the most powerful state in Europe, appear bent on giving up its newly won sovereign power?' Katzenstein's answer is telling. He sees 'a deeper transformation in both the style and substance of German *and European* politics'.[51] In other words, those institutional limitations on sovereignty and power politics abroad, and upon popular sovereignty at home, we should add, became paradigmatic for Europe.

Within Europe, the predisposition to multilateralism, the pursuit of 'soft power', the independence of the Central Bank, the pre-eminence of the Constitutional Court all in time became models for European policies and institutions; in Germany, the diffusion of power among the different branches of Government put a much greater stress upon consensus-building than upon all-out victory in party political debate – and this method is also the model for Europe's 'codetermination' of policy between the Commission, Council and Parliament; furthermore the displacement of ambitions from national pride to economic success, the turning away from public life to the private and domestic sphere, that marked West Germany in its formative, post-war years, also became the norm with which the rest of Europe caught up. A criticism made of Germany was that it was an economic giant, but a political pygmy – while other European powers, Britain and France, were political giants but economic pygmies. The way that the proposition was posed it seemed that Germany would have to change, and assume greater political authority, in line with its economic influence. But in time it has become clear that Germany's preference for moderating its own political influence under multilateralism was not a pathological weakness that put her outside the norm. On the contrary, today, it is British and French pride that seems to be out of step. Germany's diplomatic modesty is not an exception, but the emerging norm. Instead of being a *question* or a *problem* that tasked Europe, Germany had become an *answer* and a *solution* for Europeans. Pointedly, Germany is of all states most at home in the European Union, because the European Union is most like the apolitical post-war Germany that the allies constructed.

In most European Union institutions, consensus-building is the norm. The Commission operates to the rule of collegiality. The parliament is among the least combative of elected assemblies. Technical expertise generally over-rides political position-mongering. Those forums are shaped by the fact that they are removed from the hotter issues of national politics. One European institution, though, stands out. The European Council, where leaders meet is marked by some bitter clashes. Those clashes themselves, paradoxically, are a sign of the declining importance of national interests.

Grand-standing on the world stage – a sublimation of national projection

In the 1990s, with their domestic authority in decline, many world leaders found new purpose in international grand-standing. United Nations peace-keeping (and later peace-making) operations were used by politicians to reinvigorate the sense of mission that their home policy lacked. These were *performances* of national grandeur, avowedly and apparently divorced from national interest. It was a trend that was bound to impact upon the European Union, and in particular the European Council, where leaders met.

Western leaders organise photocalls in refugee camps and amongst troops regularly. John Major remembered his talk to the troops in Iraq as 'pure theatre',[52] while Boutros Boutros-Ghali caught Bill Clinton closely studying 'to learn Aristide's secret of electrifying the crowd' at his inauguration as president of Haiti, which 'the White House wanted to make an American victory celebration'.[53] In 1992 an ailing President Mitterrand had himself helicoptered into Sarajevo to break the Serb blockade of the airport. At the Senkovec Refugee Camp in Kosovo in May 1999 Tony Blair trumpeted 'this is not a battle for NATO, this is not a battle for territory, this is a battle for humanity'. Early in the Bosnia crisis, UN Secretary General Boutros Boutros-Ghali was moved to complain that the Security Council 'is becoming more like the General Assembly: it is making demands that it knows cannot be implemented'.[54] Increasingly the permanent members of the Security Council were striking propagandistic poses rather than practical policies.

What was marked about the discussion of the new humanitarian interventionism was the way that western leaders foreswore national interests in favour of a greater moral mission. Michael Ignatieff, the Foucault-scholar turned politician worried a great deal about the motivations behind the new humanitarian politics. 'When policy was driven by moral motives it was often driven by narcissism' he wrote: 'We intervened not only to save others, but to save ourselves, or rather an image of ourselves as defenders of universal values.'[55] Political leaders were finding a new sense of their worth on the international stage.

The trend among world leaders to grand-standing was not only seen in the great humanitarian disasters. The number and frequency of international summits grew markedly in the 1990s. The Group of Seven (originally created to deal with the economic challenges of the 1970s) expanded to include Russia (G 8) before a parallel Group of Twenty was pulled together in 1999.[56] Interviewing Prime Minister, Gordon Brown, at the nadir of his domestic political crisis in 2009 Katherine Viner says 'he sees his trials in a global context (perhaps so they seem less to do with him): "Every government in the world is having trouble."'.[57] Summits create the appearance of political action for leaders who are uncertain about the way ahead.

Other international forums, like the Davos meeting of business leaders also gained greater interest and attendance. The meetings of the United Nations Security Council in 2002 were also an occasion when French, German, British, Russian and American leaders indulged in some remarkable grand-standing – striking postures on the attitude towards the situation in Iraq that were addressed as much to domestic audiences as they were to the problem in hand. The striking thing, though, was that each of those leaders were struggling with a real problem of disconnect from their own electorates, which influenced their diplomatic gambits.

For the European leaders, the round of European Council summits were also part of the round of international meetings that show-cased their status as world players. Michael Franklin at the Royal Institute of International Affairs, had already mocked the idea that Britain could hang onto its sovereignty over economic conditions, counselling instead that it would make more sense to defend the distinctiveness of the British way of life, or her cultural identity:

No amount of explanation that there is nothing new in sharing of sovereignty with other countries has removed the feeling that national control has been lost. No amount of recognition that the watershed was passed when Britain formally joined the Community has reconciled some people to the past. It has only made them more determined to resist further erosion. No amount of ridicule at the fact that the British are clinging to the shadow of Sovereignty (e.g. over exchange rates) when economic realities leave them with no option has changed political attitudes, at least in some quarters. No attempt to differentiate the question of sovereignty from that of cultural identity has so far been successful in dispelling the myth that a further pooling of sovereignty in the EC will mean the suppression of the British way of life with all its distinctiveness.[58]

What Franklin could not, perhaps, have guessed, is that the pursuit of cultural identity, or the British way of life, might be even more aggressive than the defence of sovereignty, just because it is a performance, unrestrained by material interests. The moral style of political posturing has been very destructive to the European Council. At the 2002 Brussels summit, Tony Blair's point that France's support for farm subsidies discriminated against African producers was understood by Jacques Chirac as personal allegation of racism that led to a cancellation of future Anglo-French summits.

On the other hand, the growing importance of international summitry has also enhanced the status of the European Union leaders' summits. European leaders whose domestic problems seem intractable and unrewarding can find a greater feeling of importance at the photo-calls and press conferences that follow the European Council meetings. European leaders, who derive proportionately less authority from their voting publics, can find more succour in their relations to one another. In each other's company, European leaders find a degree of respect that their angry electorates are less willing to give. Speaking to an Italian magazine, Cherie Blair, partner to the British Prime Minister, recalled her 2004 holiday with Silvio Berlusconi: 'I have never had an evening like the one I had in Sardinia,' she said. 'Fireworks lit up the words "Viva Tony", and we all sang Summertime together.' She also spoke with pride of the 'friendship and trust' that existed between Blair and Berlusconi.[59]

Those federalist champions of European integration that anticipated the European Commission would continue to grow in importance, while the European Council, where member states' leaders meet would carry less weight have been surprised that the movement has rather been in the opposite direction since the Maastricht Treaty of 1993. What perhaps they did not anticipate was that the national leaders would grow more attached to their European forum, as their own domestic polities got to be less rewarding arenas.

CHAPTER FOUR

The Domestic Allies of European Integration

For many non-state actors, the European Union became a focus of activity, especially when they came up against the limitations of the national arena. Here we look at some examples of the way that non-state actors became increasingly focussed upon the European Union as a field for self-assertion, where national government proved to be intractable. Fundamentally this is a story of the failure of national polities to integrate alternative voices, but one that has the effect of pushing forward European integration.

The Italian left

The Communist Party was a strong competitor for power in Italy throughout much of the twentieth century. Where trade unions were more likely to be affiliated to the social democratic parties in northern Europe, southern European labour unions, where they were legal, often were close to the communists. Southern European workers' support for mass communist parties gave those parties much greater legitimacy than in the north. A record of wartime involvement in resistance groups put many communists close to political power in the aftermath of the Axis collapse – and they became an important source of authority. On the other hand, the stabilisation of market societies and liberal democracies under US leadership prevented communists from coming to power. The growing tension between the North Atlantic Treaty Organisation and the Warsaw Pact nations – the cold war – put communists in the position of 'traitors' in mainstream ideology. The most successful of the west European communist parties was the Italian. Italian communists' electoral success, their substantial presence in the Chamber of Deputies, and success in many city administrations made them a power in the land. Despite their considerable social weight, the Italian communists never managed to win power, failing to secure a majority in parliament, which was dominated throughout the post-war period by the Christian Democrats.

Hostility to the prospect of an Italian communist victory among the western powers was marked. US ambassador Clare Booth Luce had worked hard to undermine communist influence in the 1950s. On April 13, 1976, fearing that the Italian Communist Party might be invited to take office in a coalition ministry, Secretary of State Henry Kissinger publicly declared – just nine weeks before the coming Italian elections that the US would 'not welcome' a communist role in the government of Italy.[1] Daniele Ganser uncovered the extent of clandestine, paramilitary operations – 'operation Gladio' – conducted against the Italian left, and there is strong evidence to suggest that security forces participated in terrorist acts to destabilise Italy in the 1970s, the 'strategy of tension'.[2]

Whatever clandestine pressures stood in the way of communist success in Italy, the party still failed to win enough popular support to take power. Distrust of the communists' affiliations to the Soviet Union, and doubts about their commitment to liberal democracy were a marked barrier for many traditionally minded Italians. The Communist Party made surprising assurances of its commitment to west European institutions, even promising that Italy would not pull out of the North Atlantic Treaty Organisation if they were elected. In their efforts to calm middle class fears, the party offered programmes of austerity and social conservatism in the 1970s, as well as successive, but refused, offers of a coalition government with the Christian Democrats (the 'historic compromise'). On the other hand, impatience with the party's moderate and gradualist approach created room for a more radical challenge from the left, with groups like *Lotta Continua* – and eventually terrorist groups like the Red Army Faction – taking militants from the communists. Despite decades of mobilisation, the party failed to meet its supporters' ambitions for a communist government in Italy, which in time took its toll on support and the membership. That was the context for the Communist Party's turn to Europe.

The Communist Party of the Soviet Union encouraged west European communist parties to take part in a pan-European conference in Berlin in 1976. If anything, the Soviet party was a moderating influence, counselling communists in Portugal not to jeopardise détente by challenging NATO. But the Spanish, French and Italian party leaders were increasingly strident in their claims for a distinctive west European path to socialism, committed to pluralism and multi-party democracy, which they called Euro-Communism. In June 1976 Italian General Secretary Enrico Berlinguer told television reporters that socialism could be built in the West:

> It is better to be in this area. This guarantees us the kind of socialism that we want, to be precise, socialism in liberty, socialism of a pluralist type.[3]

Berlinguer was reprimanded privately for favouring the western alliance over the East, but avoided the worst of the soviet party's criticisms of the 'Euro-Communist' deviation, which were directed instead at Spanish leader Santiago Carrillo. Still, 'Euro-Communism' was an attractive association, since it signalled to suspicious voters that the Italian communists were independent of Moscow's domination. In fact, the Soviet party supported Italy's continued membership of the European Economic Community, and of NATO, because it was seeking a policy of détente with the West, not confrontation. Still, the 'Euro-Communist' episode suggested to the Italian party that west European links could moderate the party's pro-Soviet image.

What was more, the European parliament was a venue where Italian communists could break out of the log-jammed Italian political scene. So on 16 November 1984, the party paper *l'Unita* reported that leader Alessandro Natta met leaders of the European left: Georges Marchais, PCF, Lionel Jospin PSF, Rudi Arndt (president European group) and other MEPs of the SPD.[4] Participation in the European Union would in time become a principle for the Italian Communists.

In 1984, General Secretary Alessandro Natta, chided the government for its unpatriotic failure to defend Italian capitalism in the European Community, arguing

the need that Italy becomes an active part of the European Community policy for a more consistent and strong defence of her particular interests and her particular prospects before the heavy pressure of the economic and financial manoeuvre of the major capitalist power.[5]

The European Community recommended itself to the Italian communists as a potential middle ground between East and West, where they could imagine a future that overcame the cold war divide. In 1977, Berlinguer saw a Europe that was 'neither anti-Soviet nor anti-American'.[6] According to his successor as General Secretary, Natta, European integration would help that independence. 'Within the complete respect of the Atlantic Alliance – of its geographic limits and its defensive aims – the European Community has an objective necessity of autonomy for the safeguard and affirmation of its particular interests and aims to be achieved through its political, economic and institutional integration'.[7]

Not only did the party invest the European Union with their ambitions for overcoming the cold war rigidities, they also imagined that it could help advance economic progress: 'The European Community can and should exercise an essential contribution in the process of reorganization at an international level of the structures of production, trade, consumption'. 'We do not adopt the litanies of Europessimism', Natta added.[8]

One factor that concentrated the communists' minds on the European Union was the impasse in the Italian parliament. 'The whole legislative mechanism is jammed', they reported.[9] It certainly was jammed for the communists, who had seen the Christian Democrats share power not with them, but with a resurgent Socialist Party under Bettino Craxi. The suspicion that the party was out of step with Italy's direction was growing.[10] Within two years, the party would be confronted with its greatest ideological challenge, as the soviet system in the U.S.S.R. collapsed. A distraction from the party's own problems was provided by the Mafia investigations in Palermo culminating in a trial in late 1987, which exposed extensive corruption.[11] In the minds of the Italian communists, their own difficulties, the political corruption and the political log-jam all came together: 'The democratic system is exposed to a process of erosion' they reported 'which is all the more penetrating and dangerous because of the discredit thrown onto the institutions and the weakness induced in them by the dishonourable practices of the government parties and the phenomena of corruption and degeneration.'[12] The Italian communists experienced their own crisis as the crisis of the political system as such: 'The political system and, more generally, the state, its institutions and powers are passing through a deep crisis', they reported.[13] The following year Natta announced that the party would change its name saying 'I was convinced that the more radical the break, the more it would be possible to save and recuperate the best elements of Italian communism'.[14] The communists' prognoses were not wholly unfounded: the political system was indeed on the verge of collapse – but it was their own party's precipitate decline, despite the name change – that began the ball rolling. Still, in 1996 the new Democratic Party of the Left would participate in a ruling coalition.

In 1988, though, the Communist Party was at a very low point. But just as its prospects in national politics were shrinking, the party's new General Secretary Achille Occhetto invested the supra-national European Union with an extraordinary potential for salvation:

> The elections for a new supra-national legislature will be an occasion of great importance for the European cause; no-one can underestimate the new phase in the process of European integration, a phase which may enable the European Community to boost its economic development, face up to its great social problems with decision, starting with its 16 million jobless, and become a more active and influential promoter of vast action for progress on the world scale ... it is inconceivable, and very dangerous to think of a single European market without a European social policy, coherent economic policies, a 'European Social Space', or a European central bank and currency. Above all it is rather risky to think of a process of European unification without a parliament having powers worthy of its great role.[15]

With a role in national government more elusive than ever, the communists identified much more closely with the European Union as a vehicle for progressive change. The economic nationalism that had been the party's economic programme in the seventies was forgotten. Perhaps looking at the experience of the French socialists, the Italian communists looked forward to success in Europe as a more viable alternative than national economic planning: 'Today, then, the true question is the question of the European left, a new European left, capable of guiding the processes of transformation in our modern society, beyond the pillars of Hercules of the old Keynesian compromise.'[16]

Indeed, the programmatic rethinking in the party, led them to invest even the European multi-nationals with progressive potential. Occhetto put it that 'the basic question is whether a united Europe must be the Europe of the peoples or of the Agnellis and the Berlusconis' – to which he might be assumed to answer the former, but instead he continued, pragmatically:

> if it must be the Europe of de-regulation, or of new, shared and practised rules ... only the left has the ideas and culture to face up to the question of the relationship between democratic power and economic-financial concentration in the new supranational dimension.[17]

Occhetto was not only prepared to abandon Italy's currency and economic sovereignty, but also to embrace de-regulation and economic-financial concentration, as long as there was a role for the left to act as moderator. In the long view it might seem that the death-throes of the Italian Communist Party are of little interest. But that would be to miss out on the important role that the Italian left would play in the Europeanisation of Italy, and the enhancement of the powers of the European Union.

The Party of the Democratic Left embraced another institutional challenge to the authority of the Italian parliament, the 'clean hands' investigation of corruption – so much so, in fact, that the Christian Democrats and the leader of the new *Forza Italia* party, Silvio Berlusconi, who were often its targets alleged that the investigation was in fact a communist conspiracy on the part of the 'Red Togas' (i.e. magistrates[18]).

As participants in Romano Prodi's Olive Tree coalition, the Party of the Democratic Left (PDS) delivered up organised labour's support for the European Monetary System, and the austerity measures to meet the criteria for membership. PDS leaders Massima D'Alema and Walter Veltroni gave Prodi 'their full support' while the left 'trade union leaders Sergio Cofferati of the CGIL, Sergio D'Antoni of the CSIL, Pietro Larizza of the

UIL, played an invaluable role in persuading their members to accept the austerity measures'.[19] Everybody understood that the struggle to persuade Italians to meet the conditions for membership of the European Monetary System was a great challenge. With the Italian communists support, the challenge was met.

Scottish nationalists

In June 2009 Scots polled said that they favoured continued membership of the United Kingdom over independence by 54 per cent to 38 per cent.[20] Since the 1707 Act of Union Scotland has been a part of the United Kingdom, and in that time national independence has never commanded a majority among the Scottish people. Under British rule, says Tom Nairn, 'Scottish civil society had advanced too far, too quickly': 'The new bourgeois classes inherited a socio-economic position in history vastly more favourable than that of any other fringe of backward nationality' and so they were 'not forced to turn to nationalism'.[21] Instead, national sentiment was redirected into demands for Home Rule and a literary revival in the early twentieth century. In 1934 a moderate Scottish National Party was formed to demand self-government within the British Empire, with the Duke of Montrose as its president.[22] The Scottish National Party in the 1950s had just 2000 members and little electoral success.[23] Under the 1998 Scotland Act, powers of self-government were devolved to a Scottish Parliament, and on 16 May 2006, Scottish National Party leader Alex Salmond, leading the largest party in the assembly, became first minister.

The rise of the Scottish National Party is intimately linked to the decline of the British Labour Party, which, by the 1960s had become the largest party in Scotland (eclipsed in England, the Liberal Party continued to be popular with radically minded Scots up until the 1950s). Scottish Nationalists scored early successes in the 1974 General Election, after the British

Government had been destabilised by a series of bruising and inconclusive results. Scottish National Party support peaked in 1977 at 36 per cent. A minority Labour government held a referendum on Scottish devolution in 1979, with a proviso that at least 40 per cent of the electorate must support the move, which in the end commanded a majority of votes cast, but only 32 per cent of all voters entitled, and so fell, leaving the Scottish National Party in disarray.

In my New Left-influenced household in London, there was some glee at the Scottish Nationalists' challenge to a shaky Labour establishment. But my grandfather took a different view. He identified with Britain, not Scotland. He escaped a farm labourer's life by training as an electrician at the Working Men's Institute, and got work on the electrification of Galloway, before working in munitions during the war, and for Imperial Chemicals Industries afterwards, where he rose to be foreman. When I asked him about the Scottish National Party's successes in 1974, his judgement was curt: 'Tartan Tories'. Like many Scots of his generation, John Paterson's loyalty was to an industrial, planned and modernising Britain.

Under four successive Conservative governments in the 1980s and 1990s, drawing their support from southern English constituencies, Scots were increasingly at odds with the Westminster parliament. The Scottish National Party mocked the 'feeble fifty' Scottish Labour MPs for their inability to challenge Westminster-imposed reforms, like the 'Poll Tax' (which was tried in Scotland one year before it was made law across the UK). The years of Conservative rule, when Scots' votes against the governing party were cancelled out by English votes, lent meaning to the demand for a devolved parliament. The Scottish Labour Party's urban and industrial base was in decline, and in 1988 the radical Jim Sillars took the Labour stronghold of Govan in a by-election. The Scottish National Party won three seats in the 1992 election putting more pressure on Labour's standing as the Scottish opposition to Westminster. Labour's 1997 election pledge to offer a referendum on a devolved parliament, developed in a Labour-led 'Constitutional Convention' was an attempt to take the wind from the Scottish National Party's sails.

In its 1970s rise the Scottish National Party was opposed to the European Economic Community, which it identified with distant and centralised rule over Scotland – a point made forcefully by chairman Billy Wolfe.[24] With half of the British fishing fleet based in Scotland, the Community's fishing quotas were very damaging, and the Scottish National Party fought a popular campaign against this Westminster-Brussels agreement that punished Scots. When in 1975 Breton, Welsh, Basque and Alsatian groups set up the Bureau of Unrepresented Nations to lobby for their interests in Brussels the Scottish National Party refused to join, thinking that these were marginal movements.[25]

Still, the European Parliamentary elections did give the Scottish National Party a forum to raise its profile, with Winnie Ewing taking a seat in 1979. Tom Nairn was 'impressed by the possibilities of the European Community ... as a nexus of support' for an independent Scotland,[26] and Jim Sillars won his fellow Scottish Nationalists over to participation in the Community. Part of the nationalists' thinking was that since Mrs Thatcher seemed so hostile to the Community, it must have some advantages. Most importantly, though, the new policy of 'Independence within the European Union' had a positive impact on the plausibility of the nationalists' programme. Under the heading 'What is Scottish independence?' in the party's manifesto we read

Independence in Europe means accepting the role and responsibilities of a Member State of the European Union, in which
independent states have pooled certain of their sovereign
rights for the common advantage. Sharing sovereignty in
Europe in this way enhances Scotland's sovereignty because it

increases our influence.[27]

Like the old Home Rule demand, the qualifying phrase 'within Europe' made the prospect of isolation from the United Kingdom a lot less alarming to wary Scots. In 1989 a poll in the *Glasgow Herald* found that 61 per cent of Scots thought that an independent Scotland would represent their interests in Europe better than Westminster could (14 April 1989) – though read closely, this is a vote of no-confidence in Westminster more than it is a positive endorsement of independence.

There were supporters of Scottish independence active in the European Union itself, like Ireland's Eamon Gallagher European Commission director-general and European Community ambassador to the United Nations, as well as an advisor to Jacques Delors. Gallagher argued 'there could be no sustainable legal or political objection to separate Scottish membership of the European Community'.[28] The policy of 'Independence in Europe' was adopted at the same time that Jacques Delors promised a Social Charter to moderate the market orientation of the European Community, which appealed more to the social democratic Scottish National Party than it did to the Conservative government in Westminster. As Michael Keating says 'the Community is now seen as a mechanism for circumventing a British state itself committed to political centralisation and economic liberalism'.[29]

Most of all, though, the European Union is attractive to the Scottish National Party because it offers a political escape from the party's own impasse. Without popular support for independence, the party has to perform a difficult balancing act, where it must offer the prospect of movement in that direction to its supporters, while calming the broader electorate's fears of isolation. 'Independence in Europe' meets just that demand. The Scottish National Party is trusted by Scots as champions of their interests because popular identification with Westminster failed

– a loss of legitimacy that comes about because the mainstream UK parties could no longer bind Scottish aspirations to the British state. The European Union's appeal to this national minority in the United Kingdom is that it is an alternative seat of power to Westminster.

The German greens

The most successful Green Party in Europe is Germany's. Its origins are closely tied up with the European Union, and in particular the European Parliament: The first major Green list (there was a precursor in Schwarmstedt) was pulled together in March 1979 to contest the first European parliamentary elections.[30] One of the key and founding members, Petra Kelly, had been working for the European Union. The new list's garnering of 3.2 per cent of West Germany's votes (about a million people) surprised everyone, and gave the new movement quite a kick start. The Green Party ran for the Bundestag in 1980 and again in 1983, when they had twenty-seven members elected.

The rise of the Green Party was intimately tied up with the fragmentation of support for the Social Democratic Party. Like many socialist parties, the German party struggled with its rebellious and radical middle class supporters, especially the young. But more than most, the German Social Democratic Party lost control of those radicals, many of whom left the party, some of whom were drawn to far left activism in the 1960s and 1970s. More than the British Labour Party or the French Socialist Party, the German Social Democratic Party was closely tied into the consensus structures of the German state, lending support to repressive measures that were difficult for its more radical supporters to take. Unlike other European social democratic parties, the S.P.D. was unable to contain its 'middle class anti-capitalist left' that broke off to join the Green Party.[31] These social democrat deserters made up one important constituency for the new party, in particular making up its activists and party officials and representatives. The success of the German Green Party, then, was the first major indication of the breakdown of the post-war consensus and its left-right political party system.

Carl Lankowski describes the dead-end of the party system as it would have seemed to the Green activists, as 'the freezing of the Left-Right political spectrum, and the narrowing of the universe of this political discourse around questions of distribution of the economic pie'.[32] This was the consensus that the Greens were trying to break down, moving outside the left-right spectrum, and raising demands about industrial society that challenged output rather than sought redistribution.

From the outset, the cultural practices and outlook of Germany's 1968 rebels shaped the Green Party's attitude to power. Their party was to be an 'Anti-Party Party' from the outset.[33] On entering the Bundestag, the party's representatives disrupted proceedings with protests, speaking out of turn and without deference to the established consensus-building norms. In 1984, with German electoral success under their belts the party contested the European parliamentary elections again. In keeping with their tactics in the Bundestag, the green candidates took a jaundiced view of the European Parliament and the European Community. Brigitte Heinrich said 'we should use this fake parliament lacking legislative and executive competences as a tribune for public relations work'. 'The current goals of the EC', she added 'are to be rejected'. Her colleague Jakob von Uexküll charged that 'this dinosaur is no longer capable of being reformed'.[34]

The content of the greens' rejection of the European Parliament were largely a rejection of the centralising tendencies of the European Community, which they shared with the regional parties with whom they had cooperated in 1979, under the slogan 'a Europe of the Regions'. There was too a criticism of the market orientation of the European Community, and of its regional dominance. Greens called the European Community a 'rich man's club', undemocratic, denounced its immigration policy as 'Fortress Europe' and its outlook as 'Eurocentric'.[35]

However, with their hands at least close to the levers of power in many regional parliaments, in the Bundestag and in the European Parliament, a growing divide between fundamentalists and realists tested the greens. Before the 1989 campaign Petra Kelly declared herself 'shocked at the debate on the European election', saying 'there was virtually no criticism of the E.E.C. or the internal market' and 'the emergence of Europe as a new superpower was barely touched on'. Kelly wondered whether instead of changing the structures of society 'maybe they've changed us'.[36] Still, some greens did belatedly react to a growing disquiet about the Maastricht Treaty with a document 'Maastricht: No Way!' Even that document, though, favoured European integration, and argued for a Green European Initiative to be added to the Treaty.

Green Party spokeswoman Petra Kelly

One reason for the changes in green policy towards the European Community was that the Community was very responsive to green initiatives. Green members of the European Parliament got a hearing for their warnings over the Chernobyl and Windscale nuclear accident, won increased European Community spending on renewable energy, got bans on growth hormones in beef, and exposed a nuclear waste scandal.[37] The European Community was in fact more responsive to the green agenda than many other more intractable political debates, because their novelty meant that the Commission could act in a way that did not disturb the balance of power in member states. The European stage proved to be an effective platform for green political initiatives at a time when the party was too small to exact substantial concessions from the ruling party in Germany, or to participate in government through coalition.

Another reason for the change in green policy towards European integration reflected a growing anxiety over the national question. Though the party was moving on Europe, the standing policy of opposition did lead them to support a legal challenge to the Maastricht Treaty before the German Constitutional Court, on the grounds that the treaty abrogated Germany's statehood under the Basic Law.[38] To the party's embarrassment, though, Germany's nationalist parties also challenged the treaty on the same grounds, and the court combined the suits, making greens and nationalists co-complainant's in the case. Though the court ruled that Germany – or rather the German Constitutional Court – had final say over the terms of the Treaty, the greens made no mention of their success in their campaign literature, apparently embarrassed by their nationalist bed-fellows.[39] Further anxieties over German nationalism would wholly transform the greens' attitude to Europe.

Just as the party was moving forward in Germany, it was seriously wrong-footed by the windfall unification of the country under Chancellor Kohl. Alone among the parties in the Bundestag, the greens opposed unification, recoiling from the popular euphoria over the emergence of 'One Nation'. It was a policy stance that saw their vote drop below the threshold for representation in the German parliament, leading to years back in the wilderness. Among leading greens, Joschka Fischer made a decisive programmatic intervention in his 1994 book *The German Risk*. There, Fischer gave voice to a backdrop of disquiet over reunification that had been running beneath the mood of optimism, particularly about the appearance of national triumphalism that the celebrations voiced. Fischer's qualms about the 're-nationalisation' of Germany were not unique to the greens. His solution, a policy innovation for the greens, was further European integration:

> Since unification, democratic Germany, with its position and its potential is one of the most powerful countries in Europe west of Russia, and therefore now has the chance to anchor itself in a united Europe. In doing so, it will finally and forever put to rest the dangers inherent in its precarious "middle position" in Europe and the temptation of nationalist aspirations.[40]

Fischer's biographer, who cites this passage, makes the point that it is in fact, wholly unexceptional from the standpoint of the German mainstream. Multilateralism was intrinsic to German national policy throughout the postwar years, and Thomas Mann's nostrum of 'a European Germany, not a German Europe' was Foreign Minister Hans-Dietrich Genscher's, too.[41] It was, however, novel to the greens, who at last had a principled reason to embrace an institution that was already peculiarly and seductively responsive to their agenda. And though Fischer was not the original author of the strategy of unification within Europe, he did lend that very traditional policy a new urgency among the radical wing of German democracy that might in other circumstances have taken issue with Chancellor Kohl's national and European strategy.

In time, Fischer himself became Foreign Minister, as a part of the first Red-Green coalition government led by social democrat Gerhard Schröder. The twin-track strategy of containing the spectre of German nationalism within multilateral organisations, and advancing Europe's concerted action led to the most remarkable change both in green and German policy. The green Foreign Minister, whose party had grown through the anti-war protests of the 1980s, sanctioned the first use of Bundewehr forces outside of Germany as part of the North Atlantic Treaty Organisation actions against the Federal Republic of Yugoslavia in 1999.

The German Green Party played a key role not just in re-directing radical opposition to Europe into fulsome support; it also laid the basis for Germany's military contribution to out-of-area operations, under the multilateralist policies that their Foreign Minister Joschka Fischer re-purposed.

The British trade unions

The core of British trades union leaders were staunchly opposed to the European Economic Community, and active in the 'No' campaign in the 1975 referendum. In the 1970s British unions refused their allotted seats on the European Economic Community's Economic and Social Committee (as the Labour Party refused its seats in the European Parliament[42]). In 1983, the trade union block vote in the Labour Party endorsed the manifesto commitment to pull the United Kingdom out of the European Union.[43] By 1987, the unions had seen their party defeated for a third time in succession, and had been turned away from their traditional welcome from government (there had been too much 'beer and sandwiches at number ten', Prime Minister Margaret Thatcher had told the Conservative Party conference on 12 October 1979).

In September 1988, the Trades Union Congress invited Commission President Jacques Delors to address them. 'It is impossible to build Europe only on deregulation' he said, and '1992 is much more than the creation of an internal market'. Delors offered Europe-wide protection for employees: 'It is necessary to improve workers' living and working conditions, and to provide better protection for their health and safety at work'.[44] He also said that social dialogue and collective bargaining were key pillars of a free society, which Prime Minister Margaret Thatcher took to mean that these would be enforced at the European level.[45] Delors charmed his hosts inviting them to join him as 'architects of Europe', and delegates responded by singing 'Frère Jacques'.

Conservative Oliver Letwin paraphrased Delors' appeal to the trade unionists: 'you have totally failed to defeat the Prime Minister in this country but you have an opportunity through Brussels and Strasbourg to bring in social legislation helpful to your cause'.[46] Prime Minister Thatcher in a speech at Bruges soon after said 'we have not successfully rolled back the frontiers of the state in Britain only to see them reimposed at a European level, with a European super-state exercising a new dominance from Brussels'.[47]

The impact of the appeal was a change for the Trades Union Congress, from a broadly anti-European to a broadly pro-European stance. In fact policy change over Europe was already being discussed that summer in the Labour Party. Under the pressure of its poor electoral performance, the party was reconsidering many of its most strongly-held attitudes. On 27 June 1988 the Labour Party's economic sub-committee was looking at proposals from John Eatwell, John Smith and Gordon Brown to join the European Monetary Union as a means of shoring up Britain's (and in proposing it the Labour Party's) reputation for economic rigour.[48] Following Delors' reception at the Trades Union Congress, Smith and Brown successfully pushed the party to adopt a broadly pro-European policy, *Looking to the Future*, in 1990.

The Maastricht Treaty of 1993 did indeed include a Social Chapter guaranteeing many rights for workers. The new Conservative leader, John Major, claiming excessive costs, but probably with more of an eye to his own party's voluble euro-sceptics, negotiated an 'opt-out' clause so that the Social Chapter was not enacted in Britain. Thereafter, adoption of the European Union's Social Chapter became a key demand of the British trade unions and the Labour Party, which the latter enacted in 1997.

Since then, trade union leaders have come to look askance on their easy conversion to European cheerleaders. In 2005, the Trades Union Congress passed a motion submitted by the Rail, Maritime and Transport union that applauded the rejection of the European Constitution, rejected 'the increasingly neo-liberal policies emanating from Brussels' (particularly the 'Directive on Services') and denounced a European agenda that was 'elitist, militarist, corporate and anti-democratic'. The Communist Party's *Morning Star* newspaper looked back over the pro-European era of the TUC caustically:

> It is no coincidence that the TUC embraced the then European commission president Jacques Delors and his social chapter in those demoralised years after the defeats of the 1983 general election, the Wapping dispute, the 1984-85 miners' strike ... Only when the trades unions and the left - including the communists - began to recover at the beginning of the 1990s did sections of the labour movement come out against the big business 'single European market' and the Maastricht Treaty.[49]

Perhaps Griffiths overstates the left's recovery, but he is surely right that the unions' turn to Europe was born of a sense of fatalism that saw all their options for success in national terms closing down. In real terms, the European Union did not have that much to offer trade unions, but the belief that there was another way, around the back of an intransigent national government certainly did appeal to them.

A 'bosses Europe'?

Many of the critics of the direction Europe took from the Single European Act through to the Maastricht Treaty and beyond complain that the Europe that has been built is a 'bosses Europe'. A consensus around neo-liberal economic policy has made

Europe a creature of 'corporate lobby groups'.[50] Bastiaan van Apeldoorn focuses on the European Round Table of Industrialists as 'an elite forum of an emergent transnational class'.[51] Balanyá and his collaborators show that the European Round Table was the forum where the outline proposal for the single European market were put together, and that the organisation effectively wrote the first draft of Lord Cockfield's white paper announcing it.[52] The image of the hidden hand of big business behind Europe's market-driven unification was a strong element in the No campaigns in the referenda on the European Consitution. Understandably, the recent fiscal crisis and the determination of the European Commission to impose austerity on southern European economies lends weight to the view that the European Union is principally a big business project. Marxist economist Costas Lapavitsas and his collaborators in the Research on Money and Finance Group based at the School of Oriental and African Studies argue that 'the coordination and diffusion of neoliberal policies have consistently been at the core of the project, especially after its relaunching with the Single European Act'.[53]

There is of course little doubt that business lobbies like the European Round Table and the Union of Industrial and Employers' Confederations of Europe played a much greater role in European policy making from 1983 onwards. That much, though, is not evidence that the European Union is a project of big business. We could look at the question the other way around. What was it that led the European Commissioners to put so much faith in business lobbies? After all, that was hardly a trend that was unique to them. Rather, opening up government to input from business expertise and even bringing business into government is a well-entrenched trend.[54] It is less a sign of the big business' taking over Europe than the decline in political self-confidence. The emerging consensus on liberalisation measures was not so much a positive pro-business case as the lowest common denominator emerging between west European states in the second half of the 1980s. Uncertain of their own ability to map out a future strategy, the European Commissioners invested the business leaders European Round Table with great insight. The Round Table was influential by default – other actors, labour organisations, national policy makers, has all been defeated leaving the business lobby the last man standing. That did not mean, though, that the European Round Table was anything like a nascent transnational class. On the contrary. Its members were influenced by political considerations as much as they were by business ones.[55]

Maria Green Cowles talked to German business leaders about their attitudes to the Maastricht Treaty:

'the handful of German companies that did publicly support the 1992 project did so primarily for non-economic reasons. They did not tout the Single Market program as an important means to liberalise the market. Rather the firms endorsed the European project on political grounds – they wanted to assure their industrial colleagues that German companies were "good Europeans" and committed to further integration'.[56]

Keith Middlemas makes a similar point when he says that the European Round Table 'became animators, adjuncts to, rather than initiators of change'.[57]

The ideology of trade liberalisation in Europe should be taken with a pinch of salt. Managed liberalisation was used to reduce capacity in some industries, and to force the pace of restructuring in others. But European capitalism's addiction to government support did not end in the 1980s. Since privatisation, British Aerospace got government subsidies of £500m from the purchase of British Ordnance in 1986, and a further £600m the following year with its purchase of Rover followed by £700m government support for the European Airbus project.

Olympia and York got subsidies of £3.8 billion for their renovation of the prestige Canary Wharf project.[58] In 1988 the Bank of England coordinated a bail-out for the discredited Bank of Credit and Commerce International (BCCI). In 1992 Spanish airline Iberia Pta 120 billion government subsidy was approved by the European Commission on condition no more cash was given, but in 1995 the Spanish government gave a further Pta 130 billion. In 1996 the Commission approved a Pta 225 billion subsidy to the Spanish coal industry.[59] In 2004 it was revealed that amongst the biggest recipients of Common Agricultural Policy aid were not small farmers, but conglomerates like Tate and Lyle (£227 million) and Dutch airline KLM whose runway qualified as 'rural restructuring'.[60]

National governments continue to promote national champions, like France's support for Sanofi's purchase of pharmaceutical giant Aventis in 2004, or the German government's support for the Kirchgruppe in the face of a takeover bids from Rupert Murdoch and Silvio Berlusconi. Germany continues to protect Deutsche Telekom's monopolistic rights to the 'last mile', and to Deutsche Post's monopoly over letters.

National governments insist on their right to build up national capacity, irrespective of commitments to cut back. Three years into the New Labour administration, chancellor Gordon Brown threw off the sack-cloth and ashes of 'Tory spending plans' to grow the public sector from 38 to 42 per cent of GDP, so that nearly a third of growth was public sector growth[61] and in some regions of Britain government spending approached three quarters of output.[62] Germany, too, having insisted on a 'Stability Pact' to constrain EU spending, was the country that wrecked it, effectively claiming that its needs were distinctive, and that the EU needed Germany too much to object. Commission President Romano Prodi was mocked for dismissing the stability pact as 'stupid, like all rigid decisions'.

Business did back the European project. And business has welcomed the Commission's new determination to shift the costs of economic crisis onto the mass of working Europeans. Pointedly, though, business leaders embraced the European Union project for similar reasons to those that moved those other non-state allies of the Commission. It was the exhaustion of nationally-based strategies for business growth that led businesses to support the consolidation of the internal market in Europe. Weakness, rather than strength lay behind the business leaders' embrace of the European project.[63] Lapavitsas' rightly makes the point that over and above the neoliberal consensus among European players, 'insulation from any form of popular control and accountability is the founding logic of all the complex nexus of technocratic and expert-staffed agencies which form the backbone of the EU institutions'.[64]

CHAPTER FIVE

The Developing Institutions of the European Union

Parallel to the trend towards apolitical administration within European Community member states, there is a trend towards apolitical administration in the European Community itself. The European Union, writes Vivien Schmidt 'makes policy without politics'.[1] We can say that the contemporary institutions of the European Community are themselves an expression of that tendency towards apolitical administration (though their prehistory is somewhat different). Here we look at the Commission, the European Council – using the particular example of 'benchmarking' – and the growing bureaucratic machinery the Union has created. Lastly we will look at some of the problems that the depoliticisation of the institutions of the European Union have generated.

The forward momentum of the Delors Commission

The Commission was originally conceived of as a streamlined bureaucracy so that it would not reproduce the efforts of national civil servants, who are generally expected to action EU directives. Even today it only employs 44,554 staff.[2] The Commission was always intended more as a super civil service than a political directory. Asked who should be proposed as commissioners from France, de Gaulle offered the telling advice 'send the most stupid', meaning that it would be better if the commission was not so talented that it would become a challenge to the authority of national politicians.[3] For years the Commission was a graveyard for politicians who, if not exactly stupid, were at the end of their careers, rather than the beginning. Right back to its beginning, in fact, when Paul Henri Spaak's 'own personal

1) Jacques Delors
2) David Williamson ~~~~~~~~~~~~~
3) Peter Schmidhuber
4) Martin Bangemann
5) Vasso Papandréou
6) Sir Leon Brittan
7) Filippo Maria Pandolfi
8) Abel Matutes
9) Manuel Marín

10) Frans Andriessen
11) Carlo Ripa di Meana
12) Christiane Scrivener
13) Jean Dondelinger
14) Karel van Miert
15) Ray Mac Sharry
16) Bruce Millan
17) António Cardoso e Cunha
18) Henning Christophersen

The Delors Commission pushed European integration
forward, 1989-93

situation had changed' (he was voted out of government in
Belgium): 'The idea of presiding over an international body
whose task it would be to create a united Europe appealed to
me'.[4] Indeed the Commission of the European Economic
Community had less authority to overrule national governments
than the High Commission of the European Coal and Steel
Community.[5] Even Jean Monnet advised leaders to 'always
choose the path of least resistance.'[6]

It would be tempting to see the Commission as the institutional expression of the priority of process over sovereignty. In
some respects, it is. It is the Commission that most clearly insti-
tutionalises the non-national perspective in its oath:

To perform my duties in complete independence, in the general interests of the communities; in carrying out my duties, neither to seek nor to take instruction from any government or body; to refrain from any action incompatible with my duties.

Of course the oath is honoured as much in the breach as the observance. In 2004, when commission president Romano Prodi proposed an end to the rebate negotiated by Mrs Thatcher in 1980 he faced 'strong opposition from Chris Patten and Neil Kinnock, the two UK commissioners, who have lobbied forcefully against the proposal to axe the national rebate'. Patten used a traditional formula to represent national interests as community interests when he said 'these proposals will set back our ability to argue a positive European case in the UK'.[7]

As we have seen, under Jacques Delors the Commission found a new forward momentum, pulled forward by the vacuum left as national governments grappled with a loss of legitimacy. A poll of Commission civil servants in 2000 found 91 per cent thought the Commission's influence on the integration process very high.[8] It should be said, though, that this forward momentum also changed the character of the Commission.

The push behind the Delors commission made him look like the master of events and even lent him greater élan than he might otherwise have enjoyed. But in fact the Commission is characteristically even less in charge of events than national governments. The forward momentum of 'ever deeper union' is something of an illusion. In Pascal Lamy's phrase, the Union is like a bicycle, 'if you don't keep going forward, you fall off'.[9] By 1994 and the setting up of the reflection group at the Corfu European Council 'Europe had gone through the Maastricht ratification crisis and onto its "reform treadmill",' argue Christiansen and Reh: 'leadership and audacity were lacking; and change appeared necessary for reasons of internal crisis rather than historical opportunity'.[10] The complexity, and indecision, at the heart of the 'integration process' is borne out by the constant generation of new terms 'Asymmetrical integration, opt-outs, the pillar structure of the Treaty, plans for a multi-speed Europe, the "regatta approach" to enlargement'[11] – and you might add 'flexible geometry' to the list.

Inter-governmentalists like Andrew Moravcsik explain the loss of momentum in the integration process quite simply. The teleology of 'ever closer union' is an illusion, or an overhasty generalisation from a series of discrete treaty decisions on the part of national governments, which in no sense imply that the series must continue. But as we have seen, there is a demiurge behind the integration process, and that is the retreat from national sovereignty.

When both Britain and Italy were forced out of Exchange Rate Mechanism in 1993, American finance writer Gregory Millman boasted that the 'ERM was decisively vanquished by specu-lators'.[12] Japanese journalist Noriko Hama wrote a series of apocalyptic articles for the *Mainichi Economist,* published in a collection entitled *Disintegrating Europe: The Twilight of the European Construction* in 1996. Her report of the pessimism towards European institutions was accurate. On top of frustration over the Exchange Rate Mechanism and the high German interest rate came political opposition to the Maastricht Treaty - rejected in a referendum by the Danes in June 1992, and only narrowly supported by the French. 'Since the signing of the Maastricht treaty', wrote Stephen Tindale of the British Institute for Public Policy Research, 'the European project has faced its most severe crisis'.[13]

Most impressively, however, the Commission took the failures of 1993 as reasons for further integration, not retreat, culminating in the launch of the single currency in 1999. While Euro-sceptics were organising the funeral, the integrationists only assumed that the Exchange Rate Mechanism's collapse demonstrated the rightness of their cause:

> The significance of this episode lies in the fact that the international capital markets were effectively able to subvert the policies of democratically elected governments in major European countries, despite all the tools and resources available to national governments and despite the monetary cooperation between European countries that had been developed on an inter-governmental basis and through the EU. *This would suggest that there are severe limits to the economic sovereignty of European nation states in the late twentieth century.*[14]

According to former commissioner Leon Brittan, policy makers in the United States 'were slow to believe that it [monetary union] would ever happen'. 'Perhaps the US had been paying too much attention to the sceptical attitude of their junior British partner', he added.[15] That is as maybe, but overall the sceptics had made the mistake of thinking that it was the European Union that would pay the price for policy incoherence. In fact, it was the nation states that lacked a solution, and so the Union expanded to fill that vacuum.

What monetary union did was to put politicians out of business. Robert Mundell, the 'Chicago School' economist who helped push the Euro explained 'It puts monetary policy out of the reach of politicians,' and 'Monetary discipline forces fiscal discipline on the politicians as well.'[16]

One arena in which national leaders did forcefully set the agenda was the European Council, and so we turn to look at its role.

The European Council, post-Maastricht
The 1993 Maastricht Treaty changed the balance of power in the European Community, by giving the initiative to the European

Council. The treaty created the European Union, which combines the European Community with the additional 'pillars' of Justice and Home Affairs and the Common Foreign Security Policy. With the addition of these politically sensitive policy areas, the member states of the new European Union demanded a greater say in the formulation of policy. The institutionalisation of the European Council as the policy-making body of the European Union followed.

To many inter-governmentalists, the enhanced role of the European Council seems to confirm their claim that at heart, nation states determine the direction of the European Union, which remains fundamentally a treaty-based organisation. Some supporters of a more federalist European Union were disappointed by what seemed to them to be a backward step, a return to the priority of national egotism. However, that would be to misunderstand the way that the governments represented in the European Council have adopted the post-national methods and outlook pioneered by the European Commission. As SciencesPo Professor Chris Bickerton explains there is not a return to nation state implied in the European Union, but rather a new kind of entity, the 'member state', that draws its authority from an external sources, namely the Union itself.[17] The European Union did not just change to reflect the outlook of the member states, the member states have also changed in their attitude to sovereign claims as popular participation in their own polities has declined.

In practice, the work of the European Council is prepared by the Committee of Permanent Representatives (Coprepor) senior national officials with the status of ambassadors that meet in Brussels around five times a week. Around ninety per cent of European Union legislation passes through Coprepor.[18] Coprepor's deliberations are secret, and its documents are classed as 'non-papers' to exempt them from the European Union's open access to documents rule.

The European Council's deliberations are also secret, and shorthand minutes, known as 'Antici' minutes are also exempt, classified as diplomatic and therefore state secrets. The final Communique is the only open official record of the European Council's deliberations.

The historian, and sometime *New Left Review* editor, Perry Anderson drew out the apolitical character of these secret negotiations.

> What the trinity of Council, Coreper and Commission figures is not just an absence of democracy – it is certainly also that – but an attenuation of politics of any kind, as ordinarily understood. The effect of this axis is to short-circuit – above all at the critical Coreper level – national legislatures that are continually confronted with a mass of decisions over which they lack any oversight.[19]

The European Council system, then, normalizes the removal of policy from national legislatures and gives institutional form to the retreat from popular sovereignty. More than that, in the manner of their deliberations, the European Council, and Coprepor put such a value on consensus that sovereign ambitions are profoundly moderated, and 'depoliticised'. Anderson gives a cutting description that properly draws out the evacuation of political differences in the methods of the European Council and wider European Union structures:

> In the disinfected universe of the EU ... any public disagreement, let alone refusal to accept a prefabricated consensus, [is] increasingly being treated as if it were an unthinkable breach of etiquette. The deadly conformism of EU summits, smugly celebrated by theorists of "consociational democracy", as if this were anything other than a cartel of self-protective elites, closes the coffin of even real diplomacy,

covering it with wreaths of bureaucratic piety. Nothing is left to move the popular will, as democratic participation and political imagination are each snuffed out.[20]

This is the point made by Glarbo when he talks about the 'socialisation' among European leaders.[21] Andrew Moravcsik, taking issue with Anderson puts a rather different interpretation on the deliberations of the European Council. It is not, he says, that European publics are excluded from the debate over Europe's future, but that they are not interested in it: 'the transcendence of the nation state …today has turned out to be the project of boring bourgeois elites, not the proletarian masses'.[22]

The post-structuralist philosopher Louis Althusser's concept of a 'process without a subject' seems a rather apposite description of the working of the European Union. 'History', writes Althusser, groping for an account that will not enthrone any singular principle, ' "asserts itself" through the multiform world of the superstructures, from local tradition to international circumstances'.[23] Althusser wrote of a 'parallelogram of forces', which 'does not correspond to the consciousness of each will – and at the same time it is a force without a subject, an objective force, but from the outset, nobody's force'.[24] Sharing not much of Althusser's intellectual tradition, the historian Keith Middlemas nonethless sums up the European Union in a rather similar phrase: 'a political system without a prime mover'.[25] Antonio Negri, who collaborated with Althusser embraces Althusser's critique of the subject in *Empire*. There he formulates a conception of 'Empire', as distinct from the imperialism of nation states:

The Passage to Empire emerges from the twilight of modern nation sovereignty. In contrast to Imperialism, Empire establishes no territorial centre of power … it is a decentred and deterritorializing apparatus of rule that progressively incorporates the entire global realm...[26]

Negri's 'decentred and territorializing apparatus of rule' does seem like a good description of the dynamic behind the European Union, as does Althusser's 'multiform world of superstructures' or 'parallelogram of forces'. These are all attempts to account for history as a process without a subject, and as such, they chime with a European Union, carried forward, as it is, by the retreat from responsibility on the part of sovereign states.

One example of the way that the European Council has developed an apolitical system of administrative convergence is the Open Method of Coordination, or 'bench-marking' adopted at the Lisbon Council in 2000.

Apolitical integration: 'benchmarking'

As much as possible, the process of policy integration has been rendered apolitical. One example of that depoliticisation of administration is the process known as 'bench-marking' adopted by the European Council in 2000.

In 1994 the European Round Table of Industrialists published a document called 'Benchmarking for Policy-Makers' which identified 'benchmarking' as a means of integrating policy. The urgency behind policy integration was that without uniformity nations would be effectively bidding against each other in trying to make their legislations most welcoming to business: 'Government must recognise that every economic and social system in the world is competing with all the others to attract the footloose business'. The Round Table understood that the Commission did not really have the authority to impose uniformity, so they proposed the business tool of benchmarking as an alternative: 'at a time when the European Model of Society is experiencing some difficulties and change may be perceived as painful, the role of symbols in mobilising human effort may become more important, and benchmarking can be part of this.'

According to the Round Table 'benchmarking is not just an analytic device' but 'carries a symbolic message'.[27]

The European Council adopted 'benchmarking' as part of the new 'Open Method of Coordination' at the 2000 Lisbon Council: 'Implementation of the strategic goal will be facilitated by applying a new open method of coordination as the means of spreading best practice and achieving greater convergence towards the main EU goals'

- fixing guidelines for the Union combined with specific timetables for achieving the goals which they set in the short, medium and long terms;
- establishing, where appropriate, quantitative and qualitative indicators and benchmarks against the best in the world and tailored to the needs of different Member States and sectors as a means of comparing best practice;
- translating these European guidelines into national and regional policies by setting specific targets and adopting measures, taking into account national and regional differences;
- periodic monitoring, evaluation and peer review organised as mutual learning processes.[28]

The meaning of this curious management-speak is that the formulation of policies has been removed from the relationship between electorates, national assemblies, and governments, and re-situated in the relationship between the member states and the European Union. Furthermore, as policy formation is transported from one realm to the other, it loses its political character, and is reduced to a technical question of policy coordination. Policy decisions lose the character of a negotiated outcome between competing interests, and become instead a simply technical question of generalising 'best practice'. Just what 'best practice' is, one might think, ought to be a political question, but posed in these terms it becomes one of closer approximation to the ideal, but what gives rise to the ideal is beyond consideration, open only to intuitive recognition as 'the best'.

British Foreign Minister Robin Cook rather missed the point about 'benchmarking' when he claimed 'we have been so successful in setting the benchmarks for reform of the Commission that in Brussels there are complaints that they are being compelled to accept an Anglo-Saxon model'.[29] Cook was trying to garner popular support by boasting of British influence after Lisbon, but the whole point of 'benchmarking' is that it takes policy coordination out of the arena of national politics. Still, Cook's preening was hardly likely to be understood by most Britons, for whom the 'Open Method of Coordination' remains a closed book.

The Lisbon Summit document goes on to say that 'A method of benchmarking best practices on managing change will be devised by the European Commission networking with different providers and users, namely the social partners, companies and NGOs'.[30] As we shall see, the role of the non-governmental organizations is important for the creation of an alternative source for consultation to national political processes. But first we go on to look at the developing bureaucracy working for the European Union, and in particular the ad hoc 'technical assistance offices'.

Trend to apolitical administration

The Technical Assistance Offices are special to the Commission, a European Union equivalent of the contracting out of services that has become commonplace in Anglo-American government.[31] They are vehicles for contracted project work in specific areas of Commission activity, such as the Leonardo programme for vocational training, the Socrates educational programme and the Tourism programme. 'Outside contractors, known as TAOs, helped the Commission to run these activities'.[32]

The TAOs have been identified as a problematic feature of the Commission's work.

> Commission departments have often turned to private consultants in external "technical assistance offices" (TAOs) to help run such projects. While the use of TAOs may be a flexible means of dealing with certain Commission tasks, it is not always the most efficient. One problem is that TAOs sometimes spend too much time chasing after their next Commission contract, rather than fulfilling their current one.

What is more

> The TAOs have thus proved difficult to control. The Commission cannot say precisely how many TAOs it uses, but estimates vary between 100 and 250. Many of the instances of mismanagement and fraud identified by the Committee of Independent Experts involved TAOs. In one case involving humanitarian aid, programme funding was fraudulently diverted to pay for additional administrative staff provided to the Commission by a TAO.[33]

The problem of the TAOs comes about because the European Commission lacks the institutional means and authority to impose its will. Historically compromised, the Commission's authority is at odds with that of national parliaments and the European parliament. National-minded distrust of the Commission sets limits on the growth of a European officialdom. European Union spending is in theory limited to less than one per cent of European GDP. 'The Commission employs fewer people, for instance, than the cities of London or Paris'.[34]

To realise its policies, the Commission relies on private contractors. 'The work is contracted out to a TAO,' explains Paul van Buitenen the officer (and now MEP) who blew the whistle on the corruption at the Commission. 'The Commission has only a very limited number of permanent staff' he wrote, adding: 'But ultimately the TAO structure clearly operates as a privatized bureaucracy.'[35] Craig and Elliott estimated that the total staff employed by the Commission was closer to 100 000.[36]

In his work as an employee of the Commission van Buitenen discovered obvious breaches in propriety, where the people who won contracts were involved in drawing up the brief; tenderings were clearly not competitive at all, but sewn up before hand, and that the TAO's were not real companies, but shells created to take advantage of the Commission's need to keep its executive functions at arm's length. That Commissioner Edith Cresson was related to one of the executives of a TAO captivated the critics of sleaze. But the more remarkable thing was that the Commission felt the need to operate at a distance. That was the price it paid for its relative lack of legitimacy in the eyes of sceptical national publics, who would not tolerate the expansion of a 'Brussels Bureaucracy'.

However, as more policy initiatives develop from the centre, the Commission has extended its reach through these ad hoc bodies created when the Commission contracts out the administration of its projects. This decentralised administration, underneath the Commission's permanent civil service corresponds to the ad hoc character of the integration process. As the administration is ad hoc, so is the political process that sustains it. As well as the European Council, the Commission also draws on its widening consultation process with selected non-governmental organisations.

Manufacturing European civil society

One indicator of the declining efficacy of European nation states is the extending authority of non-governmental organisations (NGOs). The expansion of the role of these international aid and advocacy organisations is much commented on. For the

European Union, though, being itself a trans-national project, NGOs have proved a useful interlocutor between the Commission and the public, that by-passes national govern-ments, creating an alternative process of consultation. Middlemas explains that 'the Commission ... reserves the rights of access by, and consultation with, the non-governmental players which permits some of them an essentially private admission to a privileged discourse about policy'.[37] But since the relationship is *ad hoc*, there is no real openness in the relation, and no real accountability. Indeed Juan Diez Mendrano makes the point that considered as a whole (across not just the Commission, but all of the Union's institutions) 'the European public sphere is closed to civil society actors'.[38]

On the other hand, a European Commission discussion paper makes it clear just how close relations are between the Commission and those NGOs that are its preferred partners:

> At present is it estimated that over €1,000 million a year is allocated to NGO projects directly by the Commission, the major part in the field of external relations for development co-operation, human rights, democracy programmes, and, in particular, humanitarian aid (on average €400 million). Other important allocations are in the social (approximately €70 million), educational (approximately €50 million), and environment sectors within the EU. Several hundred NGOs in Europe and world-wide are receiving funds from the EU.[39]

According to Jan van Deth the 'opulent and continuous subsidies' mean that 'almost each and every citizens' group in Brussels or Strasbourg receives EU funding, and some groups are almost completely financed by the EU'.[40] In one year about half of Friends of the Earth's budget for running its 25-person Brussels office was financed by the European Union.[41] The European Union does not only fund NGOs, but consults widely with them, entrenching the institutional lines of communication between Brussels and these 'non-governmental' organisations. Twice a year, for example, the biggest pan-European environmental NGOs ('Group of Eight') meet with the head of the commission's environment Directorate-General to discuss its work programme.[42] The Group of Eight was formed in 1990 at the Commission's request and comprises Greenpeace Europe, WWF European Policy Unit, Birdlife International, Friends of the Earth, Climate Network Europe, European Environmental Bureau, European Federation for Transport and Environment, and International Friends of Nature.[43] Not just the commission, but the European Parliament also solicits input from environmental lobbies.

The involvement of the non-governmental organizations has been widely argued to supplement the European Union's democratic deficit, and as we will see David Held, Ulrich Beck and others invoke the involvement of environmental and human rights lobbies as 'European Civil Society'. On 13 October 2005, as part of the period of reflection following the failure of the European Treaty, the European Commission launched the 'Plan D for Dialogue, Democracy and Debate'. This process of consultation drew heavily upon NGOs to help '"listening better", "explaining better" and "going local" to engage citizens', it also 'decided to cofund a new series of civil society projects with a special emphasis on youth and women and on "going local"'.[44]

There have been some doubts raised about the role of the NGOs. Tony Blair complained of the NGOs 'malign tyranny over public debate'.[45] Former French Foreign Secretary Hubert Vedrine draws attention to the 'government operated Non Governmental Organisation' (GONGO),[46] and also to the small world of 'international civil society': 'to be sure there's a community for finance ministers and foreign ministers from 192 countries, for the 120,000 bureaucrats who work for international organizations, and for thousands of NGOs from all over the world'. But 'this very thin, Americanized, and globalized veneer', says Vedrine is 'not for ordinary people'.[47]

Some NGOs like Amnesty International, Medicins Sans

The Commissioners' fantasy: that they get to make laws demanded by a stylish investigative reporter backed by NGOs, in this official comic book

Frontières and Greenpeace do raise their own funds, but what they get through public subscription is also subsidized by government. Others like Agenda 21 and the European Environmental Bureau are largely creatures of government largesse. NGOs played a part in the 'anti-globalisation' protests and movement around the turn of the 21st Century.[48] The European Union, with its extensive links to NGOs saw itself as reaching out to the protests. On the eve of the 2001 Summit at Gothenberg, Swedish Prime Minister Goran Persson opened what he hoped would be a 'pre-emptive dialogue with the protestors suggesting that the EU was well placed to help tame the forces of global capitalism'.[49]

The European Commission's sponsorship of, and consultation with NGOs, creates an ersatz civil society, a sounding board against which it tests its policy ideas. As one commissioner explained to Middlemas 'you are selling an idea, you must consult with people beforehand'.[50] The NGOs give the Commission important connections to tame constituencies of acceptable and loyal opposition. The NGOs might seem like components an embryonic European civil society. But their scope is much more restricted than any European public realm might be. The function that they do perform is to side-step national administrations and organizations, offering a model of continent-wide action.

The restricted character of the European Commission's consultation process, along with the protracted depoliticisation of government competencies in their transfer from national to European settings, raises a significant problem: the public perception of the European Union in its own right.

The limits of apolitical integration

A strong anti-political mood in European member-states favours greater European integration. With national leaders' authority declining, the European Community's authority can rise.

However, there is a price to be paid for attaining change without properly engaging a public debate. Jos de Beus and Jeanette Mak of the University of Amsterdam argue that 'By top-down constructing a perception of goodness of fit between European requirements and Dutch policies, as well as picturing EMU as a primarily monetary union, public protest and worry have been effectively silenced in the Netherlands.' It is not that there is no consultation, but that the terms of the consultation take the politics out of the issue, they argue:

> Support for the single currency was "obvious" and in the "best national interest".' Thereby, objections to EMU were simply made unthinkable.

And, as they explain

> Although this has led to initial utilitarian support for EMU, it has at the same time not led to its legitimacy. On the contrary, failure of the introduction of the single currency to fulfil the promises made on its direct economic benefits has turned the Netherlands as the most 'euro-sceptic' member state of the eurozone.[51]

Increasingly, the European Union itself has become the focus of anti-political disaffection. Perhaps the clearest example of that would be the campaign against the adoption of the European Constitution in 2004.

If we look at the Eurobarometer polling on support for European integration, it is clear that this was strongest in 1991. Recalling the poll on 'how democracy works in your country?' (in chapter two) this is around the time that popular disaffection with member-state governments was at its height – outstripping satisfaction, in fact.

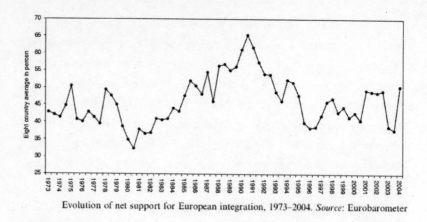

Evolution of net support for European integration, 1973–2004. *Source*: Eurobarometer

Net support (approval, minus disapproval) for European integration
dipped sharply

The eurobarometer poll shows positive support for European
integration in 2004, but in 2005 referenda on the European
Constitution in France and Holland were mostly hostile (by 55
per cent and 62 per cent respectively) – though Spain and
Luxemburg both voted in favor (72 per cent and 57 per cent).
Ireland's referendum on the Constitution was cancelled – but a
later referendum on the Lisbon Treaty rejected that by 53.4 per
cent. Jeffrey Checkel and Peter Katzenstein have a point when
they argue that 'attempts to de-politicize politics, to create
Europe by stealth, have produced a political backlash'.[52]

According to opinion polls of No voters in France, the first
reason for voting No was anxiety about the economy and society,
the second was a specific concern with the 'neoliberal' content of
the draft Constitution. In Holland and Ireland the major reasons
for opposition were a lack of knowledge of the terms of the
Constitution (which might mean an unwillingness to look at the
Constitution, though it was absurdly long – around 160,000
words[53]).

The defeat for the European Constitution is all the more
striking considering that it was supported by 'pretty much the

entire political class and the media'.[54] Perhaps the more alarming truth is that the support of the entire political class and the media counted against the Constitution, rather than in its favour. The No campaign in France was remarkable for the involvement of fringe parties of the left (and of the right), who found that they got a new lease of life by giving a voice to the popular disaffection. Campaigners also included many of the 'new social movements' that were thought to be integral to the 'cosmopolitan democracy' of the European Union's manufactured consultation process, like Association pour la taxation des transactions financières pour l'aide aux citoyens (Attac) and green activist José Bové.

Under pressure, the Yes campaign revealed an unpleasantly snooty disdain for the public whose endorsement they were claiming. Socialist leader Segolène Royal was reported as saying 'This referendum is bloody stupid', adding: 'We were bloody stupid enough to ask for one and Jacques Chirac was bloody stupid enough to call it'.[55] Leading German Member of the European Parliament Martin Schulz summed up the demoralization in the Yes camp when he said 'We must recognise that there was once a time when the pro-European movement had a heart and soul' but 'now, it is the anti-Europe movement which has the heart and soul'.[56]

As we have seen, public disengagement with the European Union is not a passing problem, but intrinsic to the apolitical development of its institutions, the Commission, its bureaucratic support mechanisms, even of the national leaders' European Council. We argue that these institutions have developed under the influence of a decline in nationally-based political participation, which amounts to a demobilization of the nation state, giving rise to a retreat from the defence of sovereignty. Though the European Commission failed to secure public endorsement in the constitution referenda in 2005, seven years later political leaders and commentators were once again talking confidently about further integration of government spending in the Fiskalpakt. Pointedly, the 2011-2012 crisis of the Eurozone did not as many expected led to any slowdown in the further integration of European institutions. It was not positive popular endorsement that led to the consolidation of the Union. It was crisis. With the failure of national governments to deal with the fiscal crisis, and the social dislocation that came in its train, the EU stepped in to fill the credibility gap. Once again the Union pushed forward less on its own positive claims than on the failures of national governments. 'What you're now seeing out of failure, not success, is the euro core integrating further,' says former British Prime Minister John Major.[57] But then in 2010 some had already been anticipated that 'the EU will thrive on Greece's troubles'.[58]

CHAPTER SIX

European Identity

In this chapter we explore the concept of the European identity as the putative basis of a European polity. We look at the ways that Europe has defined itself as partner in the western alliance, and against external forces, in the East, in the non-white world in America, and against its own history. All of these identifications, it will be argued, are problematic; and the fact that (some) Europeans should look to these problematic sources of identity is itself indicative of one of the unspoken problems of the European Union: its real existence is antagonistic to the Europe of popular national governments.

Central to the non-appearance of the European nation state is the absence of a European 'demos' – a singular people who could be the subject of the national story. Many champions of the European Union deny the need for a demos, and indeed deny that the European Union could be anything like a nation state. Others look at the European Parliament's shrunken powers and deplore the 'democratic deficit'. How can there be a singular European voice when there is no pan-european political process, but only discrete, nationally-based debates about the future of the different member states. The ambition to a Common Foreign and Security Policy contained in the Maastricht Treaty at least suggests that there might be a common European position. Kalypso Nikolaïdes has tried to make the best of the plurality of European polities. 'The EU is neither a union of democracies nor a union as democracy', she argues: 'it is a union of states and of peoples - a "demoicracy" - in the making.' The awkward coinage 'demoicracy' is explained as follows.

The EU has established itself as a new kind of political

community: one that is defined not by a uniform identity - a *demos* - but by the persistent plurality of its peoples, its *demoi*.[1]

Still, the attraction of a common European identity is not something that can be wholly side-stepped. 'The fact that we have not made much progress towards our goal is due to the absence of a European identity,' writes Oskar Lafontaine: 'To establish this identity step by step is an intellectual and cultural challenge,' (though one might have thought that identity was something that came naturally, rather than being thought out).[2] There are many ways in which Europeans have identified with one another, even if their European identification has not been as crucial as their national identification.

Europe's other

One way of looking at the question of identity is to look at the question of definition, where the boundaries of Europe are, how it conceives its limits. This could be posed as the question of what is other to Europe, or to what is Europe the other, or what is Europe not. Paul Henri Spaak, chairman of the committee that prepared the ground for the 1957 Treaty of Rome gave a sombre assessment of the European predicament on 11 December 1951, addressing the Belgian Parliament, that gives some insight into the common challenges Europeans faced.

The Europe of which we are speaking is a Europe which we have allowed to become grossly mutilated. Poland, Hungary, the Balkan countries, Eastern German – all these have gone. It is a Europe against which Asia and Africa have risen in revolt. The largest among us [UK] is at this moment being defied in Iran and Egypt. It is a Europe which for the last five years has been living in fear of the Russians and on the charity of the Americans. Faced with such a situation, we prefer to do nothing, as if history would wait for us, as if we had plenty of time to remould our thinking at leisure, take dozens and dozens of years, as if we had plenty of time to do away with our tariff barriers, to discard our national egoisms.[3]

In this short, anguished passage, all of the external challenges that might bind Europeans together are set out. Europe is challenged by Russia, by Cold War division and the loss of the East; Europe is insulted and challenged by the colonies, that are rising up against it; and Europe is dependent upon, and so at the mercy of, American charity.

White Europe

In much of Africa and other parts of the world that were colonised by the European nations, the word 'European' meant 'white', a category that had special pertinence under the colour bar that many European colonies operated. Spaak's anxieties about the colonial revolt were pertinent to the European identity before the Second World War. Then Europeans moderated their hostility to each other by putting up a common face against the non-white races. But after the war, the spell of European superiority was undermined by intra-European conflict. Racial supremacy was a policy – unremarkable before the war – that afterwards was largely discredited.[4] Further, the condition of European cooperation was the surrender of many European colonies to self-government, and to an American policing role. A degree of European hostility to non-white peoples continued to be an element of European identity, but it was too explosive to be an explicit foundation of European-ness after the war.

Conventions signed with African countries at Yaoundé in 1963 and 1969, superseded by the 1975 Lomé Convention, allocated aid to former European colonies to moderate the impact of decolonisation. Non-white migration into Europe has from time to time been the focus of social anxieties and conflicts. Under the Dublin Convention of June 1990, and then subsequently under the Maastricht Treaty European Union member states have coordinated their immigration policy to create a 'Fortress Europe' against illegal immigration.[5] Thousands of refugees held in camps at Sangatte, Calais (closed in 2007), the Campsfield detention centre at Kidlington, and Italy's aggressive coast guard actions against North African migrants all show the limits of European openness. On 21 May 2007 the Council of the European Union's Future Group presented a paper warning that 'Europe will increasingly become a region of destination for worldwide illegal immigration, organised crime and international drug-trafficking and a target of terrorist attacks'. The paper welcomed 'the development of a common European Security Strategy which is aimed, in particular at forming a "ring of responsibly governed countries from the EU's eastern borders to the Mediterranean (adopted by the European Council in December 2006).'[6] These measures show some of the deep anxieties underlying Europe's racial identity. But what is more marked is that, though many have tried, European politicians who have tried to articulate a politics of racial identity have been made themselves largely marginal to the mainstream political process.

West Europe

Throughout the Cold War the political identity of the European Economic Community was closely bound up with the demarcation of the 'free world' in contradistinction to the communist East. The Community was a subordinate association in the structure of Cold War international arrangements, where the North Atlantic Treaty Organisation (under American leadership) and the United Nations (under the permanent members of the security council) carried more weight in diplomatic terms. In NATO commander Hastings Ismay's memorable phrase his organisation was there to 'keep the Americans in, the Russians out and the Germans down'.[7] Still the boundaries of the

European Economic Community were shaped most clearly by the Cold War, not only with the exclusion of the Comecon countries (who had been refused Marshall aid), but also the diplomatically enforced status of non-alignment for the buffer states of Austria, Sweden and Finland (admitted to membership of the European Union in 1995). For the most part, the European Economic Community was studiously apolitical, derogating all high diplomatic Cold War conflicts to NATO. Between NATO and the European Economic Community, there was a division of functions: military and political power was organised through NATO and the United Nations, trade through the European Economic Community. At Philadelphia in 1962 John F. Kennedy set out the US policy without reservation

The United States looks on this vast enterprise with hope and admiration. We do not regard a strong and united Europe as a rival but as a partner. To aid its progress has been a basic object of our foreign policy for seventeen years.[8]

But Europe, bound to America, in the struggle against the East had its own limitations.

Europe v America

French distrust of the US lay behind the decision to oppose British membership of the European Economic Community in 1963 and 1965. As long as Britain was unwilling to give up its 'special political and military relations' with the US, 'what would emerge in the end would be a colossal Atlantic Community, dependent on America and directed by America' or as French political scientist Maurice Duverger put it, Britain would be a 'Trojan Horse' for American influence. French polemicist Jean-Jacques Servan-Schreiber's *La Defi Americaine*, published as *The American Challenge* in 1969 put European resentment at the US into popular language. Servan-Schreiber argued that the US was dominating its allies, and taking advantage of them.[9]

Post-war Europe enjoyed high growth rates (not least due to Marshall Aid, and US demand) for 'Thirty Glorious Years' (Trentes Glorieuses). At the Kennedy Round of the GATT, the European Economic Community aimed to put up a single negotiating team, while the US negotiators aimed to play off Germany against France.[10] Eventually Europe reversed its trade imbalance with the US. Europeans exchanged goods for dollars, which, despite fixed exchange rates were actually losing value. 'Americans used newly printed and devalued dollars to buy up European industry virtually free of charge through what was still called "American Foreign Investment",' according to Andre Gunder Frank. De Gaulle tried to cash in his burgeoning dollar reserve, leading to the collapse of the Bretton Woods system - widely understood in Europe as a failure of American leadership. 'The creation of the European Monetary System was aimed to a large extent at shielding Europe from the consequences of the decline of the dollar-based international monetary system'.[11]

Social conflict in the 1970s saw the return of radical anti-Americanism. Terror groups in Germany, Italy and Greece targeted American military and business. For its critics, America was guilty of interfering in domestic politics to favour amenable and conservative administrations, and even in supporting dictatorial regimes in Southern Europe. Intellectually, anti-Americanism was a sublimated anti-capitalism for Marxists like Ernest Mandel, Andre Gunder Frank and Tom Nairn. Nairn railed against the British Labour Party's Atlanticist leadership for 'betray[ing] the nation's independence' to the 'most distinctly "capitalist-oriented" nation on earth'.[12] Forgetting that Europe, too, was a capitalist success story, the radical anti-Americans were only putting red gloss on European nationalisms.

Europeans - or more specifically the French and Germans - balked at another bout of Cold War hostilities following the election of Ronald Reagan. Americans, meanwhile, increasingly resented European 'free riding' under the US military umbrella. European foreign policy experts detected 'a growing aspiration' in America for a 'return to the era of US supremacy and absolute leadership in world affairs'. 'This is translated in the resurgent tendency to consider every event in the world purely in East-West terms, and the use of force as the panacea for most issues'.[13] In June 1982 President Reagan prohibited European subsidiaries and licensees of American firms from delivering components for the Soviet-European Gas pipeline - taken in Europe as evidence that America was seeking to translate military authority into trade advantage. 'It violates our sovereignty', said the German Economics Minister (*International Herald Tribune*, 1 August 1982). In 1979 NATO decided to site intermediate nuclear missiles in Europe, provoking large demonstrations. German Chancellor Helmut Schmidt's support for that decision divided his Social Democratic Party and cost them the elections in 1982. By 1989, German Foreign Minister Hans-Dietrich Genscher was prepared to face down US demands for the modernisation of NATO's nuclear missiles in Germany.[14]

On 20 November 1989, a week after protestors tore down the Berlin Wall, President Bush told German Foreign Minister Genscher that German Unification was moving too fast and demanded caution. On 11 December 1989, US Ambassador Vernon Walters took part in a Four Powers Conference, at the invitation of the Soviet Union, in the Control Council Building in Berlin. Genscher protested that it was no longer acceptable to discuss Germany's future without Germany being present.[15] George H. W. Bush changed tack, and put the US at the forefront of support for unification, despite opposition from UK Prime Minister Thatcher.

Anti-Americanism did offer a shape to European identity in the later Cold War period. Radical protestors and some economic nationalists took up the anti-American theme. But it was awkward for many other European actors, establishment figures whose own status was built upon Atlanticist, Cold War structures, business leaders who wanted to trade with America, and internationalists who baulked at the chauvinistic tenor of the complaints against Coca Cola imperialism. For the most part anti-Americanism was the theme tune of the losing side in the politics of the Cold War, and the growing neo-liberal consensus in the 1980s made it seem other-worldly.

German protest against the Iraq War, 2003
- Peter Homann/bsd-photo-archiv

In August 2002, in the run-up to the Gulf War, Chancellor Gerhard Schröder announced 'We're not available for adventures, and the time of cheque book diplomacy is over once and for all'. German refusal to contribute to the costs of the Second Gulf War contrasted with the first. In 1990-91, when Germany paid 18 billion DM. The SPD Chancellor was fighting to regain ground from the CDU leader Edmund Stoiber, who had tapped a popular source of resentment objecting to US actions against Iraq.

US anger came to a head when Justice Minister Herta Daubler-Gmelin compared President George W Bush's methods to those of Hitler. According to *Die Zeit* editor Josef Joffe 'Germany no longer needs American strategic protection; at least the rent Berlin is willing to pay for this shelter has plummeted'.[16] On the United Nations Security Council German Foreign Minister Fischer, French Foreign Minister Dominique de Villepin and Russian leader Vladimir Putin stymied the American 'second resolution' authorising the use of force in Iraq.

Gerhard Schroeder, Jacques Chirac, Dominique de Villepin and Joschka Fischer breaking with America over the invasion of Iraq

The philosophers Jacques Derrida and Jürgen Habermas were interested in the way that the European anti-war protests of 15 February might be considered as an awakening of a European sentiment. Millions of Europeans demonstrated, for peace, and against America. There were precedents. In the later 1990s, many 'anti-globalisation' demonstrations took place around G-8 and other summits, which took on a more anti-American flavour following the election of George W. Bush to the Presidency, highlighting his refusal to submit to the International Criminal Court and to the Kyoto Accords. Protestors called him the 'Toxic Texan'. For west European leaders, whose own relation to their publics was tenuous, there was a temptation to play to the anti-war gallery. But anti-Americanism was not a theme that bound East and West Europe together. Many East Europeans remembered U.S. Cold War leadership with affection, not fear. More recently, they remembered that the U.S. had welcomed them into the North Atlantic Treaty Organisation while the European Union was still raising objections to their joining. Asked by Dutch television on 22 January 2003 whether his Iraq policy was creating problems with Europe, U.S. defence Secretary Donald Rumsfeld drove a wedge between Old Europe and New Europe:

> Now, you're thinking of Europe as Germany and France. I don't. I think that's old Europe. If you look at the entire NATO Europe today, the center of gravity is shifting to the east. And there are a lot of new members. And if you just take the list of all the members of NATO and all of those who have been invited in recently — what is it? Twenty-six, something like that? – you're right. Germany has been a problem, and France has been a problem.

Rumsfeld's insult was calculated, and succeeded in provoking. But it also told a truth: that Europeans were not united in their opposition to the US-led war. West Europeans were more likely to be against the war, but East Europeans were less so. Apart from the Iraq intervention, European states overwhelmingly supported and cooperated with American military actions overseas. Once again, an idea of uniting Europeans only served to illustrate their differences.

Keeping East Europe waiting

At the end of the Cold War, with the collapse of the 'People's Republics' in the East, the European Union was confronted with a problem. Throughout the Cold War years, west European states had added their voices to the demands for democratic elections and open societies in the east. The explicit outlook of west European leaders was that the people of the East were to be set free from communist domination. The first generation of non-communist leadership in the East, men like Finance Minister Vaclav Klaus in (then) Czechoslvakia, and Polish central bank chairman Leszek Balcerowicz expected their countries to be admitted to membership of the European Union – which they were in 2004. However, between the political transitions of 1993 and European Union accession in 2004 lay a long lost decade of instability and increasing – and mutual – resentment.

'The immediate euphoria following the fall of the Berlin wall had evaporated by 1993' according to the *Times Atlas of European History*: 'Europe once more seemed divided in two: an Eastern zone of instability and poverty, beset by ethnic tensions and open warfare, and a Western area, above all the EU, prosperous'. According to one report in the *Daily Telegraph* in 1991, the European Union was 'a rich man's club, against whose frosty window panes the Easterners will press their noses for a long time'.[17]

According to Katinka Barysch at the Economist Intelligence Unit

many in central and eastern Europe were disappointed with the terms of EU accession. The accession negotiations had been long and arduous. The east Europeans felt that the process had hardly amounted to a 'negotiation' – that the EU had simply imposed on them the *acquis communautaire* (the body of EU law), without giving them any say or taking into account their special circumstances.[18]

The *acquis* is some 29 Chapters of EU regulations covering 90,000 pages on everything from the movement of goods to the movement of person; from company law to educational and regional policy. East European accession states were angry that West Europeans had put special clauses into the agreement denying equal access of East European goods and labour to west European markets. Polled just before accession, only 43 per cent of East Europeans were positive about membership, and turnout in the accession states' first European election of 2004 was at a sorry 27 per cent. East European expectations of the Union had been lowered – as low in fact as west European expectations.

Perry Anderson claims that the 'implantation of political systems matching liberal norms – representative democracies complete with civil rights, elected parliaments, separation of powers, alternating governments' is 'impressive'. He writes that

Under the watchful eye of the Commission, seeing to it that criteria laid down at Copenhagen in 1993 were properly met, Eastern Europe has been shepherded into the comity of free nations.

Any difficulties in the accession process are not to down to the Union, but deeply rooted in the soil of Eastern Europe, he argues:

The reality is that from the time of the Roman Empire onwards, the lands now covered by the new member states of the union were nearly always poorer, less literate and less urbanized than most of their counterparts in the west.

Indeed, according to Anderson 'it is this millennial record, of repeated humiliation and oppression that entry into the Union finally offers a chance to leave behind'.[19] Anderson's patrician view of the eastern states shepherded towards enlightenment echoes that of the Commission. Over and again the Union has barged in telling East European governments what they should and should not do. All this telling-off is done with nice words like liberalisation and inclusion, and often the governments in question are very illiberal. Still the hidden meaning of the civics lessons from the Commission is that East Europeans are the children, the Commission the teachers.

In 2006 Hungary's 'Socialist' Prime Minister Ferenc Gyurcsany, pushing through an austerity package, was overheard saying that he 'lied morning, evening and night'. When rioting broke out in front of the Parliament building on the part of bitter electors, the European Union backed Gyurcsany and criticised the opposition. The official reprimand was that Hungary was 'rated' as the 'worst performing member member state' on the Commission's 'Internal Market Scoreboard'. The feeling was mutual: more than half of Hungarians thought that negative aspects of membership outnumber the benefits. In 2011 Hungary was in the dock again, this time President Barroso was lecturing Prime Minister Viktor Orban for his law against obscene rap music. No doubt it is unfair that Hungary's teenagers have to go on the internet to listen to Ice-T swearing, but as Orban pointed out, all European countries have obscenity laws, and many other kinds of censorship besides: the real offence was that the Hungarians had presumed to make their own laws.[20]

Also in 2006, European parliamentarians on a delegation to Poland complained that they were getting no help from their Polish counterparts (there was an election going on at the time). The European representatives were there to investigate allegations that the Polish government held 'renditioned' prisoners on behalf of the US military in its 'war on terror' campaign. It was true that the Polish authorities had collaborated with the US – but then so did Sweden, Ireland, Portugal, Greece, Spain, the UK, Italy and Germany. The real event was the European Union's justice commissioner, Franco Frattini, warning that Poland faced losing its EU voting rights. Poland has been threatened with losing voting rights, too, over its illiberal laws on homosexuality and the death penalty. Of course these are important civil liberties, but the accession process means that liberalisation is a process undertaken from the outside, under pressure to conform to the EU. Reforms that in another setting would be a real step towards freedom are instead made into a performance, like jumping through hoops. They have little meaning other than to set up a division between a show of proper, politically correct behaviour for the eurocrats, and an underlying illiberal resentment that populist politicians can draw upon. The great fear of the 'European Stability Initiative' NGO is that 'where the public consensus collapses, a political opportunity will be created for anti-reform parties, including intolerant nationalists, to challenge the European project'. That mirrors the outlook of the Union that East European states must be closely observed to make sure that they fulfil their obligations under the treaties. Perry Anderson is mistaken in thinking that the East European states have been shepherded – or in any other way found their way into – 'the comity of free nations'. Rather they have made the transition from Warsaw Pact countries to becoming 'Member States', as Chris Bickerton explains it – that is states who derive their political authority from collaboration with the institutional framework of the Union, not from the democratic will voiced by their own people. At the end of the Cold War, the European Union lost its identity as 'western Europe'. But the terms on which the East European states have been incorporated into the Union mean that any pan-European identity drawing upon the equality of nations is belied by the actually subordinate position of those countries within the Union. [21]

For and against enlargement

East Europeans had an understandable grievance over the way that the west snubbed them. Still, it should be understood that there is also a long-standing diplomatic strategy followed by those nations resistant to integration (or at least to the pace of integration) and that is the cynical pursuit of enlargement for its side-effect of diluting the union. Richard Body, the British euro-sceptic argues the case for a 'Europe of Many Circles' in his book of that name, the argument turning on the question 'whether the European Union becomes deeper or wider'. Body set out what in fact had been British Foreign Office policy since the 1950s, to slow down the process of integration, and since the 1970s, to argue for enlargement as a way of slowing it down. [22]

Attitudes to enlargement, then, are themselves a reflection of attitudes towards integration. Britons tend to favour enlargement, as do Americans: 'The United States has been an enthusiastic supporter of the EU enlargement process, even though the US clearly preferred geographic widening over functional deepening of the EU'. By contrast, the 'core Europe' of Germany, Belgium and France tended to be much more critical of enlargement. These were the battlelines in the discussion over the East European enlargement. The new member states have been described as an 'American Trojan Horse' within the union – just as was alleged against British membership before. [23]

The same battle lines were drawn over the question of Turkish accession. British parliamentarian and 'New Labour' insider Stephen Twigg argued forcefully that 'Europe should welcome the Turks'. A similiarly forceful argument was made by the US, provoking a fierce, and critical reaction from European Union trade commissioner Pascal Lamy:

It's classic US diplomacy to want to put Turkey in Europe. The further the boundaries of Europe extend, the better US interests are served. Can you imagine the reaction if we told the Americans they had to enlarge into Mexico?

Pointedly, Twigg's argument very quickly turned away from any intrinsic qualities of Turkey's onto the more problematic question, what kind of Europe? Turkish 'accession would be a dramatic step in European multiculturalism' says Twigg. 'This adds urgency to the question of European identity', he says.[24]

It is becoming clearer that anxiety about Europe's borders is in essence anxiety about Europe's own identity, projected outwards onto its external challenges. The *Economist* made it clear to west Europeans that they would not be able to go on defining themselves against the East, now that the 'soviet threat' had evaporated.

> The 'East' as a geopolitical concept is obsolete, it was a synonym for the Soviet empire. Where does that leave 'the West', which defined itself largely by contrast with 'the East'? Maybe ... bound together by a sense of external threat – fear of chaos or Islamic extremism, say, from 'the South' rather than 'the East?'[25]

Enlargement remains a difficult issue of identity for Europeans, as the ongoing argument about Turkish membership shows. But it is clear that the European Union cannot define itself against 'the East' without jeopardising the solidarity of the Union. However, one distinctive idea of Europe might be based on Europe's distinctive traditions of social welfare provision.

Social Europe

'No Europe without a social Europe', François Mitterrand.

According to the American futurologist and former advisor to Romano Prodi Jeremy Rifkin, Europe's great advantage over America lies in its prioritisation of 'community relationships over individual autonomy ... quality of life over the accumulation of wealth'. Zygmunt Bauman argues that Social State Europe is potentially the constraining force that the free market needs. Certainly welfare payments in Europe are higher than in the United States. West Europeans value their health and welfare systems and contrast them favourably with those of other countries.[28]

However, it would be a mistake to think that higher welfare spending necessarily translates into greater community cohesion. Social critics in Britain like Frank Field and David Green have shown how government welfare spending could tend to undermine voluntaristic social networks, ultimately leading to yet more atomised societies. Timothy Smith argues forcefully that pension and workers' benefits in France favour a declining indigenous core of the traditional workforce, but being distributed through work-place based organisations exclude a growing minority of migrants, women and casual workers, adding to the social divide.[28] Up until 2011 at least European governments were spending more, but without building the institutions and constituencies that gave life to the post-war welfare compromise, that money just passed through without leaving much of a mark. As we have seen, the elites' struggle to limit social expectations and to disaggregate mass social political movements in the 1980s was leading to a more individuated society.

What is more, most understand that the reform of welfare undertaken in most of Western Europe since the 1980s was jeopardising the advantages of the social state. In 1995, the French social critic Pierre Bourdieu addressed striking railworkers: 'this crisis is a historic chance for France and for all those who refuse the new alternative: liberalism or barbarism ... in fighting for their social rights, the strikers are fighting for everyone's rights'. Not just a blast from the past, Bourdieu re-purposed the socialist rhetoric of his younger days for a contemporary French audience for whom the Anglo-Saxon model of unfettered global capitalism is a danger to social cohesion. By the early 2000s 72 per cent of French people were 'suspicious' of globalisation, 65 per cent thought it a direct cause of rising social inequality and 55 per cent thought it was a threat to French jobs and businesses.[29]

In 1988 Commission president Jacques Delors emphasized the importance of the Social Charter defending workers' rights in the further development of the European Community. For the most part, though, Mitterrand's Social Europe remained a verbal protest against the privatisation of public services and deregulation of the market. Analysing poll data on European attitudes leading to the referendums that defeated the proposed European Constitution in 2005, Juan Diez Medrano notes a mismatch between elites and a significant section of the population, particularly as elites have 'remained relatively silent about the EU's social dimension'.[30] This is all the more surprising, since, as was very clear at the time, the vocal opposition to the constitutional treaty made hay attacking the neo-liberalism of the bosses Europe, contrasting that to the virtues of social cohesion. Since the fiscal crisis of 2011-12 the claims of Social Europe, of course, have been thrown into reverse. The Troika of the European Central Bank, Commission and International Monetary Fund officials setting down the law for Greece, Italy, Spain, Portugal and Ireland have made it clear that welfare spending is to be cut severely.

If Social Europe is an unlikely basis for a continental identity, perhaps the lessons of the differences over the Gulf War perhaps suggest that there is a tradition of *eirenism* or the pursuit of peace that could serve as the foundation of a European identity.

Peaceable Europe

Europe is turning away from power, or to put it a little differently, it is moving beyond power into a self-contained world of laws and rules and transnational negotiation and cooperation. It is entering a post-historical paradise of peace and relative prosperity, the realization of Immanuel Kant's "perpetual peace". Meanwhile, the United States remains mired in history, exercising power in an anarchic Hobbesian world where international laws and rules are unreliable...[31]

Robert Kagan's best-selling book *Paradise and Power* founded the view that Americans are from Mars, Europeans from Venus (Mars being the god of war, Venus the god of love). Quietly, Kagan is criticising Europeans for sheltering under America's security umbrella, without paying, their bloodless utopia under-written by American sacrifice. But many Europeans have willingly embraced the characterisation. To Zygmunt Bauman, Kagan's Hobbesian America is the past, the Kantian 'perpetual peace' of Europe, the future.[32]

According to Mark Leonard 'the law is Europe's weapon of choice in in its campaign to reshape the world'. Furthermore, says Leonard, law-governed mediation is at the core of what Europe is: 'The reason that European countries are so concerned about defending legal international norms is that the basis of the EU is itself an international treaty.' Bauman (citing Etienne Balibar and Umberto Eco) sees Europe's strength as its ability to incorporate conflicting messages, and, because mediation of different national voices is so central to European cooperation 'it has learned to make a fruitful dialogue between cultural and linguistic idioms effective without effacing the indentity of the participants'. Taking up an idea of Joseph Nye's, Leonard and Timothy Garton Ash have lauded the 'soft power' Europe exercises, how, by the appeal of participation in its law-governed prosperity, it extends its civilising mission outwards from its borders. 'The magnetism of the European Union was a signif-icant factor in Ukraine's orange revolution and EU diplomacy played an important part in its success', explains Ash.[33]

To dream of a world without war, though, is to build utopia in the here and now. When Homer said that he wished war were no part of the lives of men or gods, Heraclitus replied that Homer had forgotten that 'through war, all things come to be'. Conflict cannot be wished out of existence, nor perhaps ought it to be. More pointedly, the Kantian Empire of the law, like so many civilising missions can tip over into out-and-out fighting. With nearly 80 000 troops deployed in other countries, European nations account for the lion's share of non-US troops deployed overseas.[34] Those troops are engaged in missions to uphold law in Iraq, Afghanistan and Bosnia. To this day militarism remains a central feature of European life.

Underlying the aspiration to become a peaceable Europe is another, more troubled idea of what is Europe's distinctive identity, and that is the idea that Europe today is defined in opposition to its troubled and bellicose history.

Guilty Europe – Europe as other to itself

In the proposed European Constitution, the preamble says

> 'BELIEVING that Europe, reunited after bitter experiences, intends to continue along the path of civilisation' and that 'the peoples of Europe are determined to transcend their former divisions'

There is a view of Europe's identity that its self-criticism is what makes it distinctive, in particular the criticism of European nationalism. According to Ulrich Beck 'cosmopolitan Europe is the institutionalised self-criticism of the European path'. What he means is that the historical record of political violence and genocide in Europe, paradoxically, lays the basis for a European identity: 'radical self-critical European commemoration of the Holocaust does not destroy, but rather constitutes the identity of Europe.' The memory of the Holocaust, which might be thought to be a barrier to European pride, becomes instead a case for post-national Europe: 'the institution of future-oriented forms of memory for a cosmopolitan self-critique of Europe in opposition to national founding and warrior myths'. This argument is put too by Jürgen Habermas and Jacques Derrida in their essay '15

February, or what binds us together'. With Beck, guilty recollection becomes the argument against national sovereignty. Still, Europe might stoop to conquer. Beck, like Habermas and Derrida argues that this 'radical self-critique' might 'be what distinguishes the EU from the USA and from Muslim societies'.[35]

There is a precedent for an identity that is based upon self-criticism, and that is the identity of 'collective guilt', which was an important plank of the post-war German elite's argument – in the East and the West – that the German people could not be trusted to govern themselves. To many, though, it rather seemed to be the other way around. The foundation of West Germany was not atonement, but forgetting. In the summer of 1983 Green deputy Joseph Fischer alleged that conservatives had avoided responsibility for the Holocaust, shifting the blame away from the German people, onto Hitler, his clique, or even the Jews, and presented the Germans as the foremost victims of Nazi Germany.[36] That year Anna Rosmus' local history project exposing the Nazi ties of her hometown, *Resistance and Persecution — The Case of Passau 1933-1939* was published.

There was indeed a great temptation among Germans to avoid dwelling on the country's Nazi past, and also to emphasize the suffering of the Germans under the post-war occupation, and of those prisoners of war held in the Soviet Union, and the Germans expelled from Eastern Europe. On the other hand, there was a different response to German war guilt, which in its own way was just as much woven into the post-war outlook, east and west. The year after Fischer's angry denunciation of the right's evasion of responsibility over the extermination of the Jews, Christian Democrat president Richard von Weiszäcker made a speech in which he emphasized German responsibility for Jewish suffering. On the seventieth anniversary of the end of the war President Koehler said that Germany 'looked back with shame and horror' at the war and the holocaust of European Jewry in the Nazi Gas Chambers, conceding that it was impossible for Germany to 'draw a line under its history'. But then that was an important aspect of official response to the holocaust, too.[37]

Should we be surprised that the holocaust features so strongly in discussions of moral bonds? No. Peter Novick has shown that the discussion of the holocaust is loaded with moral significance. Novick cites the Princeton sociologist, Robert Wuthnow: 'It was the Holocaust as symbol of everpresent evil rather than the Holocaust as historical event that was of interest to persons troubled about the moral fabric'. 'In an era of moral relativity, the Holocaust museum serves as a lodestone', says John Aloysius Farrell in the *Boston Globe:* 'Americans flocking to the Holocaust museum are searching for answers - in the form of moral certainties'. Farrell added 'the Holocaust museum offers a basic moral foundation on which to build: a negative surety from which to begin.' Even the 'holocaust' itself is a peculiar coinage, meaning 'burnt offering', a religious idea of a sacrifice to God, like a mass-production era martyrdom, that made Primo Levi, amongst others, uncomfortable. But if the final solution was a moral challenge to Americans, how much more so was it to Germans?[38]

In 1946 the allies denied occupied Germany self-government on the basis of war guilt. Churchill argued, that after 'a generation of self-sacrifice, toil and education, something might be done with the German people'. The post-war authorities inherited their distrust of the German people from the allied occupation authorities. The 'defensive democracy' with its heavy limits on popular sovereignty (see above, 'from German question to German answer'), the banning of extremist political parties, are possible because of underlying assumption that Germans have a record of support for fascism. Authorities on the other side of the Berlin Wall felt the same distrust of popular mobilisation. Stasi leader Markus Wolf insisted that though 'only a small minority of Germans were actually guilty', 'all Germans who

lived willingly under the Nazis bear a responsibility for them' –
an attitude which no doubt made it easier for him to keep
records on so many of his countrymen. The German Federal
Republic also made use of diplomatic acts of atonement and
restitution to win acceptance in the world.[39]

Willy Brandt makes a show of Germany's atonement

Surprisingly, perhaps, Germany's war guilt and her atonement
for it, have become something of a model for European attitudes
to the past. Historian Elazar Barkan writes of 'the sudden

appearance of restitutions cases all over the world' in his exhaustive study, *The Guilt of Nations*, which covers the issues of German restitution, the compensation of the Swiss to holocaust survivors, the Korean 'comfort women', the extensive apologies and restitutions towards 'first peoples' and many more Barkan was intrigued by 'the willingness of the perpetrators to engage and accommodate the victims demands', suggesting that these are evidence of 'a potentially new international morality'. 'Discussions of the past have started to become rather masochistic', complains former French foreign minister Hubert Vedrine, striking a different note: 'People are constantly rediscovering tragic episodes of French history', like the Vichy regime and the Algerian war.[40]

In the terms set out in the European Treaty, the 'bitter experiences' are like the fall from Eden, the guilty pre-history of Europe, its bellicose past and the atrocities that came with it, that we are all seeking to overcome, while remaining ever vigilant of the appeal of national atavism. That is why, in Ulrich Beck's version, Cosmopolitan Europe is an institutionalised critique of nationalism.

If the European people really were to think of themselves a *guilty people* what would that mean? The German philosopher Hegel was dismissive about guilt, seeing it as a necessary corollary of a deliberate act, insofar as the deed divides the self against its mere existence to create 'over and against itself of an alien external reality'. Innocence, on the other hand 'is merely non-action, like the mere being of a stone, not even that of a child'. Here guilty reflection upon the historical past would be mere self-indulgence, and an unwillingness to act. The psychologist and founder of psycho-analysis Sigmund Freud thought that excessive guilt was a sign that the superego had become too powerful, and had started to attacked the ego. The diagnosis is not good. Excessive guilt leads to melancholia, and suicide. And in a way, this is what is happening in the performance of national guilt. The 'superego', the state, is attacking the ego, the people, who only appear to the state as 'id' ('it' in English) naked and uncivilised drives – though perhaps that is stretching the metaphor too far. Europe wallowing in guilty reflection seems close to fulfilling Bart Simpson's caricature of the 'cheese-eating surrender monkeys'.[41]

It is surprising in a way that the literature on European identity is as tortuous as it is. Europe has some remarkable claims. Historically, the European continent is the site of the birth of ancient and modern democracy, where Christianity flourished, home of the Renaissance and the Enlightenment, the crucible of liberal values and the modern free market, the scientific age, but also of socialism, Marxism, the trade union movement and much more. And today Europe is (arguably) the most productive and creative place in the world, industrially, scientifically, artistically and intellectually. One problem for the discussion of European identity is the people who are discussing it. Articulating identity is not a challenge that calls for critical thinking, but positivism, not deconstruction, but affirmation. Comparing the convention to write a constitution for the European Union to the Philadelphia convention of 1787 that wrote the American constitution, Giscard D'Estaing found that his intellectual collaborators were less like John Adams and Thomas Jefferson, more like Ambrose Bierce and H. L. Mencken – better critics than they were visionaries. Checkel and Katzenstein, Christiansen and Reh all argue European identity could never be something like a national identity, but could only be much more tentative, non-exclusive and self-critical. But that only tells us that the European project is not in the business of constructing a positive European identity, only operating as an ongoing critique of European national identities' positive exclusivity. If that is the case, the European Union's 'Other', the force against which it articulates itself, is precisely the Europe of Sovereign European peoples. The argument, made by Paul

Ricoeur is that Europe's identity should be to see itself as another – which could be read either as suggesting a remarkable degree of self-questioning, or that the peoples of Europe are that external force against which the European Union articulates its identity.[42]

In the following chapter we look at the positivist theories of European integration, first those functionalist theories that accompanied the earlier construction of the European Economic Community, and then the English School's insistence on the methodological priority of nation states.

Positivist Approaches to European Integration

Section 1
Integration Theory

The European Union has been analysed by realists, like Stanley Hoffmann, Functionalists like David Mitrany and Ernst Haas, and integrationists like Karl Deutsch. Their different approaches to the question emphasise different aspects of the process in hand, but beneath their differences certain similarities in understanding shine through. These are an interest in the depoliticisation of international conflict, and a corresponding movement away from sovereignty as the irreducible element of international relations. In this chapter, we begin by looking at the integration theorists Mitrany, Haas and Deutsch, before going on to look at the realist and inter-governmentalist analyses of European integration.

David Mitrany (1888 - 1975)

'Undoubtedly... the chief exponent of functionalism'[1] David Mitrany did military service in his native Rumania before studying sociology under L. T. Hobhouse, and political science under Graham Wallas, at the London School of Economics, before going on to write foreign leaders for the *Manchester Guardian* newspaper (1919-1922, reporting on the Versailles Conference of 1919), work on the Carnegie Endowment's economic history of World War I and acting as advisor to the Labour Party's committee on International Affairs (1918-31). He went to the Foreign Office in the Second World War, after which he continued to write and teach, as well as acting as advisor to the British Government during the negotiations in the European Council as well as working as an advisor to Unilever between 1944 and 1960, where, says Sir Frederick Pedler, 'he attended all the board meetings' and 'knew everything that was going on'.[2]

In a critique of the Covenant of the League of Nations, Mitrany suggested that 'the shock of the First World War produced an outcry for national security and the Covenant was its outcome':

> At bottom it was an attempt to apply the philosophy of laissez faire in international society, though it had never gone very far in national society. It was an attempt to provide a Common Authority to keep order between states, but for the rest not to interfere with private national enterprise.[3]

Describing his time at the Foreign Office, Mitrany explained how his outlook differed from the proponents of what we would later call a realist theory of International Relations he found there:

> The professionals at the Foreign Office, bound to their upbringing, looked at all things 'diplomatically', always shadowed by the spectre of the 'balance of power'. As a student driven by thoughts of a saner future I tended to look at things 'functionally', to look for a prospect of some balance of beneficial mutual concert. [4]

Though Mitrany contrasted his functionalist approach to the 'balance of power' politics of the Foreign Office, there was a sense in which he supported the 'balance of power' idea, praising the British position at the Congress of Vienna, inviting the Powers to declare 'their determination to unite their influence and if necessary their arms against the Power that should attempt to disturb their relations'.[5] That idea of the 'balance of power' that saw concert to constrain excessive, or disturbing nationalism appealed to him, where the other version, of a free play of national interests, did not.

Mitrany's 'functionalism' became an important concept in the study of international integration. At least consciously, it was not derived from the sociological concept of 'function' set out by Emile Durkheim. [6] What Mitrany was interested in were those social, not exclusively but often governmental activities that might be organised across national boundaries. Per Hammarlund says that the Tennessee Valley Authority, which Mitrany had studied while in the United States was one example of the 'functional approach to government' Mitrany had in mind.[7] 'The TVA', Mitrany wrote, 'seemed to me a fair prototype of joint international action'.[8] Later, Mitrany would find an exemplar of the functionalist approach in the workings of the multi-national company, Unilever, according to Sir Frederick Pedler who sat with him on the board:

> The international character of Unilever was a functional relationship extending over national frontiers, responding to spontaneous desires and natural needs. It was in fact a model of his functional approach to international cooperation...[9]

But Mitrany went further than noticing the similarities; seeing that the coordination of these activities might be an area where national competition need not hold sway. His expansion of the point is not entirely clear, though it does indicate the formulation of the concept of the functional in the 'functional theory of politics':

> Here was a rare thing in social experience - a plain demonstration of a general concept, in this case revealing the close working relation ... between the function of government and the structure of government.[10]

Ernst Haas summarises the programmatic side of Mitrany's functionalism: 'An ever widening mesh of task-oriented welfare agencies would come to pre-empt the work now done by some governments, leading eventually to the creation of a universal welfare orientation'.[11]

Mitrany's functionalism shared many of the goals of the more idealistic schemes of world federation, and later of European Federation, that were set out in the interwar years. 'Functionalist thought must be sharply distinguished from simple internationalism of the "One World" variety', writes Ernst Haas.[12] Like the internationalists, Mitrany identified 'the historical problem of our time, the chief trait of which is the baffling division between the peoples of the world'. Mitrany saw the same problem of divisiveness 'in the newly independent countries of Asia and Africa' after the Second World War. This division, he added, is 'all the more strange as in its material life the world has moved far towards common unity'.[13]

However, he contrasted his own piecemeal approach to overcoming national divisions with the European Federalists claiming his was much more effective. Mitrany quotes approvingly the assessment of Italian civil servant and Esperantist Andrea Chiti-Batelli that 'The most acute and consistent functionalists (like Mitrany) are not federalists; in a logically flawless way, they consider functionalism as the alternative to federalism'.[14]

In his memoirs, Harold Macmillan, as one of the British representatives in the European Council, contrasts the piecemeal approach pursued by the British, under Mitrany's advice, with the federalist approach of other Europeans. For Macmillan, though, and rather against Mitrany's intentions, the difference was seen as one of national advantage: '"Federation" of Europe means "Germanisation" of Europe. "Confederation" (if we play our cards right), should be British leadership of Europe'.[15]

Paul Spaak recalled that in the Council of Europe 'the British insisted again and again on what they called the "functional approach", contrasting it with the "legislative approach".' Confusing his end-goal with that of the British negotiators, Spaak continued 'Their idea was that a united Europe should be created by solving one by one the practical problems of the moment'.[16] That is, the British delegation was basing its arguments on Mitrany's functionalism.

As well as being oriented towards influencing elites, Mitrany's functionalism was socially ameliorative, in a way that distinguished it, for him, from security-based international cooperation. 'To think of peace as consisting only in the prevention of violence is to ignore the factor of social unity and growth, of life, and only to concentrate on what is an occasional disturbance of it', he wrote. Criticising the League of Nations Mitrany writes that 'the whole system was based on a conception of law and order which did not concern itself with the ordinary processes of social life'. Elaborating the distinction between strictly defined security measures on the one hand and social production or welfare on the other, Mitrany continues: 'if security is conceived merely as a matter of policing the world against the use of violence it is doubtful whether countries will long hold together on this issue, *while at the same time they strive harshly against each other in shipping and aviation, raw materials and trade.'* [17]

The implication is that beyond matters of international policing there is a dynamic towards conflict contained in the development of 'shipping and aviation, raw materials and trade', which is perhaps even more fundamental a source of conflict than army manoeuvres and border disputes. The intuition that industrial development contained the germ of international conflict was widely felt. In 1922 Louis Loucheur, in his book *Pan Europa*, proposed that 'to maintain peace, the German coal and steel industries should be merged into a single "pan-European" industry'.[18]

Mitrany does not envisage an internationalisation of industry as such, but a far more extensive cooperation on technical production and distribution. Aware of the appeal of 'aspirations for full employment and social security' and for policies 'for the benefit of the whole community', he anticipates that these will gain 'more passionate support than economic action which was merely for "capitalistic" profits'. What is more, these aspirations will be more decisive than narrowly defined security. To be successful, then, 'we must put our faith not in a protected peace, but a working peace'. Looking back over his life's work, Mitrany summed up the lesson he had learned: 'that the better promise lies in shifting whenever one can communal life and organisation towards the common need rather than the separate creed'.[19]

In 1944 he wrote that 'a socially-minded government which had made a success of its national planning might not prove very tolerant to the actions which other countries might take for similar reasons but which might upset its neatly laid schemes.' 'It should be obvious', he continued, 'that unless national planning is geared from the outset to international planning we risk a much greater and more hardset division between nations than ever before'[20] – in other words, countries that pursued national-Keynesian planned growth might create greater competitive rivalries between each other.

Ernst Haas makes some suggestive criticisms of Mitrany's work in his *Functionalism and Integration* (1964). Haas suggests that Mitrany's functionalism elevates technicians over democratic forums. First he restates Mitrany's argument: 'Functional agencies, suggests Mitrany, might be based on "equality in non-representation."' Haas elaborates,

The differentiation seems to be the Rousseauan one between the General Will and the Will of All: the manager stands for the General Will, where the politician represents the Will of All, i.e. the interests of his constituents, which are by definition selfish and therefore not necessarily geared to transforming the system.[21]

Haas has identified Mitrany's discomfort with the popular will and his preference for technocratic experts. Elsewhere he paraphrases the functionalist programme:

> International conflict is best tamed by entrusting the work of increasing human welfare to experts, technical specialists and their professional associations. Being interested in tasks rather than power, they can be expected to achieve agreement where statesmen fail ... conflict is simply sidestepped if the territorial principle of representation is abandoned.[22]

Mitrany's functionalism, as suggested here, works by *depoliticising* government. Mitrany seeks to elevate the merely technical functions of administration in the hope that they will, over time, crowd out the democratic components of government. His warnings over the nationally-based social reforms seem to be inspired by an internationalism. But conversely his internationalism might arise from an aversion to expressions of the popular will, such as state socialism.

Mitrany writes that 'by its very nature the *constitutional approach* emphasizes the individual index of power; the functional approach emphasizes the common index of need'. 'Constitutional approach' seems to mean democratic government. So, one the question of a European Parliament, Mitrany was sceptical: 'the idea of a European parliament, let alone a world parliament, elected by universal suffrage and acting on behalf and for such enormous constituencies is dangerously fallacious.'[23]

Further, he writes that the functional approach 'should help shift the emphasis from political issues which divide from those social issues in which the interests of the peoples is plainly akin and collective'.[24] But the intellectual quest for the self-evident, or non-controversial areas of administration would only obscure any truly unresolved differences.

But the very assumption of non-controversiality can only arise after political consensus has been forged. In post-war Germany, military defeat was the precondition for the widespread acceptance of international control and regulation of German industry. As late as 1956 Germans polled chose 'Germany as an equal member of a European Union' over 'the rebuilding of Germany as a completely independent nation state'.[25] Mitrany's assessment that technical cooperation moderates national conflict is not wrong, but nor is it the entire story. Before technical cooperation can be pursued, political consensus must be reached.

Mindful that his technocratic vision of European Unity was insensitive to constitutional protections, Mitrany brought the question of people's rights back in, though in a pointedly individuated way.

> With the government every day pressing its activities further into the economic and cultural fields, even sport, it was meaningless to cry out against "bureaucracy" and the "new serfdom"; all that spreading intrusion into private and communal life was simply the response of authority to the claims and demands of the people themselves. ... all once could hope to do was to find some way of protecting the citizen against abuse. To that end I bought before the public the old Scandinavian institution of the Ombudsman.[26]

Here Mitrany was way ahead of his time. The role of the ombudsman, both in member states and across the European Union has become more important as constituent assemblies have lost influence.

At its core Mitrany's distaste for popular sovereignty rests on a somewhat misanthropic view of human nature, which he set out for us, reflecting on his life in 1975:

Human nature as such cannot be all bad; but whether from

original sin or worldly sin it tends to lose control of itself when flushed with sectarian beliefs and there seems little hope that disciplined emotions can be embedded lastingly into it.[27]

Here Mitrany's functionalism and internationalism suggest a desire to put control beyond the reach of mere mortals, meshing them into a web of organisation so extensive, boring even, that they could not possible wield it harmfully. It is more closely a Tory idea of the dangers implicit in reform than at first appears. Mitrany's preference for experts over 'constitutional' bodies, or assemblies, even, should be understood in this light. So should the hostility to state socialism – less a problem because of its nationally-bounded character, than the free sway it gives to popular movements.

Ernst Haas rightly draws attention to the methodological thing-ness of Mitrany's functionalism. 'Like Saint-Simon', writes Haas, 'the functionalist would hold that the human condition will improve only when "the government of men" is replaced by "the administration of things"'. Mitrany's technicist approach to government, citing Edmund Burke's precept that 'government is a practical thing', was, he says, inspired by his teacher, L. T. Hobhouse, who taught him that 'the part of the political scientist is not to predict events but to uncover and make clear the "relations of things"'. Indeed 'all knowledge is knowledge of the relation of things'.[28]

It was for that reason that Mitrany was suspicious of constituent assemblies voicing a popular will. In 1954 he was excited by the founding of the Union of International Non Governmental Organisations with offices in Brussels and a general meeting in Dusseldorf. The claims of popular sovereignty, were dubious Mitrany thought, 'the NGOs on the other hand provide an obviously sound foundation for the growth of an informed international opinion on the issues with which they are concerned'.[29]

As he develops the argument, social change seems strangely distant from human control: 'Hence in effect the form and structure of government are in the last resort shaped by the functional "relation of things"'.[30] But what in practical terms, could this mean? Mitrany gives the example of war production:

> We had here almost a controlled demonstration of the functional 'relation of things'; showing how it was the end in view, under given conditions that determined the working of government, the tasks and organisation of administration.[31]

But the non-controversial, thing-like character of the technical-administrative tasks that war production set all derived from a prior moment of Schmittian decisionism, the declaration of war, the suppression of internal opposition which, despite being obscured in Mitrany's telling, persists as an unavoidable horizon of his 'relation of things'.

According to Mitrany's account of war production

> Here we discover a cardinal virtue of the functional pattern, what one might call the virtue of technical self-determination. The functional dimensions, as we have seen, determine themselves [with] no obvious need for constitutional division of authority.[32]

The suspicion is that this is not an administration of things, but a government over men, only one that masquerades as an administration of things to keep the levers of power beyond reach. So too the idea that Unilever's operations were simply technical is not quite true. Sir Frederick Pedler explains that Mitrany was taken on because 'his knowledge of those countries where the company had important assets, might very valuable after the war, when it would be necessary to resume control of those assets or to secure compensation for them'. 'Technical self-determination' seems to express a desire to squeeze the 'human error' out of the system, or at least to turn away from the baser acquisitive instincts of Unilever's shareholders. Fundamentally it expresses an alienation of human powers, in the form of a theory of international integration, in which the international is primarily a dimension in which human sovereignty can be extinguished.

Ernst B. Haas, (1924-2003)

As a boy Haas fled Nazi Germany before studying at Columbia University, where Franz Neumann ('a former Social Democratic apparatchik'[34]) taught him comparative politics. His studies were interrupted by service with US Military Intelligence, where he worked on Japanese translations, and later he went to Berkeley to work and study for his doctorate:

Ernst Haas theorist of European integration

> I picked European integration as my initial example, 1) because I knew the languages, so that made it easy; 2) because at that time, the mid-1950s, it was the most highly developed real-life instance of movement away from the nation state. So it was a laboratory, so to speak.[35]

In 1958, the year that the treaty of Rome came into effect, he published *The Uniting of Europe*.

In the *Uniting of Europe*, Ernst Haas indicated that the underlying trend in Europe was towards the limitation of sovereignty:

> Whereas the trend in Africa and Asia is towards evolution of ever more political groupings aspiring to statehood, the process in Europe and in the Atlantic areas tends towards the

limitation of sovereign independence, the growth of more rather than less formal bonds among national communities and perhaps towards the substitution of a new federal organism for the present national state.[36]

Like Karl W Deutsch (see below), Haas was interested in the "security community" which he though was indicated by the 'absence of violence as a means of political action among the participating groups' (setting the bar rather lower than Deutsch). But unlike Deutsch, Haas was not satisfied with integration in the non-state sphere alone. Although it is true that 'economic integration however defined may be based on political motives and frequently begets political consequences': 'Free trade cannot automatically be equated with political integration; nor can an interpenetration of national markets be so considered.'[37]

Haas's theory of integration anticipated a movement towards federation. According to Haas, 'the process of integration will eventually yield a new national consciousness of the new political community, uniting erstwhile nations which had joined.' Furthermore 'the expected overlapping of these group aspirations is finally thought to result in an accepted body of "national" doctrine, in effect heralding the advent of a *new nationalism.*' [38]

Haas continues: 'implied in this development of course is a proportional diminution of loyalty to, and expectations from the former separate national government.' However 'shifts in the focus of loyalty need not necessarily imply the immediate repudiation of the national state or government'. 'Multiple loyalties', he thought, 'have been demonstrated empirically to exist'.[39]

One question raised by Haas's theory of integration is whether his theoretical approach is sufficiently rich to capture the meaning of sovereignty of which it treats so lightly. This is especially so, considering his own criticisms of David Mitrany. Here we find that his own 'value free social science' approach has similar blind spots to those that Haas himself pointed out in

Mitrany's analysis.

Haas's definition of political community is too colourless and thin to give proper credit to the concept of sovereignty that underlies it. 'Political community', he writes, 'is a condition in which specific groups and individuals show more loyalty to their central political institutions than to any other political authority, in a specific period of time, and in a definable geographic space'. This is a description from the outside, rather than a narration from the inside, it describes the loyalty passively without any real sense of the ownership that these subjects exercise over their 'central political institutions'. And again, Haas defines 'nationalism' in that studiously objectivist social science style that was parodied by the 'Martian poets': 'For the purposes of this discussion', he wrote 'the belief common to otherwise antagonistic groups will be labelled the "nationalism" of a given community'.[40]

Later in the argument Haas goes on to insist that:

> the rationality of such beliefs is as immaterial as their precise content. The only feature of relevance is the question of whether the beliefs are entertained by the overwhelming majority of the population and can be shown to influence them in making policy.[41]

In this way, Haas puts himself outside of the direct appeal of national sovereignty, to adopt the ideal vantage point of the disinterested observer. But it is a methodological approach that abstracts from precisely that question which is at issue, *sovereignty*, or more specifically, here, popular sovereignty. Haas only considers the relationship of the populace to the national entity in so far as they invest their beliefs into it, but not in so far as they might actually exercise control over it - that much is an immaterial question of the rationality or otherwise of their beliefs.

The abstraction from sovereignty that is implied in Haas's assumed value-free approach is evident in his indifference to the distinctions between legislation and administration in the High Authority of the European Coal and Steel Community:

> Nor does the oft repeated assertion that the High Authority is merely an administrative rather than an executive agency stand up ... the difference between 'legislation' and 'administrative rule-making' is such a shadowy one that it is best not to rely on it in any study of political integration.[42]

And from the Martian viewpoint, no doubt, rules and laws appear to be much the same thing - in both cases subjects can be observed obeying them. But what is opaque from that objectivist standpoint is the law's derivation from the popular will, embodied in the elected, legislative assembly. Sovereignty is the 'value' that Haas's value-free social science is free of, which makes it particularly bad at describing the movement away from nationally based sovereignty (or for that matter towards a larger, continentally-based sovereignty).

One consequence of this methodological objectivity is the appearance of indifference to the preferability or otherwise of integration, which is described merely as a process observed, without any implication of its value. However, the mask of objectivity slips a little when Haas takes issue with the political federalism of Altiero Spinelli's Union of European Federalists, which took the issue of Federation to the people in 1954: 'with all the "sublimity" [sic] and élan of the Sorelian general strike doctrine, Spinelli posited the immediate need for recognising and organising the "European People" and making a "European Front" of dedicated and militant federalists of them, demanding the immediate abolition of the nation-state'.[43] Suddenly we are wrenched from observation to judgement, making it clear that actions that threaten integration are unwelcome. But what did Spinelli do that was so wrong? He took too literally the idea of the 'European people' and put it directly to them, presumably before the 'advent of a new nationalism' could manifest itself. Here, Haas demonstrates his own discomfort with mass political processes, and following on from that his greater affinity for elite processes.

Haas sees political integration as 'the process whereby political actors in several distinct national settings are persuaded to shift their loyalties, expectations and political activities towards a new centre, whose institutions possess or demand jurisdiction over re-existing nation states'. But that leaves open the question, which 'political actors'? As we have already seen, the Union of European Federalists are not amongst those adding to the integration process. Haas clarifies his approach in *The Uniting of Europe*: 'it is essential to specify who the actors are ... it suffices to single out and identify elites' (which he goes on to do, in the shape of political, business and trade union leaderships).[44]

Haas excuses his exclusive focus on elites in this way:

> The emphasis on elites in the study of integration derives its justification from the bureaucratised nature of European organisations of long-standing, in which basic decisions are made by the leadership, sometimes over opposition and usually over the indifference of the general membership.

In other words, the institutions carrying integration forward are themselves elite institutions, with passive memberships. 'This gives the elites a manipulative role', suggests Haas. In fact it is not just that integration is an interest of elites that is not shared by the memberships, affiliates and citizenries these elites rule and administer. Rather these memberships are often at odds with their leaders precisely on the question of integration, presumably preferring the nationally-based institutions, which are thereby more readily under their control:

> A further justification for the elite approach to the study of

integration lies in the demonstrable difference in attitude held at leadership levels of significant groups, as contrasted with their membership.[45]

In considering party political processes of European integration, Haas, adopting the approach of value-free social science, struggles to give a contrasting account of the realistic interpretation of the dynamic towards cooperation as arising out of the pursuit of national interest.

So, he writes, 'only in Holland was the essence of "Europeanism" accepted without dissent, thus becoming actually part of the content of Dutch nationalism'. Whereas in Germany 'negatively speaking, it could only be said that all pro-ECSC [European Coal and Steel Community] German parties took their stand, in part, because the treaty offered release from some allied controls',[46] or in other words, because it suited their national interest.

Haas protests that: 'The only generally valid explanation of the success of the treaty lies in the convergence not of six separate national interests, but of a sufficiently large number of separate national party positions to push the treaty over the top.'[47]

However, that is not quite what he goes on to describe, or at least, if it is, he leaves the distinction between national interest and the agglomeration of party positions under-theorised. So 'in France the SFIO [Socialist Party] was favourable because it accepted the principle of the free competitive market and Franco-German peace' while the liberals 'concurred because it gave them German coke and the hope of continuing control - via Luxemburg - over German heavy industry'; In Germany, as above, 'all parties except the SPD were favourably inclined because of common, anti-Allied motives', as well as some specific business goals; 'Italian adherence was based on a mixture of doctrine, the promise of financial aid and the assurance of raw materials and larger markets'; 'Belgian support was derived from free market motives as from the boon of foreign assistance to outdated mines'.[48]

But this description seems largely to affirm rather than deny the convergence of national interests, only deviating in that it mixes into the description some of the domestic political processes that went to make up the determination of what those national interests were. As Haas goes on to say, again tending to confirm the realist interpretation as much as any other. 'The very ambiguity of the treaty of course made this pattern of convergence possible', he writes, meaning that 'something seemed to be "in it" for everybody'. His additional qualifier, insisting that the subjects of this agreement are not nations but political groupings is not really strong enough to reverse the meaning of the above: 'a large enough body of otherwise quarrelling politicians was persuaded to launch the first experiment in deliberate integration'.[49]

Karl W. Deutsch (1912-1992)

Deutsch studied for his first degree in Prague, where he was born into a Sudetan German family, and left to study for his doctorate on a scholarship at Harvard in 1939; interrupting his studies to serve in the Organisation of Strategic Services during the war, he took part in the 1945 San Francisco conference that founded the United Nations, completing his PhD. in 1951; he taught at Yale and MIT, and was a member of the Unitarian Church.[50]

Karl Deutsch thought integration better than unification

Karl W. Deutsch's emblematic study of *Political Community in the North Atlantic Area* - a collaboration with a number of scholars - was published in 1967. Like David Mitrany, Deutsch and his collaborators understood theirs as a contribution 'to the study of possible ways in which men might abolish war'. Or, if not 'how we can prevent', then at least how we can 'avoid losing "the next war"'.[51]

However, Deutsch was not primarily interested in the administrative cooperation that preoccupied Mitrany and the functionalists. He was interested in integration, but saw this primarily as a civil society process. 'Integration meant a situation of lasting peace, and the opposite, non-integration is a condition of actual or potential war', in Arend Lijphart's account.[52] Integrated regions constitute what Deutsch calls *Security Communities*.

Lijphart reports that Deutsch and the other writers of *Political Community in the North Atlantic Area* concluding that actual political union, what they called 'amalgamation' was as likely to be problematic for integration: 'To their own surprise they found "pluralistic security communities" ... to be somewhat easier to attain and to preserve than their amalgamated counterparts'. Or 'in traditional terminology, this means that anarchy is a better road to peace than sovereign rule'. What is worse still, 'amalgamation can clearly be a negative factor' because 'efforts to achieve over-all amalgamation and the establishment of a "monopoly of violence" tended to be "more of a burden than a help" to the attainment of peace', says Lijphart, paraphrasing Deutsch's argument. Only in comparison to the pitfalls of amalgamation does Deutsch allow that functionalism might have merits: 'functionalism is an approach to amalgamation ... [which] seems to be less hazardous than any sudden attempt at over-all amalgamation'.[53]

Deutsch and his collaborators set out a scheme of conditions essential for the creation of a security community. Both amalgamated and pluralistic security communities had to meet an essential condition, namely the 'compatibility of major values', which they thought obtained between Western Europe and the North American states, noting that parliamentary socialism was still compatible with markets, where communism was not. If security communities were amalgamated, they would have to meet additional conditions: a distinctive way of life, superior economic growth, expectations of joint economic reward, a wide range of transactions, the broadening of elites, links of social communication, greater mobility of persons. The bar for amalgamation, then, was set quite high. But there more basic conditions which were favourable for all kinds of security communities amalgamated or pluralistic: A reluctance to wage fratricidal war, an outside military threat, strong economic ties, and ethnic and linguistic assimilation (and the external 'Soviet threat ... seems now to be serious', wrote Deutsch and Edinger).[54]

What was distinctive about Deutsch's work, according to Arend Lijphart, was 'the rejection of the state-as-unified-actor approach'. Lijphart saw Deutsch following the view that 'nation states were only one class of associations to be related to each other and to various sub-, trans- and supranational associations'. As a consequence 'the idea of keeping separate the study of domestic and international politics was no longer a valid one' and 'any difference in the treatment of state and non-state actors in world politics' was then unnecessary.[55] Donald J. Puchala agrees that Deutsch 'never really conceived of international relations strictly as interactions between states'. Deutsch's 'convictions about the attainability of lasting peace' put him in a minority along with David Mitrany and the world federalists, according to Puchala. Carving out a niche for integration studies in the wider study of International Relations was a challenge. As Puchala says, 'by the 1950s, with the eclipse of the early idealism about the United Nations, political realism also became the dominant paradigm for the study of international organisation, thus leaving integration theory as a distinct, rather isolated, philosophically unorthodox subculture within international relations'. Over time, though, integration studies came into its own, says Puchala: 'the integrationists' earlier curiosities about international collaboration via transnational processes within settings of interdependence have become central concerns of international relations and new avenues for theoretical growth'. For those reasons, thought Puchala, 'the "post-realist paradigm" that integration studies thrust upon our discipline ... will remain prominent in international relations'.[56]

Puchala suggests that the empirical event of European integration provoked 'two generations of scholars to proliferate abstract explanations of what was happening': 'Federalists, functionalists, neofunctionalists, and transactionalists - all mutually critical and highly self-critical'. But then 'whatever had been happening in Western Europe apparently stopped happening'. And 'to the intellectual embarrassment of the scholars involved "integration theory" offered no satisfactory explanation'. It was in that climate that: 'some suggested that the so-called integration theories were probably not theories at all but post hoc generalisations about current events'. Worse still 'others suggested' the theories 'had been moralizations and utopian prescriptions' only.[57] Puchala considers that Deutsch was far from being the worst offender, his version of integration studies being more of an empirical case than an integration theory. Still, the evidence was that in the 1970s integration had foundered on the rocks of trade war and other national disputes.

Andrei Markovits and Warren Oliver take issue with Deutsch's unspoken assumptions in favour of social peace. They quote his definition of politics as the 'dependable coordination of human efforts and expectations for the good of the society'. But this is wholly inadequate, according to Markovits and Oliver:

this conception of the political neglects many of the commonly accepted features of politics in much other social theory. Such phenomenon as the class struggle and the class nature of the state, the tensions between rulers and their staffs, or the dynamic of acceptance and rejection of claims to legitimacy are neglected or glossed over, as in Lasswell's question of 'who gets what, when and how?' Perhaps the greatest lacuna of is the begging of the question of how the 'goals of society' are themselves defined.[58]

To Markovits and Oliver the rationality that political science appeals to 'runs the risk of an ahistorical description of social change, and a tendency to allow [the political scientists] own normative preferences to intrude upon the interpretation of the action observed'.[59]

In a similar vein, Robert Pfaltzgraff writes:

> In his writing on integration, Deutsch has evolved a theoretical framework based on a consensual approach. Integration occurs as peoples ... find areas of commonality of interest and expectations of joint reward. Force is consigned to a minimal role. ... we find little place in Deutsch's writings for the coercive capabilities which are often employed in the integration process. To understand the unification of Germany without the 'blood and iron' of Bismarck; the unification of the United States without the conquest of the South in the Civil War; the building up of modern Russia without the force employed by the Tsars and their successors; or ... the preservation of the Congo by the defeat of secessionist movements is once again to ignore an important set of variables.[60]

With his basic schema Deutsch and his co-researchers look at the contemporary problem, which, though not so difficult as the East-West problem is by no means simple: 'peace *within* the North Atlantic Area'. The account they come up with is a fascinatingly tentative picture of integration in the West:

> We come out with the core area (US and Canada) ... [where] all fourteen of the conditions are to be found ... If the UK and Ireland are added, only the conditions we have called "mobility of persons" is missing. ... having crossed the ocean barrier we next cross the linguistic barrier (dropping the conditions we have called "ethnic and linguistic assimi-

lation") and find that the Scandinavian countries and Benelux can be added with only a slight reductions in the number and intensity of integrative conditions. When we move to a fourth level, quite a drop occurs by adding West Germany, France, Austria and Switzerland. Finally the longest drop of all occurs when Spain and Portugal are added.[61]

Even in 1968, the assumption that America is the core area against which all others should be measured is a little out of date (the European Economic Community had already sent a single negotiator to the Kennedy Round of the General Agreement on Tariffs and Trade in 1964). Between Ireland and Britain migration was great, but a willingness not to wage war was not. Deutsch et al might have thought that it was easier to create a security community with democratic France than fascist Portugal, but NATO thought the opposite, the former being outside of the NATO command structure, the latter being a loyal and valued ally.[62]

Integration theory took off post-war because it mirrored the real course of events. Post-war national leaders did work together to rebuild Europe out of the ruins. Mitrany's functional theory found an echo in the pooling of goods and skills Europeans undertook under American leadership in the 1950s and 1960s. Mitrany, and after him Haas, were out of love with national claims, that they saw as so much trouble. They felt closer to the experts and elites that could sort out practical challenges. By the time that Karl Deutsch looked at integration, the limits were clearer. He saw common goals in civil society as a better option, because political union was already being challenged by the late 1960s. The earlier stage of European integration carried integration theory forward, but it crashed against the trade wars and defence disputes of the late sixties and seventies. The theory of integration was less compelling and scholars once again started to take national differences as their starting point.

CHAPTER SEVEN

Section 2: Europe in the Realistic School

The British Committee

In postwar Germany everyone just accepted it as a 'good thing', in part by way of atonement, in part as a way of escaping history.

France saw integration as a way of controlling Germany, and of acquiring maximum influence in Europe.

Italy - always conscious of her fragile national unity - wanted an 'ism' the whole country could support.

For Ireland, integration represented economic revival and a way to escape from Britain's shadow.

For Spain, Portugal, and Greece the union offered a way to consolidate their democracies, to modernise, and achieve prosperity.

Our continental partners see a decisive escape from their histories and an ever-brighter future. We see the opposite: a diminished Britain, imprisoned on a smaller stage with unreliable fellow actors.

(then European Commissioner Chris Patten)[63]

To see the European Union as the outcome of contrasting national interests, as British Commissioner Chris Patten does here, is to see it in a framework best outlined by the 'English School' of international theorists.

In 1954 Kenneth Thompson an academic and officer of the Rockefeller Foundation who had organised a committee of American International Relations scholars (including Hans Morgenthau, George Kennan, Paul Nitze and Reinhold Neibuhr) wrote to the historian Herbert Butterfield inviting him to set up

a corresponding group in England. Butterfield invited a select group, which would become known as the British Committee on International Relations (or more loosely the English School) chaired by Martin Wight. Though he was not invited to join the committee,[64] Edward Hallett Carr, who had done much to found the discipline of international relations in Britain, and was a considerable influence on American scholars,

E. H. Carr saw conflict between nations as inevitable

too, was a great source of reference for the British Committee. Carr's book *The Twenty Years Crisis* (1946) if not always acknowledged, anticipated most of the committee's views on the errors of 'utopianism'.

A Christian supporter of the Peace Pledge Union, Martin Wight (1913-1972) became a conscientious objector in the Second World War after graduating in Modern History from Hertford College, Oxford. Wight worked on Arnold Toynbee's encyclopaedic International Survey at the Royal Institute of International Affairs (RIIA) and for the colonial expert Margery Perham, for whom he prepared three books on colonial legislatures. In 1946 Wight reported on the United Nations inaugural conferences at Lake Success for the *Observer*, returned to the RIIA, before becoming a reader in International Relations at the London School of Economics.

Wight's defining paper for the British Committee was titled 'Why is there no international theory?' The core of the paper is a defence of the specificity of a theory of international relations: 'by "international theory" is meant a tradition of speculation about relations between states'. Throughout, Wight argues one should resist the temptation to put other kinds of study in the place of the study of relations between states, such as the emergence of world governments, or the problems of foreign affairs. 'Virtually no political thinkers have made it their business to study the states-system, the diplomatic community itself'. Wight repeated E. H. Carr's complaint against utopianism that 'in progressivist international theories, the conviction usually precedes the evidence'. Wight saw International Theory putting itself on surer footing when it was 'transformed into a doctrine of the autonomy of the national will, a counterpart to the theory of the rights of man' and where it sees 'the will of sovereign states as the exclusive source of international law, and defines international law as nothing but such rules as states have consented to'.[65]

After 'Why is there no international theory?' the clearest statement of the English School's outlook was Martin Wight's *Power Politics* (1979, but a shorter version was published by the RIIA in 1946). In *Power Politics* Wight set out the structure of International Society, or what he called the 'states system'. Its essential element was the nation: 'A power is simply a collection of human beings following certain traditional ways of action' and 'the word "nationalism" describes the collective self-assertion of a nation'; the powers were either great, meaning that their interest were world-wide, or minor powers; 'The subjects of international law are states, not individuals' he wrote, adding 'it is states alone that are international persons'. From that it followed that 'international society is the sum total of those who possess international personality', that is, states. Like Hegel, and Carr, Wight emphasized that international law has no judiciary or government, relying on 'the states themselves' for its enforcement. Relations among states would tend to for a 'balance of power'. There were no permanent allies or enemies.

This was in short, the realist account of relations between nations. It was one that de-emphasized the trans-national organisations, like the European Economic Community. Indeed, since the Treaty of Rome had been signed only two years previously, one might think that it was, if only unconsciously, a spur to the formation of the British Committee: but there is precious little evidence that they ever discussed it.[67]

The British Committee *were* very interested in what they called the European System of States – but what they meant by that was a system of 'sovereign states, political authorities which recognize no superior' but that also 'each must recognize the validity of the same claim by all the others'.[68] Here the 'realist' doctrine of the primacy of sovereign states was clearly stated. Michael Howard made the point in a 1946 paper to the Committee on disarmament:

> The best form of international organisation that we have yet been able to contrive is still consists only of a loose association of sovereign states each of whom will consult its own interests before consulting whether to fulfil its international obligations or not.[69]

In particular, the Committee asked itself the question whether the European States System could be extended beyond Europe's boundaries, even to encompass the world. This was the question posed in a collection edited by Hedley Bull and Adam Watson, *The Expansion of International Society* (1984). There is a suggestion of an underlying anxiety that beyond the zone of peace that the States System achieved, there was a zone of war.[70] Asking the question whether the United Nations did achieve the generalisation of the States System was a way of asking whether those states that for doctrinal reasons challenged the 'foundations of international society' could be incorporated. This was to see the System of States as a moderating influence, as Wight asserts when he says that 'international revolution has never long maintained itself against the national interest', and takes a cynical comfort from the fact that 'under Stalin Soviet Communism was largely transformed into Soviet imperialism'[71]. Still, Hedley Bull worried that the enlargement of the system might have costs:

> The revolt of non-European peoples and states against
> Western dominance and the expansion of the states system
> beyond its originally European or Western confines, have
> produced an international system in which the area of
> consensus has shrunk by comparison to what it was in 1914.[72]

The question that did not seem to occur to Wight was whether
the European system of states, having secured its geographic
limit, might succumb to change from within. Wight's student, the
Australian Hedley Bull (1932-85), on the other hand, was
sensitive to the challenge that transgovernmental institutions
gave to the states system. Bull's *The Anarchical Society* is an
elegant restatement of the British Committee's theoretical reconstruction of a society of sovereign states that repeats E. H. Carr's
worry about the 'danger in the confusion of prescription and
description'. Bull rejects the charge of 'state-centrism' thinking
like Wight and the British Committee 'the primacy of the states
system is for the time being assured'. Still, in Bull's telling, there
is a suggestion that the perfection of the states system might also
be the point at which it faces being challenged by different
means of world organisation.[73]

For all his loyalty to the British Committee outlook, though,
Bull, writing rather later, was much more alert to the challenge to
the states system. Bull points out that the role of international
law has been enhanced, suggesting a higher authority than that
of the will of states.

> Since the nineteenth century the predominant doctrine
> among international lawyers has been that the only true
> source of international law that is the consent of states – either
> their express consent, as in that part of international law that
> is contained in international conventions or treaties ... or their

implied consent, as in international customary law.

But Article 38 of the Statue of the International Court of Justice gives over and above those sources of international law 'the judicial decisions and the teachings of the most highly qualified publicists of the various nations' and also 'the general principles of law recognised by civilised nations'. Bull demurs these last two 'appear to allow some scope for the treatment, as a valid part of the international law, of rules to which the states contesting an issue before the Courts have not given their consent – or in relation to which it may be difficult to demonstrate that these states have given their consent.'[74]

As international law has expanded, Bull argues, so there have become recognised subjects of the law that are not states, but other actors:

> The status of subjects of international law is also accorded by many authorities to groups other than states: the United Nations and other universal or near universal intergovernmental organisations; regional intergovernmental organisations such as professional and scientific associations, non-profit making foundations and multinational economic organisations.[75]

Responding to the functionalist theories of transnational cooperation, Bull points out that 'the perspective of technical management has intruded into international life in a number of areas'. He gives as an example of 'the discussion of economic affairs within the European Economic Community'. After all 'no other regional association can match the record of the E.E.C. in measures of economic integration actually accomplished'. Still, Bull argues 'the presentation of international problems as problems of technical management often merely obscures the true position, which is that states have different interests'. It is, he says, indicative that 'in a number of areas of international discussion the conciliator or negotiator has given place to the technical expert'. The enhanced authority of regulators and officials that are celebrated in the functionalist theory strike Bull as an evasion of the political questions of national interest.[76]

Asking whether the European Economic Community might represent the transcendence of the States System altogether Bull argues that is not necessarily the case: 'if the process of integration of European states were to lead to the creation of a single European state, the upshot would be to reduce the number of sovereign states but to leave the institution of the sovereign state precisely where it was before'. After all, Bull says

the movement for European integration reflects not only the ambition of some Europeans to 'transcend power politics', but also the ambition of others to create a unit that, in a world dominated by states of continental dimensions such as the United States, the Soviet Union and China, Europeans can engage in 'power politics' more effectively. [77]

Though the creation of a European super state might be a strategy for a more effective pursuit of power politics, says Bull, it could also be seen as the emergence of a different kind of state altogether: 'it would be a sovereign state whose tendency to engage in "power politics" (in the sense of the pursuit of power as an end not merely a means) had been emasculated':

It may be argued that a European state that arose in this way, while it would still be a sovereign state, would at least not be a nation-state, and that being free of the nationalist drives and ambitions that have brought nation-states into conflict with each other in the past, it could be expected at least to be more restrained and law abiding than the state which had surrendered their sovereignty to it.[78]

Here Bull anticipates some of the ideas of the post-national Europe argued by Jürgen Habermas (see below), or Robert Kagan.[79] Still, he argues, the European superstate is not a reality, indeed 'Western Europe, while it is not amalgamated into a single state, is not a power at all'.[80] Perhaps, he suggests, the *period of transition* is more important than either its starting point as a Europe of nation states, on the one hand, or its implied end point of European superstate.

> It is possible that the process of integration might arrive at the stage where, while one could not speak of a European state, there was real doubt both in theory and in reality as to whether sovereignty lay with the national governments or with the organs of the 'community'. ... From such a position of protracted uncertainty about the locus of sovereignty, it might be a small step to the situation of a 'new medievalism', in which the concept of sovereignty is recognised to be irrelevant.[81]

Under the heading 'A New Medievalism' Bull writes 'We might imagine for example, that the government of the United Kingdom had to share its authority on the one hand with authorities in Scotland, Wales, Wessex and elsewhere, and on the other hand with a European authority in Brussels and world authorities in New York and Geneva' – which is arguably where we are in 2012. Thirty years before Jan Zielonka argued that the European Union was a case of 'neo-medievalism', Bull writes: 'If such a state of affairs prevailed all over the globe, this is what we may call, for want of a better term, a neo medieval order'.[82]

Still this is a possibility that Bull raises without enthusiasm. He was deeply – and persuasively – sceptical about the higher claims of transnational actors and institutions. Bull argued that the common good of humanity was not something that could be elaborated outside of a process of political reflection, and that the only such process was the society of sovereign states. Outside of such a nationally-based political process, the claims of transnational actors could only be wanting.

'There is indeed no lack of self-appointed spokesmen of the common good of "spaceship earth" or "this endangered planet"', he wrote: 'But the views of these private individuals, whatever merit they may have, are not the outcome of any political process of the assertion and the reconciliation of interests'. 'Nor', he added 'do the spokesmen of non-governmental groups possess authority of this kind ... to define the interests of mankind is to lay claim to a kind of authority that can only be conferred by a political process'.

Bull continues:

> The world society or community whose common good they purport to define does not exist except as an idea or myth ... the great mass of mankind does not have the means of interest articulation and aggregation ... Insofar as the interests of mankind are articulated and aggregated, and a process of political socialisation and recruitment moulds a universal political system, this is through the mechanism of the society of sovereign states.[83]

So while Bull is prepared to consider that he is looking back over a system of states that has reached its apogee, he does in the end think that the alternatives are not strongly rooted. We can see that he assumes a given idea of what a proper political process is, which is the mediation of competing interests, leading to the framing of consensual political agreement. These are assumptions that can work alongside democratic societies, though they do not necessarily demand as much. At the core of Bull's view is that the system of sovereign states is a reality, while the alternatives are at best weakly founded. Indeed Bull argues that the emergence of a transnational society could only come about through something like a revolution: 'the very issues over which governments have control, and do not seem to be likely to relinquish control, in the absence of vast changes in the social order'.[84]

Hedley Bull was the last major participant in the British Committee to address the question of Europe and the states system, though the committee's intellectual influence continued to be felt. Though not a part of the English School, one scholar whose work parallels some of the outlook of the committee is the economic historian Alan Milward.

Alan Milward (1935-2010)

The European Economic Community was driven by national motives, argued Alan Milward

Alan Milward made a reputation writing about Europe's war economies, and was from 1993 an official historian to the British cabinet office. His 1992 book, *The European Rescue of the Nation State*, gives a broadly realist analysis of the process of European integration. Milward reverses the usual argument that the European Union was a transcendence of nationally-based political power: 'Integration was not the supersession of the nation-state by another form of governance as the nation state, but was the creation of the European nation-states for their own purposes, an act of national will'.[85] Milward's prioritisation of economic motivations over diplomatic histories is a useful corrective, though one that might veer too far the other way. Still, his history is rightly celebrated for its insight into the national interests that favoured the formation of the European Economic Community between 1954 and 1964. Unfortunately, Milward's reluctance to comment without having thoroughly researched the records leaves us waiting for the promised history of the later integration process.

In a chapter in the collection *The Frontier of National*

Sovereignty (1993), Milward has more to say about the latter revival in European integration under the Delors Commission. There he argues that it was the growing consensus around neo-liberal economic policies that lead to changes – though still insisting that the source of these changes was national:

> It was only with the emergence of a gradual agreement on the need for internal market liberalization, at first within the states themselves, that there actually were any national policies that could more effectively be advanced through the integrationist framework.[86]

In the same essay, Milward draws attention to the creation of the European Council in 1974 as evidence of the continuing priority of national governments in deciding Community policy.

There is an 'envoi' at the end of *The European Rescue of the Nation State* that does throw out some thoughts on the more recent history. There he indicates that the conditions that led to the Treaty of Rome no longer apply. 'Since all history is change, that rescue [of the nation state, post-war] could only be temporary and the process of economic development itself has ended the political consensus which sustained both nation and supranation after the war'.[88] In the lead up to the Single European Act, however, Milward suggests another basis on which integration might move forward:

> The smaller role for the machinery of national government in the new consensus allowed a greater relative role for the Community; the European Commission could appear as a more potent agent of deregulation of markets precisely because its supranationality gave it a greater scope and effectiveness.[89]

Milward's indication that the common ground that governments have found in more recent European developments rests on their removal of more political functions from the national democratic framework is very suggestive. As he writes: 'in internationalising policies they [nation-states] are seeking to restrict the force of postwar democratic pressures'.[90]

The English School in retrospect

Plainly much contemporary work in International Relations theory is at odds with the state-centric focus of the British Committee. Still, the stubborn persistence of the sovereign nation-state as a form of social organisation – particularly in the European Union itself – suggests that *realism* is still pertinent. On the other hand, a failure to reflect upon the actual growth in the weight of transnational institutions suggests a blind spot in the theoretical architecture of the system of states set out by the British Committee. We might think that the system of states theory is not so much wrong, as partial, or one-sided, capturing only a part of the equation.

The British Committee might be accused of conservatism, in their bias towards states. But just as much, those who challenge state sovereignty ought to justify their bias towards change. It might seem compelling to researchers today that scholarship ought not be a handmaiden to power, but it did not strike the British Committee as a weakness that its ideas were developed in tandem with the Foreign and Commonwealth Office and even the Treasury. On the contrary, Herbert Butterfield boasted of those connections to Kenneth Thompson of the Rockefeller Institute.[91]

We might ask whether the British Committee did enough to enquire into the very foundation of their own theory, the nation state, and specifically the concept of *sovereignty* itself. It seems odd that the very foundation of the whole conceptual development of the system of states, the sovereign state is the one thing that is not energetically investigated by the British

Committee. Sovereignty, the imputation of personality to territory, is such a strange thing, that the Committee, resting so much of their theory upon it, might have interrogated more.

Wight writes about the personification of power as a curious custom: 'It is a consequence of nineteenth century nationalism that we personify a power calling it "she" and saying that *Britain* does this, *America* demands that, and the *Soviet Union's policy* is something else'. Wight warned that

> This is mythological language, as much as if we speak of John Bull, Uncle Sam or the Russian Bear. 'Britain' in such a context is a symbol for an immensely complex political agent, formed by the permanent officials of the Foreign Office, the Foreign Service, the Foreign Secretary, the Prime Minister, the Cabinet, the House of Commons, the living electorate and the dead generations that have made the national tradition, combining and interacting in an infinitude of variations of mutual influence.[92]

But this aside does not really take us so far. On the one hand Wight translates the personification of power rationally, by saying that it is just shorthand for 'the British government says' – though that might open up as many questions as the more poetic image of John Bull. On the other hand, Wight opens up a whole other meaning of the sovereign state when he adds the 'dead generations that have made the national tradition' into the many components of the 'immensely complicated political agent'. That there are agents at all, still less that their agency should be vested in territory is not really explained here, only described.

By 1985, the British Committee was no longer, but more broadly scholars with a similar realist outlook (notwithstanding the interesting distinctions made between the English and American versions of realism made by Dunne and others[93]) were beginning to look very closely, and critically at the process of European integration. Many of these scholars were based in America, like Stanley Hoffmann, and Andrew Moravcsik.

Stanley Hoffmann

Born in Vienna in 1928, Stanley Hoffmann lived in Paris graduating from the Institut d'Etudes Politiques and later teaching at the Ecole des Hautes Etudes en Sciences Sociales, before teaching at Harvard University from 1955. He was chair of Harvard University's Centre for European Studies from 1969 to 1995. Hoffmann's writing is combative in style, rather than affecting an academic objective distance. Though he stands on the ground of *realist* international relations theory, he is unapologetically judgemental and critical – critical of the European Union as a project, which he contrasts unfavourably with the United States.

Stanley Hoffmann scorned moves to a European super-nation

Hoffmann's assessment of what he calls the 'Monnet method' of functional integration (and by implication the 'functionalist' theory that reflected on it) is damning: 'a type of mind-expanding drug which makes those who take it believe that Europe's unity will proceed thanks to step-by-step concrete bargains and independent, expert "supranational" therapy'. But functional integration, challenges Hoffmann 'does not provide an answer to the question: where do we want to go?'[94]

What Hoffmann meant was that functionalist account of the European project – and let it be said, he thought that the functionalist account was a real insight into the process of elite integration itself – was anti-political. Functional integration 'puts form over content, substitutes procedure for substance, sacrifices direction for motion'. Assuming the plurality of competing interests Hoffmann insists that 'there is no escape from politics' and that 'there is only the politics of consensus and the politics of conflict'. But consensus, Hoffmann insists cannot be created by avoiding hard choices. 'The Monnet method may seize a weak consensus and make it strong, but it cannot create it', writes Hoffmann. On the contrary, 'the recourse to supranational integration by governments means only that they choose to conceal the embarrassment of dissension behinds the businesslike façade of supranationality'– and here Hoffmann makes the mistake of assuming political contestation as a given, for all time, whereas in fact it has greatly weakened, making supranational organisation more achievable.[95]

Insofar as it was successful, says Hoffmann, European integration was a mirage built on plenty. 'The method has worked in the area of welfare alone', he wrote. Hoffmann takes issue with a suggestion by Ernst Haas that politics could be removed altogether, as the government of men gave way to Saint-Simon's (Claude Henri de Rouvroy, comte de Saint-Simon, 1760-1825, utopian socialist) administration of things: 'For Haas's (or Saint Simon's) vision to be true, we would have to imagine a world of plenty and nothing less'. But, objects Hoffmann 'split it into states again and national politics is reborn'. Politics, to Hoffmann, is the managing of competing interests, so 'introduce scarcity into the distribution of any goods and domestic politics – the manipulation of men by men for the allocation of what is scarce – re-emerges'.[96]

Hoffmann sees Europeans corrupted by not just by plenty, but also by long years of peace (the very things that seems to recommend the European Union to its supporters). The community was, writes Hoffmann, 'for many of its enthusiasts, including the disciples of Jean Monnet, going to be the exemplary civilian power'. But taking the more pacific route did not remove the need for security, 'security was left to NATO'.

This is a complaint against the European Union that has had currency among America's political leaders. It is not just that Europeans enjoy plenty, but that their plenty is unearned. 'The fertile desert of Europe', writes Hoffmann 'spurns adventures and savours the delights of consumption and production'.[97]

With that cynical insight that realist thinkers often bring to bear, Hoffmann reads the persistent national rivalries that are hidden beneath the false consensus of the European Union, which he describes as a 'cobweb of interests and relationships'. This passage anticipates both Commissioner Patten's account of the national differences that drive Union forward, in his 2002 interview, and also the 'inter-governmentalist' theory of European integration put forward by Andrew Moravcsik (below):

[In the Cold War] the French devised a policy that tried to combine the maximum of possible independence and the development of a European entity that would "contain" West Germany as did NATO, but would also be capable of resisting America's supremacy. France would offset the Federal Republic of Germany's economic dynamism with its independent nuclear force and its unique capacity to lead the Community, given the inhibitions that handicapped Bonn in this respect. The Germans saw in the Community a way back to respectability, an avenue of influence and a provider of support for Germany's legitimate national aspirations. The British latecomers endorsed it as a field of influence (now that decolonisation was over and the Commonwealth had faded) and as an instrument for the containment of both France and Germany's anti-American thrust and leadership ambitions. For Italy it was a highly desirable way of keeping out of power a Communist Party whose own radical embrace of European integration was deemed incompatible with its support of Soviet politics.[98]

In this compelling rhetorical performance, all of these masked national interests work, curiously, not to pull Europe apart, as the theory might seem to suggest, but in fact work to bind it together, albeit in a dysfunctional way. Hoffmann goes some way to explaining this as he characterises the sovereign states of Europe as something more complicated than merely interest-maximising agents that one might expect to find in a realist theory. European states are coping with something more than ordinary appetites; they are coping with *guilt*. 'All the Europeans have skeletons in their closet' writes Hoffmann, 'Europe tries to escape from its past'. While France hides failure with pride, he says, Germany has tried to exorcise their past 'by exorcising nationalism altogether' (recalling Margaret Thatcher's complaint against German neutralism, see chapter three). Germany's 'political elites' says Hoffmann 'remain committed to European unity as insurance against the temptation of adventurism and as a reassurance to the rest of the world'. [99]

Still, thinks Hoffmann, these are not sufficient bases for continued solidarity. In 1995 he recalled that 'in 1964 I wrote that the European consensus was negative; I do not think that there is one today'. Europe's difficulties revolve, predictably, around its immature relationship to the American hegemon. 'Western Europe suffers, paradoxically, both from the legacy of the post war habit of dependence on American leadership', writes Hoffmann 'and from the decline of' American predominance.[100]

One objection to Hoffmann's work is that its considered conclusions rather closely shadow the mainstream interpretation of US national interest. Indeed, between them Ernst Haas, Karl Deutsch and Stanley Hoffmann do appear to describe the evolution of US policy towards Europe from favouring the European Payments Union in 1949, to seeking cooperation under NATO in the 1960s, to a growing dissatisfaction with Europe the economic rival and security freeloader in the seventies and eighties. Still, for all his combative style of presentation,

Hoffmann gives a good theoretical account of Europe's development, and it does not follow that the vantage point of the US is
necessarily a bad one, even if the agreements were more than
coincidence. Still, the anxiety remains that Hoffmann's realism
passes off normative judgements (the preferability of Europe's
disunity) as objective conditions (the primacy of the nation state)
– a complaint laid by Noam Chomsky.

Hoffmann is acute, too on the institutions of the Union, and
their relation to the underlying complexities of the peoples and
elites of Europe. Tempting for anyone interested in integrating
the differing theories of European integration, Hoffmann points
out that the institutions themselves mirror the different
emphases of the competing schools of thought on Europe So
Hoffmann, distinguishes between:

> those who saw the EEC, the EC or the EU as an entity moving
> towards some kind of Federal Europe under the leadership of
> partly supranational institutions (Commission, Parliament,
> Court of Justice) and through the process that Monnet had
> created and Ernst Haas turned into a theory, and those who
> believed it would amount to little more than a Europe des
> États, in which the intergovernmental bodies (the Council of
> Ministers, the European Council) would dominate.[102]

Where one would have to fault Hoffmann, is that his conclusion
that European unity was a chimera seems so clearly contradicted
by the pooling of sovereignty in pan-European institutions. Here,
one has to return to the point that Hoffmann has assumed what
he ought to show, that political contestation will continue to
disrupt the apolitical-functional integration. The record seems to
indicate the opposite, that a more muted political contestation
has created the conditions for a greater degree of European
integration. One scholar working along similar lines who has
taken great interest in the process of 'integration' is Andrew

Moravcsik.

Andrew Moravcsik and intergovernmentalism

Andrew Moravcsik, is Professor of Politics and International Affairs, and Director of the European Union Program, at Princeton University's Woodrow Wilson School since 2004, having been a professor at Harvard University before that. Moravcsik developed an approach that is a much-modified realist theory of international relations and of European integration, *intergovernmentalism.* He is also husband to Hilary Clinton's former foreign policy advisor Anne-Marie Slaughter.

In his book *The Choice for Europe* Moravcsik argues that European integration can best be explained as a series of rational choices made by national leaders'. Contrary to the federalist argument 'the integration process did not supersede or circumvent the political will of national leaders'. In fact 'it *reflected* their will' (Moravcsik's emphasis). He insists that the development of a distinctive theory of European integration is unnecessary, because

Washington insider Andrew Moravcsik argues that inter-governmental agreement is the basis of the European Union

'the behaviour of European governments is *normal'* – meaning that European nations pursue their national interests just like any other nation. In fact 'European integration exemplifies a distinctly modern form of power politics'.

Moravcsik departs from the orthodox realist view in that he makes the governments not the sovereign nations the agents of international relations (or what is, in effect, intergovernmen-talism). By focussing on actual governments and their choices, Moracsik seems to evade the more metaphysical idea of The Nation. Still, Moravcsik might be said to bring the idea of the nation back in, as a necessary fiction. 'The assumption [Moravcsik's, that is] that states are unitary maintains that each act in the international negotiations "as if" with a single voice', he writes. Furthermore, states are rational, acting 'as if' they were pursuing preferences with given means. Moravcsik says that, through the political process, national preferences are forged, that these preferences are put forward in interstate bargaining before being enacted in institutional choices.

Unlike the predominant, realist account of European Union – which is to say, Hoffmann's – Moravcsik downgrades what he calls 'geo-political' and still more so 'idealistic' influences on national preferences. Hoffmann, according to Moravcsik argues that 'the geopolitical interests of individual states must be traced to national values, historical analogies, and "lessons of history" distilled in the minds of leaders, political elites, and the mass public'.[105] Moravcsik does not discount those entirely, but he does think that more prosaic commercial motives have been decisive much more often in interstate bargaining in the European Union.

Moravcsik admits that his stress on the economic motivations as an explanation of has an obvious objection: 'Most economists have viewed most of the major goals pursued by the EC over the years … with scepticism if not with outright hostility' (by 'most economists' he means mainstream, neo-classical economists). [106] To accommodate that objection, Moravcsik argues that the economic decisions that influence governments are 'political economics', where producer lobbies and other special interests are more decisive in a way that they are not in neo-classical economic theory. Indeed Moravcsik's account of the many stages in European integration depends so much on the inordinate influence of producer lobbies, that it is hard to avoid the conclusion that at some deeper level, he sees the whole project as a departure from the normal outcome of market equilibrium, and a distortion of the laws of the free market. Still, his explicit point is to show that the Union is not a disproof of rational choice theory – at the level of interstate bargaining – but evidence of it.

Moravcsik is diligent in testing his thesis against the historical record of the interstate bargains of the original Treaty of Rome (1958), the consolidation of the Common Market (1958-1969), the debates over monetary integration (1969-1983), the Single European Act (1984-1988) and the Maastricht Treaty (1988-1991). The result is a strong empirical as well as a theoretical account of the development of the European Union. Still, putting so much evidence into the balance, it is clear that his singular explanation is strained by the many events he tries to fit into it. In particular, his assumption that rationally choosing states would willingly 'pool' – or give up – their sovereignty seems like a tall order. Moravcsik hopes that that can be explained by the way that states seek to constrain their rivals by mutually agreeing to pool sovereignty. And throughout *The Choice For Europe* Moravcsik returns often to the idea that governments might, for internal reasons, seek to bind themselves and their successors in agreements that limit sovereignty, without ever convincingly showing how that might arise out of a rational and unitary state preference.

Moravcsik writes at length on France's more favourable view of monetary integration (their willingness to accept German terms) under François Mitterrand in 1983, following the failure of his nationally-based Keynesian reflation strategy and the political Union of the Left that had brought him to power. Rejecting the arguments that Mitterrand was following geo-political imperatives of 'tying Germany into Europe' Moravcsik insists that the decision was the best available economic policy – devaluation – and that the rhetorical appeal to 'European ideology' only came afterwards: 'The most that can be said for geopolitical ideology is that it provided an expedient way for Mitterrand to justify the abandonment of the Socialist experiment'. But Moravcsik is wrong to play down the significance of

François 'Mitterrand's effort to refashion his political image and discourse as "European"', which he says is in the end 'an adaptation to the only economic course perceived as realistic'. France's economic difficulties were real enough, but the historic defeat of the left programme was of more moment. Mitterrand's rhetorical flights were emblematic of the collapse of a political movement that would have a far greater influence on France's ability to formulate national preferences.[107]

Moravcsik struggles to account for the behaviour of Mitterrand, French President from 1981-1995. Mitterrand's foreign policy is 'opaque and superficially contradictory', and disturbingly interested in *the prestige of France* (Moravcsik's italics); his rhetoric is 'deliberately deceptive' and 'blame avoidance'; his leadership style is 'opaque and contradictory', or, quoting Hoffmann 'Gaullism by another name', 'a "notoriously Machiavellian" politician of whom it is said "his greatest constant is inconsistency"'. What these comments tell us is that Moravcsik cannot fit Mitterrand's actions into his theoretical framework of preference formation. And given that Mitterrand was France's longest serving president, we might think that it is Moravcsik's framework that is unequal to the task, rather than Mitterrand. What Moravcsik struggles to explain is that Mitterrand committed France to the European Monetary System and then later to the single currency for what seem to be intangible, and economically unsound reasons. But those things that Moravcsik considers 'opaque and contradictory', 'blame avoidance' and attempts to 'refashion his political image and discourse as European' are very much what politics, for Mitterrand, after 1983, was about. Curiously, to a theorist focussing on the political will of national leaders, François Mitterrand's interests as leader were advanced by offering up French sovereignty to the European Union.[108]

Moravcsik has similar difficulties accounting for British Prime Minister Margaret Thatcher's '"deep-seated prejudice" against the EC'. Thatcher, he says, opposed monetary integration on 'ideological grounds' – as if ideological grounds were somehow not the business of political leaders. Her opposition to monetary union left her 'increasingly isolated' in the years after 1983, says Moravcsik, though she was in fact re-elected in 1987 and was Britain's longest serving Prime Minister since Lord Liverpool in 1827. Moravcsik says that Thatcher ought to have been more influenced by the Confederation of British Industry that favoured participation in the Exchange Rate Mechanism. But that is because he puts too little weight on Mrs Thatcher's need to keep the 'Thatcher revolution' going once it had succeeded in 'rolling back socialism' in Britain by challenging 'socialist Europe'. It should also be said that Mrs Thatcher's position was not entirely a departure from the Foreign Office's long-standing attitude to Europe, which is to neither support wholly nor oppose, but to do the minimum necessary to stop being forced out while still slowing integration as much as possible. Disturbing as it might seem to 'the assumption that states are unitary' political leaders often pursue sectional interests that appear to be at odds with those of 'the nation' – which is after all just an abstraction, whose best approximation is just that political process that throws up these eccentric choices.[109]

Moravcsik sees producers' lobbies as central to the formation of policy preferences towards integration. He claims that in the negotiation of the Treaty of Rome the government-funded boosting of farm prices was 'less controversial, for taxpayers were considerably less well organized than farmers' and that 'the power of farm groups was considerable'. But that is not quite true. In the aftermath of the Second World War, farmers as a social group had been crushed by the effective nationalisation of their farms. Governments promoted food security after the war with big subsidies. Rural constituencies became important for Christian Democrat governments as a counter-weight to the urban left leaning voters. Farmers' lobbies had clout because their support was important to governments of the right, and when the socialist vote weakened in the 1980s, governments were more willing to attack farm subsidies.[110]

Moravcsik pointed out that the European Round Table (ERT) of leading industrialists, and also the Union of Industrial and Employers' Confederations of Europe (UNICE) played a major part in persuading the national negotiators to support the Single European Act.[111] The Act, signed in 1986 aimed to create a single market across Europe by 1992. Led by Phillips' chairman Wisse Dekkers the European Round Table industries were already, for the most part, firms that traded – and in many cases organised – Europe-wide. But as Maria Cowles has pointed out, the Round Table did more than shape political preferences, it substituted for an absent political process:

> The ERT, however, did not merely articulate interests. The CEOs organized themselves to become active political actors that shaped EC and, therefore, national policy agendas. They provided policy alternatives and informed public opinion. In short, the ERT assumed many of the roles that had previously been reserved for Member States. The ERT became a political actor in its own right.[111]

Here, what needs to be explained is not the role of business in shaping preferences, but the absence of the political leaders from the process of shaping preferences. For the most part, Moravcsik's leaning on the activities of business lobbies to explain interstate bargaining is an attempt to identify 'interests' that can explain national preferences – and betrays an unease with ideological or 'geo-political' motives. The result can at times look like the kind of economic determinism that would make a Marxist blush. The identification of economic motives acts as *deus ex machina* to Moravcsik's account of European integration. They take us away from the explicit statements of political leaders (which are often 'opaque', 'ideological' or 'inconsistent') to another realm that supplies the real motives that lie *behind* those leaders' odd actions – a kind of 'follow the money' investigation.

The paradox at the heart of Moravcsik's study is how to explain why sovereign states should choose to give up their sovereignty. One strategy is to downplay the surrender of sovereignty that the union represents, and Moravcsik does that by concentrating on those institutions that exemplify intergovernmental bargaining: the European Council and the treaty summits. Moravcsik continues to worry around the question (suggesting that it is not wholly settled) offering useful insights into the problem. He explains how interstate bargaining might lead to one government accepting a non-problematic limit as a way of limiting others – so for example 'Germany's desire to "lock in" a guarantee of low inflation by creating an autonomous European Central Bank'[113] is no challenge to fiscally-conservative Germany, though more of one to some of her European partners. On the whole, though, Moravcsik's most striking arguments are at odds with his own theoretical assumptions of a *unitary* and *rational* formation of policy preference. The answer that Moravcsik comes to again and again is this: that the best explanation of how a sovereign state could willingly choose to bind itself in the future, is to see that state as not unitary but divided. Namely that a part of the state, its government – perhaps on behalf of a business elite – chooses to bind the whole state, as way of putting limits on another part of the state, which might be special interests, like labour organisations, or producers' lobbies, or popular expectations over government spending.

So Moravcsik shows that one key motive for supporting the European Monetary System among French political leaders was 'to impose monetary discipline', or *'une solution de rigeur'* as it was called in internal government documents. Moravcsik argues that Nigel Lawson 'saw the EMS primarily as a means of reducing the domestic political costs of disinflation', as the government could, in Lawson's words avoid the 'political pressures for the relaxation of monetary discipline ... if we were to embrace the exchange rate discipline'.[114]

Interestingly, given his insistence that her scepticism towards European institutions was irrational, Moravcsik gives a very good explanation why it was that Mrs Thatcher was not tempted by the economic disciplining effect of the European Monetary System on wages and inflation that impressed her chancellors: 'Thatcher, in overt opposition to many of her advisors, preferred to disinflate by confronting and conquering rather than circumventing domestic opposition, whatever the short-term costs';[115] Which is to say that Mrs Thatcher preferred to pursue her goals within the domestic political arena rather than to try to use the European Community to avoid a fight. In that she had greater political resources than those European counterparts, like Bettino Craxi and François Mitterrand, who leant on the European Community to impose discipline on their domestic economies.

Like Odysseus, governments willingly bound themselves to the European mast, to resist the siren calls of inflationary spending, and inflationary wage demands – bunging their populations' ears' up with claims that there was no other way. As well as willingly submitting to fiscal and monetary discipline, governments also disavowed responsibility for unpopular decisions by insisting that these were conditions of European Union membership. Moravcsik points out that 'national politicians reduce the political costs of unpopular policies by "scapegoating" international institutions or foreign governments', or reducing 'the political cost of austerity by "shifting blame" and "locking in" policies' – such as Mitterrand's 'blame avoidance' (see above).[116] In a chapter in a Brookings Institute collection Moravcsik wrote about politicians 'blaming the EU for unpopular policies of fiscal austerity, monetary discipline, and the reduction of subsidies'.[117] This is a parallel argument running alongside his main thesis that governments' seek cooperation in pursuit of commercial advantage – but it is one that seems to offer more explanatory power. However, Moravcsik's useful identification of the way that government's shifted blame onto the European Union should be understood in a wider framework of the declining importance of national assemblies and domestic political contestation in the formation of elite preferences.

The meaning of realism

What is realism theorising? Realism theorises the independence of states. Put another way, realism explains just why it is that sovereignty finds national limits. It is a theory to explain the inability to generalise the rule of law and government, and, against the usual view, is a theorisation of the toleration of difference. When Fitzroy Maclean questioned the wisdom of backing communist insurgents in the Balkans, Churchill challenged him: 'Are you going to live there?' No, replied Maclean. Churchill replied: 'Neither am I, so had we not better leave the Jugoslavs themselves to work out what sort of system they are going to have?'[118] Churchill knew that Maclean's question was academic – Britain lacked the resources to take responsibility for governing Yugoslavia, so it handed over power to which ever authorities were in a position to rule.

Secretary of state Henry Kissinger formalised the realistic policy of 'détente', saying 'we cannot gear our foreign policy to the transformation of other societies' and 'peace between nations is also a high moral objective'.[119] The US army, and the US government, was in no position to take authority over Eastern Europe – and struggled to help stabilise Western Europe, which was the reason that the US accepted the common European tariff boundary. That was the meaning of the British Committee's research project into the limits of the states system. Wight had explained that the subordination of the 'revolutionary state' to the states system represented a stabilisation of the world order.

They were interested to know if that stabilisation could embrace the different realms of the less developed, or 'Third World'. If society, and more specifically, polity developed evenly, geographically, then there would be no national differences, no distinct nation states, and no other sovereign governments to recognise. But it does not, and there are.

Realism and the European Union, the record

The 'realist' school of International Relations gives a good account of the process of interstate bargaining that gave rise to the European Union. But its conception of sovereignty is unreflective – gifted from political philosophers of the past, and unequal to the challenge that the 'post-national' thinkers were about to make. The realists and intergovernmentalists were lifted by the growing disparity between functionalist accounts of integration and the actual, and conflictual record of European inter-state relations. But they were not prepared for the vigour of the critique of nationalism that came from structuralists and constructivists.

Worse still, taking as it does, the nation-state as presupposition, the realist school of international relations is not well disposed to analyse transition from a political system based upon nation states towards one where the nation state is of less importance. If it can be shown that this is indeed the case, then the realist theory risks redundancy. What if nations cease to exhibit the property of self-aggrandisement?

What the realist and intergovernmentalist theories struggle to explain is how it could be rational for a sovereign state to limit its future action, or bind future governments through the surrender ('pooling') of sovereignty to super-national institutions. As Ben Rosamond puts it 'intergovernmentalism has to find an answer to the question of why it is that states should invest in an enterprise that results in a *de facto* clipping of their policy autonomy'.[120] Despite the creativity that Andrew Moravcsik has brought to this question, the answer is still elusive. The answer might be that the state must be *divided* to see a rational advantage in self-denial. That is, that one part of the state sees an advantage in binding the whole nation because it wants to bind another part of the nation. If, for example, elites, fear the challenge of substantial lobbies within the nation, they might prefer to enter into agreements that set specific limits, limits that cause the elite relatively less difficulty, but act as a barrier to claims by powerful lobbies.

In July 1940, French minister Paul Baudouin claimed that 'the total revolution of France has been prepared by twenty years of uncertainty, discontent, disgust, and latent insurrection'. He was describing the 'National Revolution' under which the collaborationist Vichy Regime used Germany's occupation to reorder French society on a traditionalist basis, with the left firmly shut out. 'The war has burst open the abcess', he explained, 'this possibility of doing something new thrills men of every walk of life'.[121] For some, who felt the left's influence in the 1930s to be a burden, it was better to make peace with the German occupation and accept the constraints that imposed upon radicalism, than to put too much store by self-determination. On a more moderate scale, Andrew Moravcsik shows us that some European ministers were happier to tie their own hands in wage and monetary policy, the better to face down social demands.

If states were divided in the 1930s and the 1980s, are they divided today? Not so forcefully, it must be said. Social conflict is much quieter than it once was. But if there is not the active challenge to elites that there once was, there is all the same a marked divide between elites and populations. Juan Diez Mendrano says that there is marked 'disagreement between political elites and a significant segment of the population on the values that should sustain the European project'.[122] Most pointedly, there is a chasm of ignorance between elites and populations, for the simple reason that elites have a less organic relation to their populations than once they did. Elite distrust of 'populist' movements leads them to invest greater authority in the Brussels- and Strasbourg-based institutions of the European Union than the unpredictable and argumentative national parliaments.

Perhaps those theories of European integration that emphasize its social side can provide a further insight into the process. In the next chapter we look at the constructivist and other post-positivist theories of European integration.

CHAPTER EIGHT

Post-Positivist Theories of European Integration

Europe and the constructivist theory of international relations

The major challenge to the realist theory of international relations is made by scholars who emphasize the social construction of reality, known as 'constructivists' (in the humanities the same views are more often called 'social construction' or 'social constructionist', and 'constructivism' in International Relations has nothing to do with the preceding school in architecture also called 'constructivism.).

The theory of social construction has various philosophical roots, but primarily comes from Edmund Husserl's phenomenology. In his essay *The Origins of Geometry*, and in the *Crisis in the European Sciences*, Husserl overturned empirical theories of objectivity, bracketing the question of whether there was an external reference point for knowledge, and looking instead at the inter-subjective construction of social reality – 'in this regard we speak of the intersubjective constitution of the world'. Following Husserl, the Sociologist Max Scheler wrote in the 1920s of 'the fundamental fact of the social nature of all knowledge and of its preservation and transmission, its methodological expansion and progress'. [1]

The Frankfurt Institute, under its directors Max Horkheimer and Theodor Adorno popularised German sociology and, in a radical form, the sociology of knowledge, in America after the war. For the Frankfurt Institute, the social nature of thought is counterposed to its *naturalisation* at the hands of the positivists. Furthermore, naturalistic social theories are taken to be conservative, imbuing the status quo with the character of a natural given. Setting out their own 'critical theory' the institute challenged positivist thinking because it

> seeks to reduce society to the purely natural, it no longer aids in the liberation from the compulsion of the institutions, but only furthers a new mythology, the glorification of the illusory primal qualities, to which is attributed what in fact only arises by virtue of society's institutions. The extreme model of rendering society 'natural' in such a false and ideological fashion is the racist insanity of national socialism.[2]

The British philosopher Peter Winch drew upon both sociology and Wittgenstein's later work in his *Idea of a Social Science and its Relation to Philosophy*, first published in 1953. There he develops the idea of socially constructed meaning in opposition to a naturalised and eternalised meaning. He writes that the

> criteria of logic are not a direct gift of God, but arise out of, and are only intelligible in the context of, ways of living or modes of social life. It follows that one cannot apply criteria of logic to modes of social life as such. For instance science is one such mode and religion another; and each has its criteria of intelligibility peculiar to itself.[3]

As Winch has it, 'ideas cannot be torn out of their context ... the relation between an idea and context is an *internal* one' and 'the idea gets its sense from the role it plays in the system'. The sociologists Peter Berger and Thomas Luckmann, drawing on Scheler make the point that there is no real substrate that explains beliefs, writing, playfully, that 'rural Haitians *are* possessed and New York intellectuals *are* neurotic'.[4] An exchange between Max Scheler, an early enthusiast of the phenomenological method, and his Marxist friend Georg Lukacs sheds some light on how it worked:

Once during the first world war Scheler visited me in Heidelberg, and we had an informing conversation on this subject. Scheler maintained that phenomenology was a universal method which could have anything for its intentional object. For example, he explained, phenomenological researches could be made about the devil; only the question of the devil's reality would first have to be "bracketed." "Certainly," I answered, "and when you are finished with the phenomenological picture of the devil, you open the brackets – and the devil in person is standing before you." Scheler laughed, shrugged his shoulders, and made no reply.[5]

The social constructionist programme of scepticism towards the external referent of objective reality underlying subjective ideas was given a distinctive overhaul by those philosophers called postmodernists or deconstructionists. Jean-François Lyotard was commissioned to write a report on knowledge by the Conseils de Universities of Quebec, where he summed up modernism as 'any science that legitimates itself with reference to a metadiscourse ... making an explicit appeal to some grand narrative, such as the dialectics of Spirit, the hermeneutics of meaning, the emancipation of the rational or working subject or the creation of wealth'. But postmodernists, he argued, must show 'incredulity to metanarratives'. French philosopher Jacques Derrida, reworked Husserl's *Origins of Geometry* to show that even the intersubjective cannot constitute reality 'since the Logos and the Telos are nothing outside of the interplay of their reciprocal inspiration'. Derrida's project of deconstruction has excited and irritated scholars ever since, inspiring many open-ended critiques.[6]

Social construction theory was never really a single school of fellow collaborators, but its main propositions had a growing influence over sociologists, and later historians, anthropologists and literary critics. For students of international relations, the impact of social construction was probably first felt in the re-imagining of nationalism. The sociologist Ernest Gellner was generally critical of social construction theory, but in his influential work on nations and nationalism, his scepticism towards primordial ideas of the nation did lead him to see nationalism as an ideological construct. 'Nationalism is not the awakening of nations to self-consciousness,' he wrote 'it invents nations where they do not exist'. The Marxist historian Eric Hobsbawm, too, emphasized the historical creation of nations in his *Nations and Nationalism*, though he qualified Gellner's account of nations 'constructed essentially from above' with a greater sympathy for popular nationalism 'from below'.[7] All the same, the research project that Hobsbawm undertook, published as the collection co-edited with Terence Ranger, *The Invention of Tradition* (1993) drew attention to the manufactured rituals and myths that lay behind apparently primordial ideas of nation. The anthropologist Marshall Sahlins wittily drew out the point by showing that not just third world national myths, but the European Renaissance also was a 'self-conscious tradition of fixed and essentialised canons':

> When Europeans invent their traditions – with the Turks at the gates – it is a genuine cultural rebirth, the beginning of a progressive future. When other peoples do it, it is a sign of cultural decadence, a factitious recuperation which can only bring forth the simulacra of a dead past.[8]

But Sahlins' irony was misplaced. The growing emphasis upon Europe's invented tradition was not intended to be a lionisation, but a critique. In 1983 Benedict Anderson wrote *Imagined Communities*, which opened up its analysis of the construction of national ideology in Indonesia to a generalised theory of invented nations. Anderson proposed the definition of a nation 'an imagined political community – and imagined as both inherently limited and sovereign'. Five years earlier, the Columbia literature professor Edward Said had published his influential *Orientalism*, where he showed that 'without examining Orientalism as a discourse, one cannot possibly understand the enormous systematic discipline by which European culture was able to manage – and even produce – the Orient'.[9]

Plainly, saying that nations were a social construct was more than just a methodological proposition – it meant a downgrading of the nation state, challenging its claims to an essential nature, bringing out instead its passing and artificial character. The new theoretical approach mirrored a changed attitude to nationalism, which had been the outlook of the educated classes in the nineteenth and early twentieth century, but was now increasingly out of favour, as it was more likely to be associated with plebeian and demotic movements.

John Gerard Ruggie

Born in Austria in 1944, John Ruggie is Kirkpatrick Professor of International Relations at the Kennedy School of Government, Harvard University, and the UN Secretary General's representative championing human rights in the business sector. Ruggie was also instrumental in the development of a constructivist theory of International Relations. As he explains in the autobiographical introduction to *Constructing the World Polity*, Ruggie had already identified the research agenda of the institutionalisation of international relations, before he was familiar with social constructivist theory, drawing on it as it seemed to offer the best insight into his project. Foremost among his concerns is the potential supersession of the system of states. The modern system of states, he argues 'may be fluid and in the process of being remade'. Furthermore, mainstream International Relations theory might be missing the changes because its bias towards states and against changes that go beyond the redistribution of power between states.[10]

Ruggie writes

we are not very good as a discipline at studying the possibility of fundamental discontinuity in the international system; that is, at addressing the question of whether the modern system of states may be yielding in some instances to postmodern forms of configuring political space.[11]

Here, Ruggie is following the postmodern lead given by Jean François Lyotard. He expands the point:

I have argued that disjoint, mutually exclusive, and fixed territoriality most distinctively defines modernity in international politics and that changes in few other factors can so powerfully transform the modern international polity. What is more, I have tried to show that unbundled territoriality is a useful terrain for exploring the condition of postmodernity in international politics, and I have suggested some ways in which that might be done. The emergence of multiperspectival institutional forms was identified as a key dimension in understanding the possibility of postmodernity.[12]

Ruggie's ambitions for International Relations theory finds a focus in the European Community, because he has high hopes for what it might become. 'Take first the EC, in which the process of unbundling territoriality has gone further than anywhere else,' he writes. But his disappointment for the current state of International Relations theory is also writ large in the articles on Europe. So he writes of his fellow International Relations scholars' work on the Community: 'In none of these theoretical perspectives is there so much as a hint that the institutional, juridical, and spatial complexes associated with the community may constitute nothing less than the emergence of the first truly postmodern international political form'.[13] Ruggie is saying to his fellow International Relations scholars, 'get with the program, guys!' His approach, though, is not as critical of these new trends as it ought to be – as critical as it is of the states system they purportedly supersede.

Ruggie is resistant to the idea that the European Union might become some kind of super-state, because that would be to see things only as a recreation of the national state model: 'There is an extraordinarily impoverished mind-set at work here, one that is able to visualize long-term challenges to the system of states only in terms of entities that are institutionally substitutable for the state'. Rather he says 'There is no indication, however, that this reimagining [Jacques Delors' Single European Act, he means] will result in a federal state of Europe – which would merely replicate on a larger scale the typical modern political form'. So 'a very different attribute of the EC comes into view: it may constitute the first "multiperspectival polity" to emerge since the advent of the modern era'.[14]

Interestingly, Ruggie, while looking forward to the supersession of the nation state is less than enthusiastic about 'globalisation' when it means the diminishing power of national governments in relation to the world market. Ruggie seeks to distance himself from that neo-liberal argument: 'The orthodox liberal position that these developments somehow imply the growing irrelevance of states is ... "fundamentally misplaced" '.[15] But it is not immediately apparent that the trend to diminish the authority of nations is different from the growth of cross-border trade.

Barry Buzan

John Ruggie's critique of state-centric theories of international relations has been taken up by Barry Buzan. For Buzan 'the focus on the competition between nation states as an inherent feature of the anarchic international system is the hallmark of realism'. Buzan takes the long view of history to show that far from being ever-present conditions of human existence, nation states are institutions of a relatively recent creation. Realism is unduly 'state-centric' and 'presentist', Buzan argues. In his debate with social realist dramatists in 1959, the surrealist Eugene Ionescu joked of Kenneth Tynan that he was 'a realist, with all four feet firmly on the ground'. Buzan's sees realism in the study of international relations in much the same light. Equipped with state-centric lenses, realists cannot see the worldwide social processes that pass them by. According to Buzan, a 'new type of entity' the European Union commends itself because it 'is experimenting with a new form both of unit and subsystem structure, where the sharp inside/outside features of the modernist era are blurring into a mixture of the domestic and the international'.[16] Ruggie and Buzan could be accused of being over-reactive to change, and underestimating the inertia of the states system, even in relation to the European Union. Still, the have set out a challenging research agenda, which has encouraged a variety of different groups of scholars, such as those who collaborated at the London School of Economics, and those working with Thomas Christiansen – as well as Alexander Wendt.

THE LSE GROUP

Anthony Giddens, David Held and Ulrich Beck have been exchanging ideas for some years. Standing at the crossroads between sociology, political science and international relations, they have developed theories of de-traditionalisation, of a 'risk society', the 'End of Left and Right' and cosmopolitan democracy. Anthony Giddens, Baron Giddens since 2004, has been an important advisor to the former British Prime Minister Tony Blair. All had posts at the London School of Economics where Giddens was director between 1997 and 2003. Between them they elaborated an important story about the limits of nationalism and the potential for cosmopolitan society – especially as it relates to Europe – drawing on the background in critical theory they share.

David Held

Born in 1951, David Held was Graham Wallas Professor of Political Science, as well as co-director of the Centre for the Study of Global Governance at the London School of Economics until he left for the University of Durham. According to Held 'the states of Europe' give the best example of the supersession of sovereignty. What is it that is leading to the supersession of national sovereignty? Held is clear: 'the globalisation of production, finance and other economic resources is unquestionably challenging the capacity of an individual state (whether democratic or not) to control its own economic future'. Held dismisses the argument made by Hirst and Thompson that globalisation is not as profound as has been argued, and in particular he resists the alternative explanation 'that economic globalization is ... an ideological veil that allows politicians to disguise the causes of poor performance and policy failure' – but as we shall see, it is indeed the case that politicians use the ideology of globalisation to disguise policy failure.[17]

On top of the economic processes of globalisation, argues Held, there is the proliferation of international governmental organizations (IGOs) and international non-governmental organizations (INGOs)

Growth of international organisations[18]

	1909	1996
IGOs	37	4667
INGOs	176	25,260

Having identified the growth of international organizations as the decisive factor, Held holds that 'The European Union provides an important ... illustration of the issues posed by international organizations'. Among international organizations, the European Union stands out: 'the impact and efficacy of the EU reaches further than that of any other kind of international organization by virtue of its right to make laws which can be imposed upon member states' says Held, adding 'accordingly the member states of the EU are no longer the sole centers of power within their own borders'. What is more, the changes in the European Union mean that 'any conception of sovereignty which assumes that it is an indivisible, illimitable, exclusive and perpetual form of public power – embodied with in individual state – is defunct' (one might object that not even the most hardened realist would argue for limitless and eternal power). The attraction for Held is that this post-national world offers up a vision of what he calls cosmopolitanism.[19]

Like Ruggie, Held is reluctant to see his post-national world too closely identified with the growth in world trade, and so he triangulates a third position –cosmopolitanism – that is neither economic globalisation or nationalism. 'We live today at a funda-mental point of transition', says Held. On the one hand 'there are clear tendencies which are combining to weaken democracy and accountability within and beyond [sic] the nation state'. As he says, there is 'the progressive concentration of power in the hands of multinational capital, and the weakening of the role of states faced with global market processes and forces'.[20] However, for all his warnings of the concentration of power in the hands of multi-nationals, Held has no love of nationally-based democracy:

the spreading hold of the regime of international sovereignty has compounded the risks of arrogance in certain respects. This is because, in the transition from prince to prime minister or president, from unelected governors to elected governors, from the aristocratic few to the democratic many, political arrogance has been reinforced by the claim of the political elites to derive their support from that most virtuous source of power – the *demos*.[21]

Welcoming restrictions on the 'democratic princes', Held declares 'political alternatives to this state of affairs might be developed by deepening and extending democracy across nations, regions and global networks.' What could democracy outside of the context of the nation state mean? Held is not very clear: 'Such a process can be referred to as the entrenchment of democratic autonomy on a cosmopolitan basis – or "cosmopolitan democracy" for short'. Means to hasten the emergence of this 'cosmopolitan democracy' might include 'strengthening the administrative capacity and accountability of regional institutions like the EU'. It is not quite clear why strengthening the *capacity* of the European Union would help democracy, but it has certainly been a lot easier to strengthen its capacity than its accountability. Held hedges his bets, saying 'a cosmopolitan democracy would not call for a diminution *per se* of state capacity across the globe': but that is exactly what he means, 'arguing for a layer of governance to constitute a limitation on national sovereignty'. The cure for the disease of the decline in democracy, then, is a further limitation on democracy.[22]

The rationale for such reforms, that cosmopolitan democracy would enhance, not limit democracy is largely speculative. 'Democracy has to become not just a national but an international affair', says Held. But just how that might happen is largely unstated, or where it is, put in the future conditional tense. Apparently 'a cosmopolitan polity would need to establish an overarching network of democratic public fora, covering cities, nation-states, regions and the wider transnational order'.[23] Picture the scene: 'Come to the Overarching Network of Democratic Fora! Standing Room Only!' But there is no reason to imagine the scene, it has already begun in the European Commission's post-2005 'D for Democracy' consultation process (above) – though no-one yet has dared to suggest that that might be a substitute for national assemblies.

Held's projections for a future cosmopolitan democracy are little more than bullet points scribbled on a white board, but that is because the real punch in his *Models of Democracy* is an attack on democracy, at least the democracy we know: 'The explosion of interest in democracy in recent times has all too often conceived of democracy in terms of liberal democracy, assumed that democracy can only be applied to "governmental affairs" and presupposed that the nation state is the most appropriate locus of democracy'.[24] Invited to abandon the existing structures of nationally-based democratic government in favour of much more tentatively outlined and as yet untested models of cosmopolitan democracy, European publics might think that they are being asked to buy a pig in a poke.

With a background in critical theory, Held has criticized the 'positive philosophy' that tends to 'affirm the existing order against those who asserted the need for negating it': 'Instead of making the individual and the conditions under which he or she lives the object of critical reflection, positivist methods duplicate the reified consciousness of their object'. Clearly Held maintains a critical stance towards the *status quo ante*, the states system. But might he not be guilty of adopting an affirmative, or positive approach towards the emerging order of super-national governance? According to Held, the view that social change springs from law-like developments, which he attributes to Karl Marx, is flawed: 'the subject is denied an active role in the making of history'.[25] But where is the role of the subject in the transition from the states system to cosmopolitan democracy? As Held tells it, it seems to be a social process whose inevitability lies outside of any human – or at least popular – intervention.

One keen student of Held's work wanted to follow 'a cosmopolitan theory of global justice, which supports the legitimate exercise of political power on the basis of David Held's cosmopolitan principles'. Those principles, it turned out, did not include such a strong commitment to democracy, as the student,

Saif al-Islam Gaddafi, whom Held had advised on his doctoral thesis, returned to Libya to defend his father's dictatorship. The younger Gaddafi threatened democracy protestors 'we will fight to the last minute, until the last bullet.' Professor Held said he was shocked that the Saif Gaddafi, whom he found to have 'a deep commitment to liberal democratic reform' had become 'the enemy of ideals he once proclaimed'. Except that the ideals he had learned from the LSE professor were exactly those that held 'democracy' to be a word that could be twisted in any way that suited elites. Professor Held was criticized for advising that the LSE take contributions of £1.5m from the Gaddafi foundation, which led to the resignation of the school's Director, and Held's own departure for Durham.[26]

Ulrich Beck

Born in Stolp (now Slupsk in Poland) in 1944, Ulrich Beck is director of the Institute for Sociology of Munich University and *British Journal of Sociology* Professor at the London School of Economics. Beck's sociology of risk and the new modernity is very widely ranging, but has in recent years laid the basis for more speculative accounts of a new politics, and especially a European cosmopolitanism.

In his 1986 book the *Risk Society: Towards a New Modernity* (1994), Beck argued that the unintended consequences of modernity – manufactured uncertainties, like pollution – outweighed the intended product, wealth. The accumulation of risks frustrated planned change. 'The motor of social change is no longer considered to be instrumental rationality, but rather the side-effects: risks, dangers, individualization, globalization.' Agents of change, then, were not to be found in class-based collectivities, but a new 'solidarity from anxiety' that comes with action against environmental degradation. The old modernity of rational action gives way to a new reflexive modernisation that dissolves the old traditional order. This new reflexive modernity, with its complexity and generalised risk, comes spontaneously, as a 'revolution without a subject'. Beck expands the point, explaining that the subject of social change cannot be the working class, as the Marxists argued. 'Among the many questions concealed behind this [transformation to a risk society] is also that of the *political subject*', he says, adding: 'What corresponds to the political subject of class society, the proletariat – in risk society is only the *victimization of all by more or less terrible dangers.*' Grand schemes of social planning, too, must give way to the reflexive politics: 'one is no longer concerned with attaining something "good", but rather with *preventing* the worst: *self-limitation* is the goal which emerges'. Perhaps conscious that this argument posed the question of reflexive modernisation rather negatively, Beck has argued a more optimistic case for an 'unexpected renaissance of a political subjectivity' in citizens groups and non-governmental organisations.[27]

In his book *Cosmopolitan Vision* (2006) Beck argues that nation states are redundant in the face of a cosmopolitan reality. Beck rejects what he calls 'methodological nationalism' that 'assumes that a space defended by (mental) fences is an indispensable precondition for the formation of self-consciousness and for social integration'. Methodological nationalism is a characterisation of the realist theory of international relations, but Beck intends it more widely as summation of the failings of social theory. His witty inversion of the claims of realism is to insist that cosmopolitanism is real and national thinking an illusion. The 'autonomous nation state ... was a feature of the first but not the second modernity'. It is, he says, an 'historically irreversible fact that people from Moscow to Paris, from Rio to Tokyo, have long since been living in really existing relations of *interdependence*'. Setting the bar rather low, Beck argues that 'If the nation is essentially a nation of people influenced by the same newspapers, it also becomes problematic in the age of globe-spanning television and telecommunication.'[28]

Perhaps protesting too much, Beck rejects the charge that cosmopolitanism is an elite choice, 'grand hotel cosmopolitanism' or 'business lounge cosmopolitanism' – plainly he is aware that for many citizens of European nations cosmopolitanism is a happy prospect for elites, but not for them. So Beck suggests that there might be a good and a bad cosmopolitanism, or 'deformed cosmopolitanism'. 'Really existing cosmopolitanism is not achieved through struggle' Beck acknowledges, 'it is not chosen' and 'does not come into the world with the reflected moral authority of the Enlightenment, but as something deformed and profane' a 'side effect'. Deformed cosmopolitanism – swine flu, terrorism, economic globalisation – happens to us. Those pressures tempt us to respond by retreating into national defences, but, argues Beck, the more intelligent solution comes when 'the causes and agencies of global threats sparks new political conflicts, which in turn promote an institutional cosmopolitanism in struggles over definitions and jurisdictions'.[29]

Holding that cosmopolitanism is the reality Beck has to account for the persistence of national forms of organisation, which he does by characterising them as a kind of false consciousness, 'zombie categories' that persist without real content: 'the façade of persisting national spaces, jurisdictions and labellings, while national flags continue to be hoisted':

The British behave as though Great Britain still existed; the Germans believe that Germany exists; the French think that France exists; and so on. But these state-organized national containers have long since ceased to exist as empirical realities.[30]

Here one feels that the wish has become father to the thought. To argue that nation states are of declining importance is one thing, but to say that they do not exist tests credulity. It suggests a method that forces a division of the phenomena into the cosmopolitan real and the national illusion, but gives too little grounds to the illusion. 'Everyday life has become cosmopolitan in banal ways; yet the insidious concepts of nationalism continue to haunt peoples' minds unabated' he writes.[31]

However, Beck does give some ground to national sensibilities when he argues that 'a cosmopolitan Europe would have to safeguard the coexistence of ethnic, religious and political identities and cultures'. He says 'Europe teaches us that the political evolution of the world of states and of concepts and theories of the state is by no means at an end'. For that reason Beck takes issue with the 2004 proposal for a European Constitution. 'Those who seek a single constitution for Europe would abolish Europe' writes Beck. The constitution is emblematic of the error of 'a national Greater Europe, a federal superstate'. Beck faults social philosopher Jürgen Habermas, a supporter of the constitution, for proposing 'a "European people" qua subject of a postnational democracy', arguing that this amounts to a contradictory 'theory of the postnational nation of Europe'.[32]

But Beck did not reject the European Constitution *before* the Dutch and French referenda failed to endorse it. On the contrary, he saw the constitutional process as a positive development, part of 'the struggle for a political Europe, one that is more than just a conglomeration of nation-states that jump at each other's throats at regular intervals.' His goal back then was 'a constitutional scheme that affirms different cultures and facilitates peaceful coexistence': 'In order to achieve this, the European continental ethos of democracy, the rule of law and political freedom needs to be renewed and cultivated for the transnational era.' More definitively, in an article coauthored with Anthony Giddens on the defeat of the constitution, the two declared 'we write as supporters of the constitution'. As we shall see, Beck is not the only critic who, on being denied a European constitution by the voters, has decided that those grapes were sour, anyway.[33]

So, after the referendum, Beck acknowledges that 'there is no doubt that the current state of the European Union merits criticism' – but he is not ready to give ground to the critics who lead the campaign to vote down the constitution. 'The concept of a cosmopolitan Europe makes possible a critique of EU reality that is neither nostalgic nor national but radically European', writes Beck, arguing that 'much of the current state of the EU is un-European' and the cure is 'more Europe'. In other words, it is right to criticise European integration, but only from the point view that it does not go far enough. The point of view that Beck most definitely rejects (one we ought really to take seriously) is this:

> Could it be that the rallying idea of Europe is merely a front for the very opposite of all that Europe stands for, namely a rejection of democracy, freedom, separation of powers, transparency and political accountability?[34]

If Beck is wrong, though, and the Union is indeed hostile to democracy, freedom and accountability, then he is in a hole, and really ought to stop digging. But he thinks otherwise, that the shortcomings of the European Union are only that it has not gone far enough. In his *Guardian* article Beck endorses Tony Blair's call for a 'Europe wide debate on this issue' – which we now know is the Lisbon Treaty, a debate largely restricted to elites and policy wonks, that set down the main planks of the European Constitution behind the backs of those European citizens that voted against it in 2005. When Beck lays claim to the concept of democracy, though, he is at the same time redefining it. Beck argues that popular rule is not necessarily a good thing:

> Dictatorship from below, the dictatorship of the majority, is a real possibility and it uses democratic methods. Democracy

and totalitarianism are not mutually exclusive.[35]

In 2009, Beck saw salvation for the European Union in financial crisis: 'I thought: my God, what an opportunity!'[36] Perhaps if they were not willing to vote for a European Constitution, Europeans could be terrified into one. Fundamentally, Beck's concept of democracy is not one in which the demos rules. His recoil from the idea of a collective subject and downgrading of political action to attempts to find security in the adaptation to uncontrolled events leaves little room for popular sovereignty – and it is this truncated vision of democracy that he perceives in the development of European cosmopolitanism.

In the court of Muammar Gaddafi, Anthony Giddens (far right)

Anthony Giddens

Anthony Giddens, Baron Giddens, born in 1938, former director of the London School of Economics made the transition from professor, to public intellectual to government advisor, with his collaboration with British Prime Minister Tony Blair. Blair's faction in the Labour Party used the issue of Europe to re-define party policy, characterizing the 'old Labour' policy as backward-looking and nationally bounded.[37] In office, Blair's support for Europe cooled somewhat, as it clashed with the projection of British national interests.

Giddens' intellectual development precedes his relationship with politicians, following his well-received books *Capitalism and*

Social Theory (1971) and *New Rules of Sociological Method* (1976), where he circumvented the debate among sociologists about the primacy of structure or agency, by arguing both were equally important. In *Beyond Left and Right* (1994) Giddens' thinking more closely paralleled that of the future prime minister, such that Giddens is often credited with coining Blair's political philosophy of 'The Third Way' – between statist socialism and free market capitalism. There were precedents: in 1976 Libyan ruler Muammar Gaddafi outlined a 'Third International Theory' in his *Green Book*. In Giddens book *The Third Way*, the academic again rehearsed themes that were being heard in the government, following Blair's election in 1997. In *The Third Way*, Giddens rejects the realist theory of International Relations, that 'nations and power blocs, acting in the selfish pursuit interest of their interests, are the arbiters of power in the world arena'. 'It is obvious' he says 'that this is a self-defining theory': 'leaders who think in such a way will act in such a way'.[38]

Following Held, Giddens sees 'major forms of cosmopolitanism coming from below' from 'groups such as Greenpeace or Amnesty International' – the kind of non-governmental organisations that the European Commission identified as another source of authority to nation states. More explicitly than either Ulrich Beck or David Held, though, Giddens reconciles his cosmopolitanism with the reality of nationalism. Cosmopolitanism is not the end of nationalism, but an amendment to it. Rather we need 'a more cosmopolitan version of nationalism' to keep the 'divisive aspects of nationalism' in check. Giddens coins the oxymoron 'cosmopolitan nationalism' to describe his argument. (It will be remembered that Diogenes first said 'I am a citizen of the world', or *cosmopolites*, after being exiled from Sinope.) Anthony Giddens cites 'talk of "rebranding Britain" and Cool Britannia' as evidence that national identity can be 'actively shaped, in a dialogue with other identities'.[39]

The European Union says Giddens, is 'ahead of the rest of the world' and 'pioneering forms of governance that do not fit any traditional mould'. Giddens concedes that 'the EU has become increasingly important in the lives of its citizens at the same time as it is losing popular support'. That was a thought that ought to have been dwelt upon. But in truth it was only raised so it could be laid to bed. Most importantly, thinks Giddens, the Union plays a role socializing European states into a more cosmopolitan order: 'Member countries of the EU have a strong motivation to behave like cosmopolitan nations outside as well as within the European context'.[40]

Giddens, Beck and Held, the groups of scholars collaborating at the London School of Economics, were interested in the European Union first and foremost because it seemed to them to be a realisation of the trends in non-majoritarian, 'sub-politics' (Beck) or civil society (Held) and the transcendence of the nationally-based 'first modernity'. But they tend to amplify those trends that fit their research programme and downplay or dismiss those that do not, leaving many of their more provocative propositions too speculative.

Jürgen Habermas

Born in Düsseldorf in 1929, Germany's foremost public intellectual Jürgen Habermas studied philosophy and sociology under Max Horkheimer and Theodor Adorno at the Institute for Social Research in Frankfurt and in 1981 published the *Theory of Communicative Action*, which located reason not in the knowing subject but in structures of communication.

Habermas explains:

> By "interaction," on the other hand, I understand *communicative action*, symbolic interaction. It is governed by binding consensual norms, which define reciprocal expectations about behaviour must be understood and recognised by at least two acting subjects. Social norms are enforced through sanctions.

Their meaning is objectified in ordinary language communication. While acceptance of technical rules and strategies depends on the validity of empirically true or analytically correct statements, the validity of social norms is grounded only in the intersubjectivity of mutual understanding of intentions and secured by the general recognition of obligations.[41]

In his work Habermas has been very critical of the atavistic conception of the nation as a realization of the *Volksgeist*, or 'Spirit of a People', arguing instead for a post-traditional conception of patriotism towards the democratic structures of modern states. In the essay 'What is a People?' Habermas looked at the philological conception of nationhood, saying that the Volksgeist 'always directed toward a real or imagined past, poses insurmountable difficulties for the future-oriented intentions of liberal republicanism' and risks 'the fatal dialectic of inclusion and exclusion'. In *Between Facts and Norms*, Habermas develops a concept of modern statehood that derives its authority not from the singular voice of The People, but from the communication between people: 'To the extent that we become aware of the inter-subjective constitution of freedom, the possessive-individualist illusion of autonomy as self-ownership disintegrates'. Habermas' demotion of The People as author of the nation is related to his own philosophical development. According to Habermas's follower Axel Honneth 'Habermas ... dropped the notion of a unified subject of history', such as the Marxist 'self-emancipation of labour' – and so too, the People.[42]

In this Habermas was drawing upon the ideas of Martin Heidegger as much as of the Frankfurt School. Heidegger had written in 1926 that mass man 'is not something like a "universal subject" which a plurality of subjects have hovering above them'. Heidegger thought that mass man would never be a collective Subject, and Habermas agrees. Habermas developed his own theory of intersubjectivity studying Heidegger and Georg Lukacs, though he decided that in the end, Lukacs's collective subject 'wouldn't work'.[43]

Taking issue with another champion of 'the We', Habermas argues that 'Carl Schmitt's existentialist notion that "the Political" consists merely in the self-assertion of a collective identity over and against other collective identities ... the ontologisation of the friend-foe relation' is 'false' and 'dangerous'. More than that, national rights must be reconceived as arising out of mutual recognition, and an implied demotion of the self: 'The self-understanding of modernity ... has been shaped by an egalitarian universalism that requires a decentring of one's own perspective' Habermas argues. 'It demands one relativise one's own views to the interpretive perspectives of equally situated and equally entitled others'. This line of thought runs parallel to the idea of seeing 'oneself as another' that we came across in Paul Ricoeur and Emmanuel Levinas's ideas, and the guilty, self-reflective version of European identity.[44]

There is a link between Habermas's ideal of a constitutional state and the allied reconstruction of Germany post-war, which he describes as a catalyst of democratization: 'Allied victory ... sparked the democratic developments in the Federal Republic of Germany' and in Japan, Italy and eventually Portugal and Spain, he adds). Certainly, the Federal Republic's constitution included many features – the dispersal of power across the Lander, the Constitutional Court and the Bundestag, as well as the independent Central Bank and limits on military expansion – chosen to limit German power that would later become models for Europe's 'post-national' institutions. Though as we have seen, the 'defensive democracy' the allies put in place was criticized for setting limits on popular sovereignty.[45]

Habermas sees the realist theory of international relations as not so much wrong, as outdated, undermined by changes in the real world: 'This conventional model is less and less appropriate to the current situation'. The changes that supersede the realist theory of international relations are primarily the changes that come with economic globalisation, which are leading to a 'disempowerment of the nation state'. And here, Habermas has a more cautious response to globalisation than Held or Beck, particularly in his essay 'The Postnational Constellation', first published in German in 1998. There, Habermas sees that with economic globalisation '"Keynesianism in one country" is no longer a possibility' as the 'implicit threat of capital flight' acts as a restraint on national governments' spending plans. He sees the aggressive assertion of nationalism – as in campaigns against refugees or drug traffickers – in the face of globalisation as a dead end, but equally claims that the Beck-like 'politics of self-liquidation – letting the state simply merge into postnational networks – is just as unconvincing'. Habermas concedes a 'certain charm to the relentless processes of dissolution that characterize organized modernity' that Beck has embraced, but warns that they can also lead to attacks on the welfare state, greater unemployment 'a fragmented society and the loss of social cohesion'.[46]

Like Held, Habermas wants to believe that social democracy can be recreated at the world level, as it has been restrained at the national level: 'the foregoing analysis suggests the transnational task of bringing global networks under political control'. But as he explains, the track record of global governance is not promising. Though agreements about lowering tariffs on trade are successful, positive measures like the Tobin tax (James Tobin's proposal of a small tax on international financial transfers to create a global fund for developing countries) have failed to materialize. Of the networks and standing conferences of intergovernmental and non-governmental organisations Habermas is realistic: 'These new forms of international cooperation lack the degree of legitimation even remotely approaching the requirements for procedures institutionalized via nation states'. Habermas adds that 'while the postmodernists are convinced of the fading of the classical world of states' just as neoliberals want the market to take over from government 'we should be just as cautious with these progressivist visions of opening as with the regressive utopias of closure'.[47]

The best test – the 'exemplary case' – 'for the conditions for a democratic politics beyond the nation state', thinks Habermas is the European Union. Foremost among his questions is 'whether the European Union can even begin to compensate for the lost competencies of the nation state'. Habermas rejects the Eurosceptic case 'eulogizing the virtues of the dearly departed nation-state' but still thinks that their criticisms are not answered by post-nationalists, most importantly the question 'whether the European Union has any real hope of regaining the political capacity for action that nation-states have forfeited'.[48]

Habermas' doubts, though, are not a rejection. On the contrary, in *The Postnational Constellation* he sets out the conditions that will meet the objections. Habermas endorses his former student, the political scientist Claus Offe's qualification that 'a strengthening of the governing capacities of European institutions is unthinkable without an expansion of their formal democratic basis of legitimacy'. Intriguingly, Habermas goes on to sketch a new European constitutional settlement that not only incorporates the 'intergovernmental' aspect, but also grants it greater weight than the European Parliament. He envisages an upper chamber like the European Council of Ministers which 'would have to hold a stronger position than the directly elected parliament of popular representatives, because the elements of negotiations and multilateral agreements between member states that are decisive today cannot disappear without a trace'. On the other hand, something like the European parliament would have to foster governmental restraints on the free market, because 'positively coordinated distribution policies must be borne by a Europe-wide democratic will-formation, and this cannot happen without a basis of solidarity'.[49]

Interestingly, Habermas downplays the argument put by Euro-sceptics that 'there is no such thing as a European people, and thus also no force capable of generating a European constitution'. This, he says, 'only becomes a fundamental objection through a particular use of the concept of "a people"'. Here, Habermas is well-prepared to lower the bar for what constitutes a people, because of his own development of the post-traditional citizenship, owing allegiance not to blood ties, or atavistic history, but to a lawful constitution and democratic polity. Habermas mocks those who see 'the democratic state primarily as a duty-imposing authority demanding sacrifices from its dominated subjects'. This is a pre-enlightenment view of the state, he says, with a 'publicly demanded *sacrificium*'. Duties are not distinct from, but arise out of mutual recognition. Military duty and capital punishment – which stood as Hegel's pre-eminent examples of the ethical life of the State – 'cannot be defended' on these grounds. (Though, education, being 'based on the fundamental right of the children' can be enforced 'even against the resistance of the parents'). It is this post-traditional conception of the state, that cannot compel its citizens to fight, or hang them, but can make them send their children to school, that allows Habermas to imagine a less emotional bond to society that would still meet the fulfillments of something like a European people – an intersubjective Europe, in fact, rather than a collective subject Europe.[50]

In their manifesto 'February 15, or what binds Europeans together', the late Jacques Derrida and Jürgen Habermas sought to connect the anti-war movement to European identity (February 15, 2003 was the date on which the largest European anti-war demonstrations were coordinated). It will be remembered that the US Secretary of State Donald Rumsfeld played off 'new Europe' (meaning those East European states that were applying for EU membership) against the less supportive 'Old

Europe' of France, Germany, and Belgium. Controversially, Habermas and Derrida seemed to argue the case for a European hierarchy, seeing 'core Europe' – France and Germany – at risk of failing to carry the east European states: 'The avant gardist core of Europe must not wall itself off into a new "Small Europe". It must – as it has so often – be the locomotive.' Here was an echo of Jacques Chirac's irritation at the independent actions of the accession states over Iraq (he said they should 'shut up', 18 February 2003) – but however revealing of Derrida and Habermas' underlying belief in the superiority of 'core Europe', 'What binds Europeans together' explicitly argued a much more downbeat connection.[51]

Deconstructionist superstar, Jacques Derrida

What binds Europeans together, apart from challenging the U.S., it seems, is working through the experience of loss of Empire; 'with the growing distance of imperial domination and the history of colonialism, the European powers also got a chance for reflexive distance from themselves', the write. Interestingly, back in 1992, Derrida was less convinced of the worth of guilty self-reflection as a moment in European identity formation, which, he said, 'took on the appearance of a confession': 'avowal, guilt, and self-accusation no more escape this old programme than does the celebration of the self'. In 2003, though, Habermas and Derrida's Europe is an anti-identification, in which overcoming 'a bellicose past' teaches the lesson that 'the successful history of the European Union may have confirmed Europeans in their belief that the domestication of state power demands a *mutual* limitation of sovereignty, on the global as well as on the nation-state level'. The point of the European Union is to formalise the de-limitation of a potentially aggressive national sovereignty – it is an institutionalisation of the critique of sovereignty.[52]

Alexander Wendt: bringing the state back in

Born in Mainz, Germany in 1958 Alexander Wendt is Ralph Mershon professor of international security at the Ohio State University. Wendt has championed the Constructivist theory of International Relations. His work draws on the analytic philosopher John Searle, summarized in Searle's *The Construction of Social Reality* (Searle's book might be read as a rear-guard action against the 'Post-Modernists' to save the proposition of an objective natural world by allowing the social construction of the social world).[53]

A weakness in the speculative essays on the historical redundancy of the states system offered by Ruggie and Held is the truculent and persistent fact that nation states continue to be the dominant mode of public organisation across the world. Wendt's *Social Theory of International Politics* does not project the wholesale supersession of the nation state, but rather subsumes the realist outline of the states system into a constructivist theory. You might say that Wendt's constructivism is more 'moderate' than Ruggie's or Held's. Wendt starts with the acknowledgement that 'States are the core of any international system, since they constitute the distinct entities without which an "inter" national system by definition cannot exist'. Still Wendt is reluctant to abandon the sphere of international relations to the play of material interests, insisting that social relations are 'ideas all the way down'.[54]

Wendt's innovation is to treat *states* as *subjects*. That way world society remains a social construct, the construct of its members, primarily states. Though Wendt appears to give much ground to the realist account, in one important respect he reverses its polarity. It is not that states precede the states system, which arises out of their interaction; the states system, he is arguing, creates states as states:

In the contemporary states system states recognize each

other's right to sovereignty, and so the state-centric "project" includes an effort to reproduce not only their own identity, but that of the system of which they are parts: states in the *plural*.[55]

Wendt accepts that states have sovereignty through their relation to their publics:

> sovereignty is an intrinsic property of states, like being six feet tall, and as such it exists even when there are no other states

but that is not enough:

> This property becomes a right only when other states recognize it.

He explains

> Rights are social capacities that are conferred on actors by others' permission to do certain things.[56]

Because mutual recognition is the key to the initiation of states into the states system, Wendt puts much more store than realists do by international law: 'Far from being an epiphenomenon of material forces, international law is actually a key part of the deep structure of contemporary international politics'. It is the inter-national system that confers on states their special status. As Wendt says of the 'hegemonic' power – 'a state cannot *be* a hegemon ... any more than a person can be a master without a slave, or a wife without a husband'. Though in some ways Wendt is recreating the system of states theorized by the English School, Martin Wight would not have gone this far. Wight quoted Hegel (quoting Napoleon) saying that 'the Revolutionary French Republic at the height of its victories needed "recognition as little as the sun requires it"'. And further quoting the Russian Statesman Gortchakoff 'a great power does not wait for recognition, it reveals itself'.[57]

Still it is important that Wendt does not see sovereignty as exclusively a property of the states system, but rather insists that the internal dynamics of sovereignty are of weight, too. 'The density of interactions remains much higher within states than between them', he cautions. 'I do not claim that states are constructed *primarily* by international structures,' he writes: 'Much of the construction is at the domestic level, as Liberals have emphasized, and a complete theory of state identity needs to have a large domestic component'. Still, Wendt adds 'these identities are made possible by and embedded in a systemic context'.[58]

Wendt challenges the realist assumption that states are self-seeking, on the grounds that it universalizes just one way that states act: 'Sometimes states are egotists and sometimes they are not'. The implication here is that the ordering of the states system can constitute states as combative, or cooperative: 'Conflict is no more evidence for materialism than cooperation is for idealism; it all depends how conflict and cooperation are constituted'. Following John Ruggie, Wendt sees the 'Westphalian culture' less as a law of nature, more as a set of rules that dictates the behaviour of the players: 'it constitutes states as the individuals with the right to play the game of international politics, but does so in a way that makes each state seem to be the sole proprietor and guardian of that right.' The shortcoming is that 'Westphalian states are possessive individuals who do not appreciate the ways in which they depend on each other for their identity, being instead "jealous" of their sovereignty and eager to make their own way in the world'.[59]

Wendt, it seems to me, captures an important aspect of the changing character of international society, and gives useful insights into European integration, particularly if he is read as describing a *changing condition* of the international order. Comparing the weight of the domestic and the international in forming state identity, the former is in decline relative to the latter.

Wendt points to the transformation of egotistic states into cooperative states – 'the fact that France and Germany have become friends has dramatically altered the European landscape'. But he also wonders whether the logic of egoistic identity will overwhelm the European Union: 'this stress on egoistic identities has sometimes been so great that state have merged their bodies in a new *corporate* identity (the US in 1789, Germany in 1871: the European Union today?)' Still, Wendt is drawn to Europe as an example of the way that 'in the European Union some states have managed to form a collective identity' which is not egotistic but 'a level of collective interest that goes well beyond "Realism"'.[60]

There are some pointed weaknesses in Wendt's approach. He is wordy to a fault, digressing on questions of epistemology and natural science at length. His characterization of 'egotistic' states would sound less pejorative if he called them self-reliant; and contrasting cooperation with conflict is perhaps prejudging the outcome – who would embrace conflict? We might, object, though, that the conflict is in the world, not in the theory. Still Wendt captures a definite transition. Since 1983, let's say, inter-governmental relations have become more important for European (and world) leaders, while relations between the public and those leaders have declined in importance. Those horizontal relations among leaders, the international conferences and summits, participation in international organizations (and international conflicts, too) are a greater source of confidence and identity than the vertical relations between the rulers and the ruled, which are, by contrast, diminishing in vigour, characterized by scepticism and distrust.

In this sense one might argue that Wendt's account of the

construction of state identities in the society of states has come to be truer over time. As governing elites got less of their authority from their relations to their publics, they got more from the developed relations between them – their cooperation given institutional form in the international organizations that David Held holds up as evidence of the supersession of the nation state. And in Europe, this international cooperation has gone furthest, attaining the form of a permanent governmental body. Wendt's insistence that the international setting – over and above the domestic pressures – creates the framework for identity formation is more true, and truer over time, of the states of the European Union.

The social construction of Europe

One group of scholars who developed a constructivist account of the European Union were gathered together by Thomas Christiansen, Knud Erik Jørgensen and Antje Weiner, their papers collected in a volume titled *The Social Construction of Europe*.

One point of view Christiansen rejects is that 'the European Union can best be understood as a post-modern text, and perhaps as a post-modern polity' (Ian Ward quoted in *The Social Construction of Europe*). But Christiansen maps out a middle ground between post-structuralism and realism. As with Wendt just what it means to argue that post-structuralism is a bridge too far is not immediately obvious, but suggests a reluctance to admit radical indeterminacy. The authors signal a desire to meet their inter-governmentalist rivals (mostly Andrew Moravcsik) halfway, meaning that, like Wendt, they grant a large role to inter-governmental agreement as a source of the European Union's authority. What then does the 'constructivist' method have to offer? Christiansen says 'a social constructivist approach would not seek to ignore or invalidate the rationalist search for "member state preferences", but that it addresses the wider question of how state preferences have come to be socially constructed'. Thomas Diez is more adventurous, arguing that 'attempts to capture the Union's nature are not mere descriptions of an unknown polity, but take part in the construction of the polity'.[61]

'Postnational constitutionalism' it is claimed shows the advantages of the social constructionist account. So, for example, Jo Snow says 'the European constitutional ship has to be constantly rebuilt at sea'. Snow cites Tully's 'very strong critique of modern constitutionalism as fostering imperialistic practices'. She cites Richard Bellamy and Dario Castiglione, too, writing that 'the European Union has highlighted the inadequacies of certain key concepts of constitutional and democratic thought outside the context of relatively homogeneous nation states, such as the sovereignty of the people and the link between citizenship and rights'. According to Snow 'constitutionalist ideas are not capable of simple transmission to the supranational level'. Snow points out that the European Court of Justice has tended to construct the existing body of treaty law as a constitution. According to Snow, the Court's approach to the constitution is insufficient: 'overall this conception of the EU legal system as constitution lacks the degree of clarity in relation to its external or internal contours as well as the degree of coherence, consistency or completeness which one would normally associate with "a" constitution in the classic sense.'[62]

Diez worries that the 'emerging "Euro-Speak" that focused on subsidiarity and flexibility' arising out of the Maastricht Treaty 'serves to reify the "nation state" as a central concept in politics'. Though one might object that it was not the words that reified the nation state, but the reified nation state that demanded these words. Diez complains that the democratic deficit charge 'has haunted the EU since its inception'. Acknowledging that 'its citizens claim that the EU is far too bureaucratic, technical, distant, and its decision-making procedures too transparent'. But this, he argues is a fault of the theoretical construction of the Union 'as a monster of bureaucracy concerned with the technical matters that increasingly affect the everyday lives of its citizens without their formal consent, while the nation state carries with it the ideals of self-determination and democracy'. What is this in the end, though, but an expression of frustration with the way that the debate has crystallized out? Diez protests that the common view takes no account of the way that 'non-governmental organizations are heavily involved in the making of EC policies' – though it is not obvious why the involvement of lobbying organizations would bring the Union closer to popular accountability. And he says that most directives come from member state governments, but again, that is not the same thing as democratic control, since member state governments, according to majoritarian democratic theory, have authority over their own nations, but the Union has no comparable source for its sovereign authority over the citizens of Europe.[63]

Martin Marcussen, Thomas Risse, Daniela Engelmann-Martin, Hans Joachim Knopf and Klaus Rocher collaborated on an investigation, 'Constructing Europe?', subtitled 'the evolution of Nation-State identities' sponsored by the Deutsche Forschungsgemeinschaft and the European University Institute, Florence. They formulate a constructivist equivalent of the Patten/Hoffmann list of national positions – though restricted to Britain, Germany and France, now re-imagined as social identities constructed in relation to an *Other:*

When speaking about the political order during the Cold War, the élites in the three countries collectively shared an "Other", communism and the Soviet Union. Moreover British political élites have continuously considered "Europe" as the friendly "out-group", whereas German élites have seen the countries' own catastrophic past as "the other", and French political élites have traditionally added the US to their list of "others".[64]

As well as developing the analysis of the way that Britain formulates its identity in relation to Europe, and Germany to its own past, Marcussen and his collaborators have an interesting account of how President Mitterrand overhauled de Gaulle's vision of France's *mission civilisatrice* to put it into a European context: 'France is our Fatherland; Europe is our Future', Mitterrand, *Le Monde*.[65] One can see how the constructivist theoretical framework lends itself to a look at an idea like 'identity' – though in truth, the English School always did acknowledge the weight that 'prestige' played in international relations' and Stanley Hoffmann, too is at ease talking about French pride. But more to the point, the discussion of 'identity' takes these constructivists right back to some state-centric preoccupations that had been argued were weaknesses in the realists' arguments.

One very useful contribution to Christiansen's collection is Kenneth Glarbo's essay 'Reconstructing a Common European Foreign Policy'. Glarbo is serious about his intellectual debt to social construction theory, which he reconstructs with reference to the sociologist Alfred Schutz, Peter Berger and Thomas Luckmann, as well as the school of 'symbolic interactionism'. More contemporaneously, Glarbo follows Wendt in reconstructing the state-centric (or perhaps it would be more accurate to say that it was diplomat-centric) approach of the realists, arguing that constructivism gives a better account of the formation of the Common Foreign Security Policy. Certainly, it is an intellectual framework that helps Glarbo focus on the different techniques of negotiation, such as the 'Gymnich meetings' (foreign ministers, face-to-face without fixed agendas or diplomats, 'their informal format was meant to cultivate personal friendships and an esprit de corps among ministers'). Glarbo quotes Simon Nuttall's argument that policy coordination has become a means of *socializing* national leaders into a common outlook: socialization 'is real, and has become an effective substitute for traditional bilateral diplomacy among the Twelve'. This is right: European leaders increasingly derive not just authority, but also their outlook from their relations to each other.

Particularly fascinating is Glarbo's suggestion that different theoretical approaches, constructivist and realist are appropriate to different periods in the development of inter-European relations. Glarbo grants that 'social construction did not entirely sum up EPC [European policy coordination] formal matters during its formative years' and that 'national interest also prevailed during the early 1970s'. However, he says, 'common typifications began to materialize – and hence spurred on – symbolic exchanges on the first areas for concerted action'.[67] So, fascinatingly, we get the result that the realist, state-centric theory is truer of the earlier period, and Glarbo's symbolic interactionism sheds more light on the later period, where 'concerted actions' that were ideological exercises in bonding between European governments as much as they were actions in pursuit of common interests. It is an argument that suggests that European leaders have indeed changed their perspective since around the time of the Single European Act – where before 1985 they formed their goals with an eye to domestic expectations of national interest, but after then they were increasingly drawing confidence not from the national mandate, but from their relations to one another in the realm of high diplomacy. However, given the relative weight of the institutions involved, it seems more likely that it is a change in the way that nation states are organized that has enhanced the role of European policy coordination, than that European policy coordination that has changed the way that nation states are organized.

Glarbo makes an interesting case for the enhanced role of socialization and confidence building measures among European leaders, which we can see draws on the research agenda of constructivism, with its emphasis on inter-subjective identity formation, and the importance of norms over interests. However, we should note that it is a far from flattering picture of the inner workings of European policy cooperation. Glarbo's image is of an elite bureaucracy that has insulated itself from democratic accountability. Where national interests are 'referenced', he says, this has the character of a performance for 'achieving leverage in CFSP [Common Foreign and Security Policy] negotiations, but also for maintaining credibility and status *vis-à-vis* domestic and international publics'.[68] Given the optimistic association of constructivism in International Relations theory argued by John Ruggie, we seem to have come a long way towards the recreation of the cynical and secretive world of diplomatic maneuvering that had been thought to be the perspective of the realist school of IR.

To take the project outlined in the proposition that Europe is a social construct seriously, one ought to approach 'Europe' – by which is generally meant the European Union – with the same critical tools that were brought to bear on nation states. The European Union is indeed a transient human institution, subject to historical change, just as nation states are. We have argued here that the meaning of the European Union has indeed changed as European elites have derived greater authority from their relations to each other than they have from nationally-generated democratic mandates. But frustratingly, the critical-theoretic tools that the social constructionists bring to bear upon 'Westphalian sovereignty' seem to be a lot less incisive when they are applied to the European Union. One rhetorical strategy often repeated in the social constructionist investigations into Europe is to characterize critical thinking as 'Euro-scepticism', which has the effect of closing off more challenging analyses.

Thomas Christiansen and unconstituted Europe

Thomas Christiansen is professor of European Institutional

Politics at Maastricht University and editor of the *Journal of European Integration*. In his co-edited collection *The Social Construction of Europe* Christiansen included a response from the main inter-governmentalist critic of his constructivist collaborators. Andrew Moravcsik made a stinging criticism of the papers for their methodological meanderings, suggesting that among the constructivists, 'meta-theory was not the solution, but the problem.' 'Philosophical speculation is being employed not to refine and sharpen concrete concepts, hypotheses and methods, but to shield empirical conjectures from empirical testing'.[69] Perhaps with Moravcsik's challenge in mind, Christiansen's most recent work, *Constitutionalizing the European Union*, written with Christine Reh of the University College London, and published in 2009, pushes the methodological discussions into the background, and concentrates instead on an empirically supported account of the growing body of treaty law.

Constitutionalizing the European Union has many interesting things to say about the way that the dialogue among heads of state, ministers and official creates layers of shared meaning that create a foundation for the whole entity. Still, there is a weird sleight of hand in the shift from writing a Constitution to what Christiansen and Reh call the process of 'constitutionalizing Europe': 'we understand Europe's constitutional order as evolutionary, rather than as the product of an explicit and deliberate constitutional moment'. According to Christiansen and Reh:

> both the Convention and the Constitutional Treaty are best understood as embedded in Europe's long term process of implicit and incremental constitutionalisation, and not as the *futile, historical attempt at fixing the Union's* finalité politique'.

The word constitution has a double meaning for constructivists. More than a piece of paper, or even a founding document, *constitution* is the iteration of Europe that brings it into existence.

Voting down the European constitution those Europeans, the Dutch and French electorates might be said to be deconstructing the European Union – at least the one that was put to them. That 'No' vote is the background to Christiansen and Reh's downgrading of the ' *futile, historical attempt at fixing the Union's* finalité politique'. Retreating from the singular constitutional act, Christiansen insists that the 'constitutionalisation of Europe need not necessarily result in a formal "capital-C Constitution"'. But tweaking the spelling, lowering the case or any other sleight of hand will not shift the central problem that without some kind of public affirmation, the law on which the Union rests is treaty law, between states, not the constitutional declaration of the European people.[71]

Christiansen's argument that the attempt to create a constitution was an error would be more convincing if he had made it before the failure of the Dutch and French referenda. But what we find him saying in August 2005 is optimistic about the appeal of a constitution: 'because we are speaking about a European Constitution, the people – the *people* – would push decision makers and institutional actors to further reform the Union and thus lead the way to a genuine European constitution.' It seems as if Christiansen, like Beck, has decided that those constitutional grapes are sour, now that they are beyond his reach, and that he much prefers the more attainable constitutiona*lizing*.[72]

That Europe has no definitive constitutional document ought not to be a problem, say Christiansen and Reh, even though most European states do have constitutions, because 'the UK a notable exception'. This is a point that Ulrich Beck also makes in support of the idea that Europe does not need a singular constitutional document: 'Great Britain, for example, does not have a constitution; yet it speaks at times with a genuinely European, genuinely democratic, cosmopolitan voice'. Still, Britain's lack of a single constitutional document has long been identified by liberals – and champions of the European Union in Britain – as a profound failing. Furthermore, the British constitutional scholar A.V. Dicey's case for the superiority of the British system was that a sovereign parliament was a surer champion of the rights of Britons than a legal document, whereas the case for the European Constitution draws its authority not from an elected parliament, but from the European Council and the European Court of Justice.[73]

If Europe's constitution were not to come through a declaration of the European people, where would it come from? Citing the adjudication of the European Court of Justice, Christiansen and Reh suggest that the treaties between member states ought to be 'seen as substantively akin to a constitution' (the position that Snow rejected, see above). But the authoritative source of the treaties is the bargaining between heads of government, not the collective will of the European people as such. The peculiar result of the constructivist research project as far as it applies to the European Union is that the Union is not constructed by society, as we might understand it, but by a 'society' of national leaders and officials, judges and others authority figures.[74]

In the collection Christiansen co-edited in 2001, *The Social Construction of Europe*, Rey Koslowski highlights the optimistic meaning of rational constructivism that 'since man has himself created the institutions of society and civilization, he must be able to alter them at will so as to satisfy his desires and wishes' (quoting F. A. Hayek, unexpectedly). Koslowski goes on to make the argument that constructivism might also follow Hume's theory that institutions are 'the result of human action but not of human design'.[75] It is a point that recurs in the constructivist theories, as Wendt explains, 'social kinds confront members of the relevant collectives as seemingly natural facts' – a phenomenon which he calls, after Berger and Luckmann,'reification'.[76] In Beck's reflexive modernity it is explicitly the case that unintended consequences dominate, and the best that we can hope to do is to mitigate, or organize around them. The constructivist criticism of realism that it renders the human institution of the states system as if it were a law of nature seems to lose its bite, as the constructivists in turn reify the institutions of the post-cold war order as being beyond our control. With the constructivist theory of Europe the trajectory of the enquiry is to deconstruct the nation state, but then to treat the institutions of the European Union in an uncritical, positivist way; the job of researchers is to amend their theories to give the best account of those institutions, but not to look at them in turn as transient social organizations.

Jacques Derrida (1930-2004) and another Europe

Born in Algiers, Jacques Derrida worked most of his adult life as a philosopher, director of studies at the École des Hautes Études en Sciences Sociales in Paris investigating phenomenology, structuralism, and founding a project of 'deconstruction' as indicated earlier in our discussion of social construction. With François Châtelet and others he co-founded the Collège international de philosophie in 1983. While many of his colleagues were drawn into the political struggles of the 1960s, mostly on the left, Derrida largely stayed aloof from explicit political affiliations and did not embrace the events of May 1968. He did work quietly on behalf of East European dissidents, like those in the Charter 77 group. His elevation to a public figure came charming an American audience by exposing the pretensions of European 'structuralist' theory at a conference at the John Hopkins University, sponsored by the Ford Foundation. Early on, those who ran across Derrida understood that he was not radical, but something of a Cold War liberal. His interest in 'reactionary' thinkers like Heidegger and Nietzsche was noted by the left-wing *Humanité,* and later became a sticking point with the radicals at *Tel Quel.* Even giving papers in US colleges, more radical US academics were disappointed that Derrida's 'End of Man' was not tempered by the hopes of 1968: 'the pessimism of Professor Derrida's conclusion goes contrary to this hopeful mood'. In time, though, as many left wing certainties fell into disgrace, Derrida's star rose among radicals in Europe and America. Whatever Derrida intended for it, his project of deconstruction became a slogan for radicals seeking to unpick the ideologies of nationalism and other mainstays of conservative belief.[77]

Around 1991, when the Eastern Bloc was disintegrating, there appeared to be a resurgence of atavistic nationalism in the East, and the map of Europe was rapidly changing, Derrida turned to some more explicitly political themes, and in particular reflected on 'today's Europe'. Even here, though, Derrida's elliptical style of essay writing resists any direct political application. Derrida writes at a time when, as he says, there is 'a feeling of imminence, of hope and of danger, of anxiety before the possibility of other wars with unknown forms, the return to the old forms of religious fanaticism, nationalism or racism'.[78]

Derrida caricatures the position, particularly marked in his native France, and in the rhetorical claims of the French Commission Chief Jacques Delors that 'Creating Europe is a way of regaining that margin of liberty necessary for "a certain idea of France".'[79] As Derrida re-words it 'the logical schema of this argument, the backbone of this national self-affirmation, the nuclear statement of the national "ego" or "subject," is, to put it quite dryly:

> "I am (we are) all the more national for being European, all the more European for being trans-European and international; no-one is more cosmopolitan and authentically universal than the one, this 'we' who is speaking to you."'[80]

This way, Derrida points out, the European project (certainly as it is outlined in France) is at the same time a national project, the statement of the *national 'ego' or 'subject'*. That is to say that

Derrida calls the European project into question *because* it is the realisation of national egotism, just as the realists would argue.

Derrida pursues the point, talking about the competition for the title of European Capital of Culture. Taking a French Foreign Affairs Ministry text of 1988 as his starting point, Derrida takes issue with the argument that 'It is the task of *culture* to *impose* the feeling of unity, of European solidarity' and that in this, France has a 'determining role ... by teaching others to look to France as a creative country that is helping to build modernity'.[81] As Derrida says, dismissively, 'this is state talk.' But more than that it is indicative of a broader levelling trend:

> The best intentioned of European projects, those that are quite apparently and explicitly pluralistic, democratic and tolerant, may try, in this lovely competition for the 'conquest of spirit(s),' to impose the homogeneity of a medium, of discursive norms and models.[82]

Here Derrida, looking primarily at cultural policy insists European cultural identity 'cannot and must not be dispersed into a myriad of provinces, into a multiplicity of self-enclosed idioms or petty little nationalisms, each one jealous and untranslatable'. But on the other hand 'it cannot and must not accept the capital of a centralising authority'.[83]

In 1992, at least, Derrida was conscious that Europe itself might represent a kind of unwelcome closure, and argued 'it is necessary to make ourselves the guardians of an idea of Europe, or a difference of Europe, but of a Europe that consists precisely in not closing itself off in its own identity and in advancing itself in an exemplary way towards what it is not'. And here Derrida is developing his critique of identity and the subject in relation to Europe. So he says that what is proper is for Europe 'not to be able to identify itself, to be able to say "me" or "we"; to be able to take the form of a subject only in the non-identity to itself or, if you prefer, only in the difference with itself'. Or in relation to European culture, the point is 'what is proper to a culture is not to be identical to itself'. Again, these are the lines of thought, of 'non-identity to itself' that lead to the concept of 'oneself as another', of an alienation from self, or self-doubt that seems imbedded deeply in the deconstructionist account of European identity.[84]

However, in an apparent reprimand to the popular versions of 'deconstruction', and particularly the critique of 'Eurocentrism', both of which were popular on the university syllabuses, Derrida looks forward to a new 'Europe beyond all the exhausted programs of Eurocentrism and anti-Eurocentrism'. He adds 'we today no longer want either Eurocentrism or anti-Eurocentrism'.[85] Here Derrida is cautioning his fellow-thinkers not to close down the argument, or to give away too much, by falling into a crass assault on 'Eurocentrism', but rather to keep open the idea that a self-reflective Europe might be a positive gain.

Derrida is particularly critical of the apparent victory of liberal capitalism at the end of the Cold War, as trumpeted by the Rand Corporation associate Francis Fukuyama in his influential essay 'The End of History' (which drew obliquely on Hegel's *Phenomenology of Spirit*). Derrida disdains 'the Hegelian moment wherein European discourse coincided with the spirit's return to itself in Absolute Knowledge, at this "end-of-history" that today can give rise to the prating eloquence of a White House advisor when he announces with great media fanfare "the end of history"'.[86] Derrida goes on to scorn Fukuyama's argument that history has come to an end

> because the essentially European model of the market economy, of liberal, parliamentary and capitalist democracies, would be about to become a universally recognised model, all the nation states of the planet preparing themselves to join us

at the head of the pack, right at the forefront at the capital point of advanced democracies, there where capital is on the cutting edge of progress.[87] (The ironic tone in this passage is clearer in the cumulative impact of the essay)

Derrida argues that in the place of the old dogmatism of communism in the east, there is a 'counter dogmatism that is setting in today' that would ban 'even the critique of certain effects of capital or of the "market" as the evil remnants of the old dogmatism'. Arguing the case for a 'new critique of the new effects of capital' Derrida, alluding to his own quiet activism for East European dissidents, writes 'Is not this responsibility incumbent on us, most particularly those of us who never gave in to a certain Marxist intimidation'.[88] Resisting the stampede to free market Europe is as strong a compulsion for Derrida as was that to challenge the 'totalitarianism' of the left.

Years later, in his last years, in fact, Derrida again took up the question of Europe, but by that time the balance of power had shifted. Europe no longer seemed to be a vehicle of market-led uniformity, or indeed of national egotism, but of difference, as he anticipated – specifically of difference from the American hegemonic project of the war on terror. These were the themes that Derrida developed in the essay, co-authored with Jürgen Habermas, 'February 15, or what binds European together'.

POSTMODERN EUROPE
Jan Zielonka's European empire

Professor of European Politics at the University of Oxford and Ralf Dahrendorf Fellow at St Antony's College, Jan Zielonka was born in 1955 and graduated in law at Wroclaw, teaching there and then in Leiden, Groningen and Florence. 'The enlarged European Union is likely to have soft borders in flux, rather than hard fixed external borders', according to Jan Zielonka 'Multilayered and multicentred government will be the norm' he continues, and 'pan-European identity will be blurred and fragile with no truly European demos'. According to Zielonka 'the union will resemble an empire', but not the superstate that the 'Eurosceptics' fear, because 'the European Union is not becoming a superstate projecting its ever-greater power all over Europe and beyond'. Rather 'it is becoming a polycentric polity' with 'its multilevel governance system of concentric circles, fuzzy borders and soft forms of external power projection'. Not a 'Fortress Europe' but a 'Maze Europe'. Zielonka sees the enlargement to the east in 2004 as 'an enormous import of diversity': 'The last wave of enlargement has not made the Union look more like a state', he writes 'on the contrary, enlargment has resulted in more layers of authority, more cultural and legal pluralism, more diversified and cross-cutting institutional arrangements'. What the European Union looks like is a medieval Empire – 'the system we knew in the Middle Ages before the rise of nation states, democracy and capitalism'.[89]

Zielonka thinks that the 'frequently deplored "democratic deficit" of the European Union is also in part the result of unclear arrangements'. There is of course a question of democratic accountability, and even of rights, created by ambiguity, and this, thinks Zielonka, is the reason for the demand for a European constitution:

the set of gradually accumulated European laws containing a quite complex set of mysterious formulations confront European actors with an ever greater challenge of comprehension and interpretation. The recently undertaken efforts to simplify the European treaty systems in the form of a new constitution represent a response to this increasingly untenable situation.[90]

Attempts to formalize the structures of the Union only tend to institutionalize diversity. So, writes Zielonka, 'homogenizing tendencies in the process of European integration have also made it necessary to develop and "legalize" the concepts of subsidiarity and flexibility'. So Zielonka argues that 'enlargement will increase *variable geometry* within the Union'.[91] He expands:

> there are currently three geometric objects in the monetary union: members of the euro-zone (twelve), members of the new Exchange Rate Mechanism (ERM II) (one) and members with floating exchange rates (two). With the Eastward enlargement we are likely to have a fourth geometric object: members with currency boards (currently Bulgaria and Estonia have currency boards.[92]

In saying that the complexity of the Union is 'increasingly untenable' does Zielonka really mean that the structural ambiguity is a bad development? Not really. He writes 'a certain degree of diversity is ... unavoidable' and 'I argue that there is no need to demonize it'. On the contrary 'not all types of diversity need prove detrimental to the process of European integration'.[93]

Allowing that the Union's complexity militates against democracy, understood as majoritarian rule, Zielonka plays down the problem:

> The Majoritarian principle is only one pillar of democracy in Westphalian states; the other is constitutionalism with its emphasis on bills of rights, territorial or functional devolution of power, the independence of the judiciary, and some other institutions such as central banks and regulatory bodies.[94]

This is effectively to dilute the meaning of democracy. The protection of civil rights are plainly related to the idea of democracy, or are even preconditions of democracy, but democracy is not civil rights, but popular rule. As he pushes the point further, to identify independence of central banks and even the judiciary (which is not independent of the executive in the United States), Zielonka conflates some exigencies with democratic rule that arguably are the very opposite of democracy. The effect is to downplay the absence of popular sovereignty in the European Union. Zielonka argues that the trend towards extra-democratic restraint upon sovereign governments is not unique to the European Union, but, as we have already seen, characteristic of our age: 'More and more decisions affecting respective national electorates are now being taken by various supranational bodies or worse by quite mysterious global economic regulatory or even judicial networks'.[95]

Further, Zielonka claims, restraint of popular sovereignty might be a good thing – even a democratic improvement – 'After all, many autocrats had come to power via democratic elections, and measures were taken to prevent the "tyranny of the majority" by introducing some tight constitutional constraints on the respective parliamentary majorities'. It is true that in Weimar Germany, under the advice of Max Weber, Article 48 was introduced allowing the President to circumvent the Reichstag – but that was not much of a constraint on autocracy, being the instrument that President Hindenburg used to suppress democratic rights in Germany. Still, Zielonka understands that this is not the 1930s and supra-parliamentary constraints need a contemporary justification, which he finds in complexity: 'More recently constitutionalism has been enhanced by the complexity of modern governance that requires special "technical" expertise in certain fields and justifies the creation of various independent regulatory agencies.'[96]

Zielonka is not optimistic about the enhancement of the powers of the European parliament to meet the 'democratic deficit'. Rather, he says, 'in the EU power is much more in the hands of non-majoritarian institutions, that is, the Commission, the European Court of Justice, the European Central Bank and the European Council than is the case in member states'. Furthermore, these democratic by-passes are increasingly used by governing elites: 'National executives are often able to bypass their respective Parliaments by making decisions in the European Council.'[97]

Plainly Zielonka's European Empire, if it is not a superstate, is an opaque, even obscurantist institution, that offers great resistance to the exercise of popular sovereignty. If we were to accept his re-definition of democracy to mean the constraint of popular sovereignty, one can see how it might thereby become a more democratic organization. But this would seem to be a case of an argument that has gotten carried away with itself, redefining democracy out existence, and renaming the growth of officialdom, democracy.

Robert Cooper

A more playful version of 'postmodern Europe' has been put forward by the British diplomat Robert Cooper, who in 2002 became Director-General for External and Politico-Military Affairs at the General Secretariat of the Council of the European Union. Cooper coined the provocative phrase 'postmodern imperialism' to describe the Union's expansion.

> The postmodern EU offers a vision of cooperative empire, a common liberty and a common security without the ethnic domination and centralised absolutism to which past empires have been subject, but also without the ethnic exclusiveness that is the hallmark of the nation state.

Cooper sees the 'postmodern' Europe as a positive development in comparison to the limitations of the balance of power system:

> a system of counter-balancing alliances which became seen as the condition of liberty in Europe ... But the balance-of-power

system too had an inherent instability, the ever-present risk of war, and it was this that eventually caused it to collapse ... The balance of power never suited the more universalistic, moralist spirit of the late twentieth century.[98]

The 'balance of power' was meat and potatoes to British diplomats, right up to the 1990s. But more recently they have been swept up in the modification of Foreign Policy that is both 'ethical' in projection and activist, rather than foot-dragging in Europe. Cooper's vision of the Union as decidedly not a balance, but 'mutual interference' mocks the Euro-sceptic complaints

The postmodern system in which we Europeans live does not rely on balance; nor does it emphasise sovereignty or the separation of domestic and foreign affairs. The European Union has become a highly developed system for mutual interference in each other's domestic affairs, right down to beer and sausages.[99]

Cooper is relatively non-committal on the form that European governance will take: 'we have to try and invent multinational democracy, which will not be exactly like national democracy' and most decidedly will not be a European superstate. Cooper lowers expectations of common institutions, and does not put much store by an enhanced European Parliament (which is where the 'realist' outlook of his predecessors meets Cooper's 'postmodern' approach), rather seeing that 'law is the funda-mental value of Europe', and law in common, therefore, is the real basis for the Union.[100]

With an eye to Robert Kagan's characterisation of the differ-ences between Europeans (from Venus) and Americans (from Mars), Cooper insists that

Multilateralism - for which the European Union stands and

which is in some way inherent in its constitution - is more than a refuge of the weak. It embodies at a global level the ideas of democracy and community that all civilised states stand for on the domestic level.[101]

Cooper is one of those who took Joseph Nye's idea of 'soft power' and made it into a positive model of European influence:

the most far-reaching form of imperial expansion is that of the European Union. In the last few years countries all across central Europe have transformed their constitutions, rewritten their laws, adjusted the rules of their markets, set up anticorruption bodies and adopted a huge volume of EU legislation - all in the interests of becoming members of the Union.[102]

It was an argument that found favour with Commission President José Manuel Barroso, who claimed of the Union 'what we have here is the first non-imperial Empire'.[103] Still, Cooper's is a curiously apolitical, quietistic model of European power and European expansion – though it certainly seems to be accurate (albeit smoothing over the real antagonisms between East European leaders and the EU). It is hard not to think that Cooper is an old-fashioned British realist playing with words like 'postmodernism' to avoid finality, in much the same way that the Foreign Office always did in its relations with Europe.

Cooper's work on the outward projection of Europe puts him somewhat out of the scope of this study, but in one interview Cooper gives a useful shorthand for the process of integration. Asked the question 'Why have European countries drawn much closer together?' Cooper replies: 'Europe — perhaps for the first time in 300 years — is no longer a zone of competing truths'. He expands 'The end of the Cold War has brought with it something like a common set of values'.[104] It is true that the diminished importance of ideological differences has enhanced consensus amongst elites. Or, put another way, the down-grading of political contestation at the domestic level has made cooperation at the pan-European level a lot more attractive. But as much as there has been a coalescence in values in European societies, there has also opened up a marked gap between populations and elites that one would hesitate to call a consensus.[105]

Mark Leonard is an enthusi-astic policy wonk, and founder of the think tank the European Council on Foreign Relations, and a Director at the Foreign Policy Centre (founded with UK Prime Minister Tony Blair's support in 1998). He took up the 'post-modern' Europe theme around the same time as Cooper and Zielonka. In his book *Why Europe will Run the 21st Century* many of Cooper's themes are rehearsed. Like Cooper, Leonard's 'postmodernism' bears some similarities to old-fashioned English school realism. Leonard dismisses those federalists who 'still dream of a country called Europe'. For Leonard, Europe is 'fundamentally different from a state', in fact it is like the credit card electronic payment brokers, Visa: 'Like Visa, it is a decentralized network that exists to serve its member-states'. And again 'Like the Banks that own and control Visa, it is the national governments that set the agenda for the future of Europe'.[106]

Mark Leonard policy wonk and postmodernist

The death of the subject and the deconstruction of the sovereign nation state

One enduring theme in the literature on the social construction of international relations is the underlying appeal to deconstruct the sovereign nation state. It is there in Ulrich Beck's cosmopoli-tanism as the assertion that the sovereign nation state is already an outmoded social form. Habermas makes the point more gently when he appeals to de-centre national egotism in favour of other-oriented approaches, making the communication *between* actors the focal point.

The great strength of this argument is that it appeals to an already entrenched social philosophy, of the 'Death of the Subject'. Sovereignty *is* Subjectivity, at the international realm.

Slovenian philosopher Slavoj Žižek opens his book *The Ticklish Subject* with this pastiche of *The Communist Manifesto:* 'A spectre is haunting Western academia...the spectre of the Cartesian subject. All academic powers have entered into an unholy alliance to exorcise this spectre.'[107] Slavoj Žižek names feminists, New Age obscurantists, postmodern deconstructionists and deep ecologists as differing intellectual trends which now coalesce in their hostility to what he calls the Cartesian subject. To understand what Žižek is getting at, let us look at the argument against Cartesian Subjectivity.

Louis Althusser says 'Ideology interpellates individuals as Subjects'. He means that subjectivity is an ideological effect of social relations that cast individuals as subjects: 'ideology has the function of "constituting" concrete individuals as subjects'. His insight was a challenge to the philosophy of 'humanism' (which he confronted in the special form of 'socialist humanism', in his debates within the French Communist Party). This is a pointed departure from conventional social science in that Althusser sets out to construct a theory of society that does not take the human subject as its starting point. In fact, he says, he wants to understand 'history as a process without a subject'.[108]

In *The Order of Things*, Michel Foucault draws this striking image:

As the archaeology of our thought easily shows, man is an invention of a recent date. And one perhaps nearing to its end. ... one can certainly wager that man would be erased, like a face drawn in the sand at the edge of the sea.[109]

Foucault's point is part of a longer discussion about the status of the human sciences, but it is hard to avoid the sense of the end of humanism that is made here. The point is not necessarily that the human species is facing extinction, but that the mode of social organization, humanism, has reached its historical limit, and core to this humanism is subjectivity.

In her essay, 'Crisis of the ~~European~~ Subject' the literary theorist and psycho-analyst Julia Kristeva characterises the 'European dynamic' as a 'global civilizing effect' on behalf of a particular 'conception of the human person and of subjectivity'. This 'identification of the subject with freedom' corresponds to free markets and liberal democracies and to the 'the Anglo-Saxon model of all out production and financial profit'. The 'free subject as it has been constructed in Europe,' the 'definition of freedom coextensive with the self', 'this European tradition of the theory and the practice of subjective freedom' all carry within them a profound shortcoming Kristeva argues. She chooses to cast this failing in psycho-analytic terms, arguing that the subject is first and foremost the Oedipal subject, as analysed by Sigmund Freud; 'the subject is free only because he is a subject animated by this twofold forbidden wish for incest and parricide'. But as problematic as that Oedipal subjectivity already is, 'in the European domain itself, *this oedipal model is in a grave crisis*'. According to Kristeva 'the collapse of paternal authority, the modern economic crisis and the reign of the image are among the essential factors' (recalling Reimut Reiche's theory that 'repressive desublimation' and the decline of the father figure were core to the authoritarian personality). Kristeva says that 'the free subject has become a mirage' and that 'clinical practice shows that many of us are in the process of losing the capacity to elaborate an inner life'.[110]

The post-structuralist critique of the subject corresponds to the closure of political options in the 1970s and 1980s. The resonance of the proposition, if not the theory, comes from the widespread disappointment with political choices. In academia, the same basic proposition has been rediscovered across the humanities, from the 'death of the author' right through to the reconsideration of consumer rationality in economics.

Those international relations scholars looking at the question of sovereignty are already predisposed to be critical, because they can see that sovereignty is a special form of subjectivity, where agency is invested in state institutions, or territory. The deconstruction of sovereignty is a work whose arguments have been long in preparation. And here the theoretical critique of sovereignty corresponds to the more mainstream discussions of sovereignty as a pathological condition.

It would be fair to say that the main analyses of European integration have been in those schools of thought that we have looked at here, the 'functionalist' (Mitrany) or 'integrationsts' (Deutsch, Haas), realists (Bull, Hoffmann) and intergovernmentalists (Moravcsik), and constructivists (Christiansen, the LSE group) or deconstructionists (Checkel, Derrida). One other notable contribution is worth considering, that of Maria Green Cowles.

Maria Green Cowles and 'Europeanization'

A valuable contribution to the study of European integration is made by a group of scholars led by Maria Green Cowles, James Caporaso and Thomas Risse. Their collection *Transforming Europe* (2001) uses an approach that looks at the question of the 'fit' between European Union reforms – embodied in European legislation – and domestic institutions in European nation states. Cowles's argument is that domestic institutions bend to European reforms and legislation, according to how fitting they are to existing arrangements. We can expect, say Cowles and her collaborators, that local application of European reforms will be distinctive, and that national legislatures and courts will respond to European legislation with a high degree of autonomy in the mode of application. A straight-forward homogenization of European institutions is not the true picture, because of the specificity of domestic enactment of Brussels-originating reform. Particularly striking in Cowles's account is the characterization of a process of *Europeanization* that is taking place within the domestic arena of European nation states.

Lisa Conant's research into the relationship between the European Court of Justice and domestic legal systems shows that where there is a strong 'fit' reform is relatively straight-forward, but where there are marked differences, change is contested and difficult. As she explains, the German Constitutional Court has for many years been used to adjudicating on political arrangements much more proactively than the British courts: 'the United Kingdom courts do not function as coequal branches of government, but the German Constitutional Court does serve as a formidable check on court action'.[112] Britain's doctrine that parliamentary sovereignty was preeminent has been a great limitation upon the powers of the courts. Under Article 249 of the European Treaty, Community Regulations are directly applicable in member states. That represented less difficulty for the German Courts, who were accustomed to over-ruling the German legislature, and so German Courts readily adjudicated on European Regulations, just as they had done on German law. But for English Courts, the immediate applicability of European Regulations found them for the first time ruling on laws that had their origin outside of the national parliament, and potentially could clash with UK legislation. UK court rulings on European Regulations changed the balance of power between the courts and parliament (in favour of the former). English courts enjoyed a right of judicial review, previously unheard of. The fit between the German Courts and the European Court of Justice was closer, so cooperation presented fewer problems. There was a misfit between English law and European, leading to a greater degree of adaptation being demanded from the English courts and parliament. (We must set aside the paradox that it was the German Constitutional Court that ruled German law superior to European, which was perhaps, only a sign that used to a greater status in relation to the Bundestag, they were not ready to subordinate to the European Court of Justice.)

Cowles and her collaborators are studying a Europe-wide process that they call Europeanization. There is something odd about the idea of the 'Europeanization' of Europe. Is it not European already? Cowles means something else – the way that European domestic societies conform to Europe-wide, or European Union created norms. But is that the best way to characterize the process? It would be truer to say that there is a Europe-wide process of depoliticisation, whose institutional effects are generalized through the forums of the European Union.

Lisa Conant's comparison of the German and English Courts in their relations to their national legislatures and the European Court of Justice is a case in point. Germany's national institutions are the outcome largely of the post-war reconstruction under the occupying powers. The great power of the Constitutional Court in respect of the Bundestag, the diffusion of power between the institutions, all stem from a view that the sovereignty of the German people must be moderated. Over the years, other European nations have become more like Germany. Britain's courts took advantage of the European Regulations to impose judicial review on a sometimes-reluctant parliament. But that was a shift in the balance of power between them that had domestic sources. The Westminster Parliament had lost authority through a series of scandals, and a perceived indifference to civil liberties; British judges acted both to create new sources of stability and to enhance their own powers. The change was domestic in origin, albeit shaped by Community Law.

In one perceptive essay, Alberta Sbragia describes the way that in Italy, the crisis amongst the political class helped a core of non-party technocrats to force through the austerity budget reforms needed to fulfill the country's obligations before joining the Euro-zone: 'the collapse of the old system of partitocrazia allowed those committed to public finance reform to define the new policy space that emerged with the serious weakening and even disappearance of the traditional parties'.[113] There was in fact widespread agreement amongst elites that Italy's finances needed to be reformed, but the extensive ties between leaders and their party constituencies made the imposition of austerity measures too difficult. It was only with the collapse of the party political system and the greater wiggle room won by the technocrat leaders, that they could force through reform in the name of Europe. The demand for reform in fact came from domestic actors, and the possibility arose under a domestic crisis. That domestic exigency, though, took on the appearance of a European demand as Italian elites avoided responsibility for the changes by casting them as such. 'Europeanization' was indeed an adoption of a European norm of tight budgeting, but that norm was in the end one that arose out of domestic demands that won out as trade unions and other pressure groups lost influence upon national assemblies.

Maria Green Cowles is well-known for her research on the European Round Table of industrialists and its significant role lobbying for the Single European Act. She showed how leading industrialists like Wisse Dekker of Phillips were key drivers of the liberalization reforms and common standards that would lay the basis for a single currency. In the collection *Transforming Europe* she continues her investigation of the role of business lobbies, looking at the role of the Trans-Atlantic Business Dialogue – a forum dominated by CEOs from Europe and America's major industries. There Cowles shows how the new forum, launched by US Commerce Secretary Ron Brown in

Brussels in 1994, upset traditional structures of dialogue between some national leaderships and their Chambers of Commerce. Cowles explains that the open involvement of company CEOs representing business interests ran across the German 'corporatist' model, where business was represented by the Bundersverband der Deutschen Industrie (BDI). The BDI was alarmed that German CEO's like Jürgen Strube of BASF and Jürgen Schrempp of DaimlerChrysler by-passed them to take a leading role in the Trans-Atlantic Business Dialogue. By contrast, in Britain, where the Confederation of British Industry's formal status had been undermined throughout the 1980s, by a Conservative government that preferred more direct ties to individual business leaders, there was less difficulty in having CEOs taking part on their own account, on the American model.[114]

Cowles' research has recommended itself to inter-governmentalists like Andrew Moravcsik and Marxists like Bastiaan van Apeldoorn for the way that she highlights the role of capitalist business leaders in the formation of European policy. This research agenda seems to mirror the theory of economic globalisation as a driver homogenizing national polities.[115] However, the enhanced role of business in government that Cowles finds in the European Round Table and the Trans-Atlantic Business Dialogue might also be seen as the outcome of trends in political adminstration and management towards greater participation by private industry. Pointedly, these two business forums, the European Round Table and the Trans-Atlantic Business Dialogue were both organized by political leaders, Commissioner Etienne Davignon and Commerce Secretary Ronald Brown respectively. The trend towards according leaders drawn from business special roles as advisors, and managers – especially in reforming roles, is well developed in Britain and America,[116] and as Cowles shows, being adopted, under the Trans-Atlantic Business Dialogue, in Germany, too. The enhanced role of those business leaders arises out of a need to draw on sources of authority that are not compromised by charges of political insider-dom. That is to say, governments lean on business leaders to front up reforms because the authority that government can command has declined. The role of the European business leaders under Wisse Dekker was to make the case for free trade across the Community, which they shared with the European Commission, which in turn needed authoritative voices for change. Those business leaders were in fact speaking as politicians.

Volker Schneider argues that the European Union was a 'relatively autonomous actor' in the liberalization of the telecommunications industries, a change that 'should not be explained by intergovernmental bargaining alone'. That is true, and the support of the Union's important business partners Phillips, Siemens, Alcatel and Olivetti gave the Commission confidence to impose change on national governments that were nervous of its effects. However, the enhanced status of those business leaders, and their authority to set out an apparently technical, non-political case, arose out of the way that Europe's domestic politics were changing. A decline in political contestation created greater room for expert policy making, round the backs of the elected assemblies, of which the Commission, with its business backers took full advantage.

Maria Cowles sets out her collection with this qualification: 'Although the causality between Europeanisation and domestic structure runs in both directions, we have chosen to emphasize the downward causation from Europeanization to domestic structure'. That is an approach that ought to be looked at from the other side. The way that what she and her collaborators call 'Europeanization' – a set of trends to a diminished role for national parliaments, and an enhanced one for appointed regulators and business – while Europe-wide, is one that has its roots deep in the domestic politics of the European states, and is causal of the greater policy convergence managed by the

European Union.[118]

European integration theory in summary

Perry Anderson complains, with some justice, that 'the field of EU studies ... forms a closed universe of often highly technical literature, with few outlets to any wider public sphere.'[119] He points to more than just poor writing, but to the way that theories of European Union are skewed by the lack of a public debate in which they could hone their arguments. Still, there is a point to the many twists and turns in the writing on the Union. The first wave of integration theory mirrored the technocratic and functional organization of Europe by elites who were, because of the social dislocation of the war, less burdened by national expectations (Britain, as one of the only countries that was not invaded, or defeated, and had not lost its global ambitions, was always something of an outsider in that). The return of state-centric theories, derived from the realism of the English Committee and its US counterparts, mirrors the rising expectations of populaces that they invested in national programmes of reform. This is the meaning of the much-commented upon 'Euro-sclerosis'. US – and British – skepticism towards the Union made the 'realist' criticisms sound shrill and ideologically motivated, so that they failed to register the way that the Delors commission had taken vitality from the collapse of national recovery programmes in the 1980s. When Andrew Moravcsik modified realist theory as 'inter-governmentalism' he was taking note of the way that not nation-states, but governing elites were the real actors, as critical publics played less of a role.

Those constructivist theories that drew out the way that elites were being 'socialised' within the integration process to derive their outlook less from a nationally-based debate, drew attention to what was new in the European Union, that did not fit state-centric investigations. The European philosophy of deconstruction found fertile soil in the dung heap of European nationalism. The hollowing out of national assemblies and ideologies was endless subject matter for deconstruction. The anticipation of a 'Third Way' by Anthony Giddens and Ulrich Beck, and indeed of a post-national constellation by Jürgen Habermas, captured the non-specific alterity of the new institutions growing out of the European Union. At the same time, the relentlessly critical frame of the deconstructionist philosophy, its default hostility to subjectivity (read: 'sovereignty' in this context) was better suited to demoting the nation state than it was to elevating a continental alternative to the nation state. In that way the academics' were like the European leaders – much better at putting the negative case than the positive one. The process of integration is the effect of a diminished national sovereignty, consequent on declining political contestation and a diminution of the subject of the 'national epic', the sovereign people or General Will.

With the budgetary crisis of 2011-12 writers of critical accounts of the European Union have mostly tossed the body of European integration theory off to one side, and started again on a blank page. Their accounts take the financial problems and Eurozone difficulties to be proof of ready-made theories, whether of the foolishness of policy-makers seeking to buck the market, the presumed German conquest of Europe or the emerging crisis of capitalism. None of these are wholly wrong, but rather right in the way that a wide enough spanner will fit every nut, yet without getting a hold of any. Theoretical understanding of the European Union has to deal with the emergence of this new governmental formation, its technocratic and procedural expansion, and the way that it develops negatively, out of the decay of national institutions, polities and civil society. Without understanding, Europeans will carry on being unwitting objects of the integration process, and never become the subjects of their own story.

Conclusion

National sovereignty did not emerge on the basis of popular elected assemblies, but democratic contestation gives the fullest realisation of the formation of a national interest. Democratic contestation has not disappeared but persists both as a means of selecting governments and a ritual of policy debate; but that should not distract us from the way that the compass of ideological differences has closed, and the party political debate is increasingly bound up with personalities or symbolic debates as policy has converged around a consensus of regulated but free markets, with modest welfare states, and a broadly liberal political outlook. Policy convergence corresponds to a marked decline in public participation, specifically in party political affiliation, but also in broader national institutions, like military service, church attendance, trade union membership and so on.

At its core the transformation that was taking place in the 1990s was an exhaustion of political projects. Perhaps this was most dramatic for the Communist project, disproved, as it were, by the failure of the Soviet countries to offer working people security or prosperity, let alone control. But Keynesian solutions, too, had been proved a failure, by the inability of the French and Greek Socialists to offer a national strategy of recovery. Their attempts to boost the economy by boosting spending were wasted as consumers took advantage of liberalised European markets to spend their additional wages on German and Italian goods. The national economic policy of 'Keynesianism in one country' was no match for liberal capitalism.

At the same time the Conservative drive to free the economy from socialist controls proved to be a grave disappointment. The idea was that once the shackles of government regulation were removed the healthy entrepreneurs would leap free. Instead Western Europe's timid capitalists proved to be peculiarly risk averse - unwilling in fact to invest unless governments planned the projects and guaranteed them against any losses as well. The victorious free market floundered in the 1990s as growth petered out, this time without any labour movement to blame for pushing up wage costs. National capitalism was as great a disappointment as state socialism.

The ability of governing elites to elaborate national interests depends upon their capacity for inward self-reflection. In the modern era, the process of working out the national interest happens through political contestation, typically through party political elections and debates in parliament. Of course foreign policy matters tend to play a minimal role in domestic politics, but that does not stop domestic debates from being debates about the national interest, its identity and projection. Much as it might appear that High Diplomacy is independent of domestic politics, it is argued here, the functioning of the domestic realm is a precondition of the formulation of national priorities and also foreign policy. That is important because all across Europe, from the early to mid-1980s, the programmatic exhaustion of the left shut down one side of the political debate; by the 1990s, it became clear that the right, too, had lost its *raison d'être* of facing down the socialist challenge. From 1991 onwards, in effect from the end of the Cold War, domestic political processes became sclerotic, collapsing from a profound popular disengagement with the political elite.

The governing styles of European elites have changed to take account of the new conditions. Most problematically, policy-making operates in a near void. The competition for the popular vote was an important discipline in formulating policy. Alongside the debate in the constituent assembly, this was how a modern society reflected upon itself. Consulting narrower sections of society, elites were flying blind, guessing wildly at what a popular policy might be, where once these would have been developed in a dialogue with broader social groups.

Parliamentary sovereignty was diminished in favour of extra-parliamentary sources of authority, often judicial like the Italian magistrates, or administrative, like the British Parliamentary Standards Commissioner; or even supra-national bodies like the European Commission, or the European Court of Human Rights. Social questions were de-politicised, reduced to matters of administration, to be resolved by auditors, rather than electorates. The public was consulted through market research, focus groups and questionnaires, as a passive mass, rather than being mobilised in a contest of clearly demarcated political platforms. Political ideology lost its contours of left and right, posing questions as either modernisation or not.

This argument is open to the objection, which proponents of a discrete discipline of International Relations are bound to make, that I have conflated two different things. The first is sovereignty, a fundamental term of international relations. The second is popular sovereignty, a relationship between elites and the governed, in the domestic realm. However, my argument is that sovereignty in relations between nations is informed by popular sovereignty. Elites that have a less than robust relationship with their governed classes, will necessarily have less authority in the international sphere, and behave accordingly.

The contemporary model of apolitical social administration favours cooperation between European states, and even their integration in a new European entity. Of course it can be, and is, argued that however healthy European democracies are, states still interact according to the higher diplomatic pursuit of national interest. But that would be to see national interest as the self-evident datum of economic or military competition, irrespective of the process whereby that national interest is reflected upon and understood. We find that the actual tendency is for elite actors to derive authority more from their relations to each other, than, as they once would have, from their relationship to a national constituency of support.

The history of the European Coal and Steel Community, the European Economic Community, the European Community and the European Union is less continuous than appears to be the case when all are collapsed together as so many stages on the path of a retrospective and idealised history. European integration has often been interrupted – most chronically in the era of Euro-sclerosis. What is more, the dynamics of European integration are different in different era. West European cooperation during the stabilisation and reconstruction under U.S. tutelage laid the basis for the technocratic and functionalist theories of integration. More recent attempts to characterise the process of Europeanisation in the constructivist tradition rightly qualify national sovereignty, because that is the practical transformation, the decline of national sovereignty that drives the contemporary process of European integration. Properly, that process should be understood as one that is driven by social changes taking place within each of the major European societies: the process of declining public participation and the consequent diminution of the general will, that subject of the national epic narrative, the sovereign people.

Evidence of the negative character of the European Union's forward momentum is the tortuous question of European identity, which has lingered as the problem of the 'democratic deficit', and blown up once again in the failure to win popular support for a European constitution. Attempts to articulate a European identity lack the inspirational character of truly founding constitutional moments, and have too few resources to call upon. It is telling that such intellectual attempts as have been made to pull together what makes Europe special have tended to drift into morbid self-questioning, or, yet more problematically articulate European identity in opposition to the direct participation of European publics. There can be no European identity without a European 'we', but those who are mostly closely identified with the future of the institution of the European

Union are those most resistant to any such call. That does not mean that the dynamic towards European integration will be dampened by the failure of the constitution referenda: Far from it. The dynamic for integration of governing functions within the European Union comes from the failure of national political processes – which has not been reversed.

At the time of writing, Europe is in crisis. In Greece, Spain and Portugal national budgets hover on the verge of collapse, unemployment is rising sharply, governing elites are in disarray, workers rally in mass protest, riots threaten, repression is on the rise, and far right gangs are waiting in the wings. Naturally enough, the immediate features of the crisis captivate us. To many it seems clear that the European project is being de-railed.

Still, it is easy to forget that Europe is often 'in crisis'. West Europeans often fail to notice that Eastern Europe's accession has been far from an easy ride, but rather is marked by governments that lurch from right-wing populism to a kind of obsequious performance of pro-Europeanism. Meanwhile, the south Balkan states, Serbia and Bosnia-Herzegovina remain stuck in a no-man's land of conditionality on the one hand, and OSCE control on the other.

In 2004 the European Union was confronted with its own crisis of legitimacy when successive referenda failed to win public support for the pan-European constitution that the continent's leaders assured us we could not survive without. Rejected by the voters, national elites nonetheless went ahead and brought much of what was proposed in behind the voters' backs, through intergovernmental agreement, the very thing that they said could not be done. With hindsight these events seem quaint, that there should be such an argument over constitutions, when the challenge of economic collapse was waiting to unfold. Then, defenders and critics of the proposed constitution were agreed that the reform failed of the missing social dimensions of the European Union, rubbished as a 'neo-liberal' 'bosses union' –

and yet reforms on the table today are for tighter budgets and welfare cuts. Before the waters close over that earlier crisis of legitimacy, recall that mass movements of 'No' voters were organised that defeated the governing classes and media, only to melt away once the constitution was shelved.

In 2003 Europe was the site of another kind of conflict, as millions of west Europeans protested against their governments' participation in the US-led War on Terror. Then the European leaders were effectively divided, with France, Germany and Russia combining to de-rail the US plans; and at the same time provoking conflict with the governments of Britain, Italy and many East European countries.

In the 1990s Europe was in turmoil over the way that economic recession and the costs of German reunification were pulling apart its carefully constructed 'Exchange Rate Mechanism'. Back then, when Germany was accused of exporting its recession through harsh limits on inflation it was widely thought that the European project was on the verge of collapse. Then, later in the decade, Europe was once again in turmoil over the break-up of the former Yugoslavia and the Union's failure to put forward a clear military strategy, and its reliance on US intervention to resolve the differences.

Each of these crises was gripping, some of them seemed insurmountable at the time, and most of all each seemed to be a unique problem in its own right, with its own special causes. But if we step back there is a recurrent problem underlying each manifestation of crisis, and that is the incremental shrinking of the national political arena as a place where problems are solved. Each crisis appeared insurmountable because each demonstrated the way that the public – which until now has only really meant a national public – has been witness to, and victim of events over which it has no effective control. It is the failure of the nationally-bounded political process to take control that enlarges the sense of crisis.

It is for that reason that none of the many crises that have wracked Europe over the last quarter century have led to what was expected, the arrest or break-up of the Union. On the contrary, the European Union advances through crisis management. It gets stronger, not weaker. The Union responded to each of these crises with successive measures that put more power in the hands of its institutions, taking them out of the hands of elected governments: the Exchange Rate Mechanism was replaced with the Single Currency in the Eurozone; tensions over external policy were addressed with a Common Foreign and Security Policy; the failure of the referenda on the European Constitution were answered with the Treaty of Lisbon that put in place majority voting on the Council of Ministers as well as creating a European President and Foreign Minister; the budgetary crisis of 2011-12 led straight-away to the creation of the Fiskalpakt and European Stability Mechanism, and is leading towards an integrated fiscal policy within the Eurozone where officials will control government budgets.

The Union gets stronger on each occasion, because the source of these crises is the failure of national politics (apart from the Constitutional referendum – though even there it was argued that the No campaigns were exorcising national grievances). The European Union grows to the extent that national politics fails. It fills the vacuum created by the failure of national politics. Given how destructive nationalism has been in the history of Europe, there might seem to be reasons to applaud the victory of European institutions over national ones. However, the sorry truth is that the European formation that fills the gap is one that is fundamentally hostile to democratic control of political power. Despite the rhetorical commitment to what it calls democratic norms (that is rule-governed procedures) the Union is wholly at odds with government through the formation of a popular will – the rule of the demos. It is the dying of popular participation in national assemblies and in national political life that the institutions of the European Union substitute for.

Time and again popular movements have tried to deal with the real problems that Europeans face. In 2012 it was radical movements against austerity that ran up against the brick wall of the European Union's technocratic administration. In 2006 populist movements in Hungary and Poland, in however confused a way, were trying to take control of events. In 2004 it was the 'No' campaigns that tried to deal with the way that Europe was governed. Before that anti-war movements rallied millions in Europe's capitals. To date, though, none of these has succeeded in building any lasting and deeply rooted political challenge to the impersonal and technocratic administration of European affairs. Still, the likelihood that Europeans will take control of their destinies gets stronger with each conflict.

What is not clear at the moment is within what geographical boundaries Europeans can succeed in reasserting their control. National coalitions like SYRIZA in Greece have had a marked impact, and a welcome one, though as things stand that grouping is facing a severe test of its credibility. Just as promising are the popular campaigns, like the anti-war campaign of 2003, the anti-constitution campaign of 2004 and the trade union campaign against austerity in 2012. These pan-European mobilisations are still episodic, and their organisation tending to be ad hoc rather than institution-forming. Still they are very different from the 'Grand Hotel Cosmopolitanism' that marks out elite pan-European activism. Where the latter takes refuge in an international realm that floats off from the mundane world of local needs, these more militant campaigns need to mobilise masses to have an impact. To move beyond the immediate circle of sympathisers to talk to broader groups in society, the motivated activists are bound to be confronted by a deeply-rooted hostility to politics. Whether the activists can make their appeal seem fresh and untainted by the failure of the old parties and ideologies will determine whether a campaign will be a passing enthusiasm, or the beginnings of a new movement. These are early days, of course, but anyone should be able to see that Europeans whether at a national or a continent wide level need to take back control over the government of their lives, though few can relate that to the exhaustion of the old politics.

What is clear is that if popular activism led to a revival of the contestation of our national futures, or whether the more dramatic emergence of a European-wide assertion of common interest could be possible, the barrier to any forward movement would be the institutions of the European Union itself. Europe is the most creative and productive place on earth, embracing 503.5 million people. Over the last quarter century a common European civilisation has moved from being a utopian dream into something that is palpably within our reach. Talking and writing to each other, living in one another's countries, approaching a common language (American!) trading with one another and working together, sampling one another's culture and studying across the continent, Europeans, especially younger Europeans are becoming in one sense a single people. As yet, though, there cannot be one European people, because the one dimension that is missing is the one that could unify the continent, and that would be a pan-European debate over our political future. As a terrain contested not on regional but on ideological lines, Europe could become more than a common civilisation, and move towards being a risen people, in control of its own destiny. But one thing is for certain, no such transition could ever begin without a decisive struggle to sweep aside the hollow shell of the European Union. Reforming the Union is not an option, because the Union exists to suborn the popular will.

The actual course of events will be nothing quite so logically clear. For the medium-term the continuing decline of national political life will continue to set the pace of change. Before any continent-wide popular movement can even be thought of, the immediate conditions will be a messy and more often defensive struggle to retain control of events in the face of a paralysed national politics, backed up by an impersonal and distant European administration. Sovereignty, self-government, what Georg Lukacs called 'societal self-determination' is as yet only an intermittently illuminated ideal, whether at the national or, yet more ambitiously, the pan-European level. So far the European Union has taken its strength from the exhaustion of sovereignty, and the death of politics. Recreating the conditions of political contestation could only mean a challenge to the existence of the European Union.

Footnotes

Introduction: The Soft Coup d'État

1. Call for Greek Vote Unsettles Europe, *Wall Street Journal Europe*, 2 November 2011
2. *Guardian*, 31 January 2012; *EU Observer* 17 May 2012 http://euobserver.com/19/116300
3. Miners rebel against the 'EU Occupation', *Sunday Times*, 15 July 2012
4. *Guardian*, 18 January 2012
5. *Obsolete Communism, the Left Wing Alternative*, London, Penguin, 1969, p 249
6. *Guardian*, 13 April 2009
7. *Guardian*, 20 November 2011
8. 'Why Berlin Is Balking on a Bailout', *New York Times*, June 12, 2012
9. 12 September 2012
10. Max Hastings, 'The week politics all but died of shame', *Daily Mail* 30 March 2012, http://www.dailymail.co.uk /debate/article-2123035/The-week-politics-died-shame .html#ixzz1qfsdqJUV
11. Alain Badiou, *The Rebirth of History*, Verso, 2012; Furedi, 'From Europe to America: the populist moment has arrived,' http://www.spiked-online.com/Articles/0000000 CABCA.htm, 13 June 2005

Chapter One: Pathological Nationalism

1. Till Geiger, 'Reconstruction and the beginnings on European integration' in Max Stephan Schulze (ed) *Western Europe, Economic and Social Change*, Harlow, Longman , 1999, p 36
2. Simon Bulmer, 'History and Institutions of the European Union', in Mike Artis and Frederick Nixson, *Economics of the European Union: Policy and analysis*, Oxford, University Press,

2004, p 3

3. Gerald Hackett, *Cautious Revolution: the European Community Arrives*, Westport, Greenwood Press, 1990, p 1

4. Derek Urwin, 'The European Community: 1945 to 1985', in Michelle Cini, *European Politics*, Oxford, Oxford University Press, 2003, p 12

5. Jean Monnet, *Memoirs: The architect and master builder of the European Economic Community*, Garden City, Doubleday, 1978, p 96, 97

6. François Duchêne, *Jean Monnet: The first statesman of interdependence*, New York, Norton 1994, p 181

7. Simon Bromley (ed) *Governing the European Union*, London, Sage, 2001, p 65

8. Alan Milward, *The European Rescue of the Nation State* 2nd Edition, London, Routledge, 2000; Tony Judt, *A Grand Illusion: An Essay on Europe*, New York, Hill and Wang 1996

9. Alan Milward, *The European Rescue of the Nation State*, 2000, p 3

10. José Manuel Barroso 'You don't have to love Europe.' Guardian 18 October 2006

11. Oskar Lafontaine, *The Heart Beats on the Left*, Cambridge, Polity , 2000, p 200

12. Kavaljit Singh, *The Globalisation of Finance: A citizen's guide*, London, Zed Books , p 1999, p 142, 143

13. Anthony Giddens, *The Third Way: The Renewal of Social Democracy*, Cambridge, Polity Press, 1998, p 29 citing Keniche Ohmae, *The end of the Nation State: The rise of regional economies*, London, Harper Collins, 1995

14. In Vivien Schmidt, *The Futures of European Capitalism*, Oxford University Press, 2002, p 269

15. In Norman Fairclough, *New Labour, New Language?*, London, Routledge, 2000, p 23

16. Norman Fairclough, *New Labour, New Language?*, London, Routledge, 2000, p 24, 27

17. Anthony Giddens, *The Third Way*, 1998, p 31

18. Anthony Giddens, *Beyond Left and Right: The Future of Radical Politics*, Cambridge, Polity Press, 1994, p 10

19. Ulrich Beck, *The Brave New World of Work*, Cambridge, Polity Press, 2000, p 25

20. Ulrich Beck, *The Reinvention of Politics: Rethinking Modernity in the Global Social Order*, Cambridge, Polity Press, 1997, p 74, 75

21. Paul Hirst and Graham Thompson, *Globalisation in Question*, 2nd Edition Cambridge, Polity Press, 1999, p 1

22. Colin Hay, *Why We Hate Politics*, Cambridge, Polity, 2007, p 125

23. Hay, 2007, p 125, my emphasis

24. See James Heartfield, 'State Capitalism in Britain', 24 June, London, Mute, http://www.metamute.org/en/content/state_capitalism_in_britain, 2009; Ian Bremmer, State Capitalism and the Crisis, McKinsey Quarterly, June, http://www.mckinseyquarterly.com/State_capitalism_and_the_crisis_2403, 2009

25. Geoffrey Robertson, *Crimes Against Humanity*, New York, New Press 2000, p xviii, 347

26. Kenneth Roth, Human Rights Trump Sovereignty in 1999, Human Rights Watch, 9 December, http://www.hrw.org/fr/news/1999/12/09/human-rights-trump-sovereignty-1999, 1999

27. Joelle Tanguy and Fiona Terry, 'On Humanitarian Responsibility' December 12, http://doctorswithout-borders.org/publications/article_print.cfm?id=1393, 1999

28. Brian Hanley and Scott Millar, *The Lost Revolution: The Story of the Official IRA and the Workers' Party*, Dublin, Penguin, 2009, p 429, 450

29. Tony Wright, *Citizens and Subjects*, London, Routledge, 1994

30. See James Heartfield, '1648 and all that', *Critique*, Volume 35, Issue 3 December 2007, pages 445 – 455

31. As reported by E.J. Dionne et al, 'Liberty And Power: A Dialogue On Religion And U.S. Foreign Policy In An Unjust World, Executive Summary', Pew Forum, at http://pew forum.org/publications/books/liberty-execsum.pdf, 2004, p 2-3

32. *Prospect*, December 1995

33. Norman Bailey and Criton Zoakos, 'After the End of History', 19 July, available at http://www.igeg.org/BaileyAfterTheEndOfHistory.html , 2004

34. Alan Milward, *The European Rescue of the Nation State* 2nd Edition, London, Routledge, 2000, p 2

35. Nicholas Dykes, review of Thomas G. Paterson *On Every Front: The Making and Unmaking of the Cold War* in *Free Life* (the journal of the Libertarian Alliance) No. 22, April 1995

36. Justin Rosenberg, *The Empire of Civil Society: A Critique of the Realist Theory of International Relations,* London, Verso , 1994, p 11

37. Fritz Heider, *The Notebooks*, Vol. 3, Book 6 (M. Benesh-Weiner, ed.) New York, Springer, 1989, p 42

38. F. V. Aguilar Jr., 'The dialectics of transnational shame and national identity', *Philippine Sociological Review,* 44(1-4), 1996, 101-136, p 106

39. Benno Teschke, *The Myth of 1648: Class, Geopolitics and the Making of Modern International Relations,* London, Verso Books, 2003, p 171

40. Teschke , *The Myth of 1648,* p 225; James Heartfield, '1648 and all that', *Critique,* Volume 35, Issue 3 December 2007, pages 445 – 455

41. Krasner, *Sovereignty: Organised Hypocrisy,* Princeton, University Press, 1999, p 19

42. German Constitutional Court, 1993

43. Krasner, *Sovereignty: Organised Hypocrisy,* p 9

44. See G. W .F. Hegel, *Phenomenology of Spirit.* Oxford, University Press, 1977, p 166

45. Agnes Heller, *Renaissance Man*, New York, Schocken Books, 1981, p 32

46. Evgeny Pashukanis, *Law and Marxism: a General Theory*, London, Pluto, 1989, p 95

47. Lewis Mumford, *The City in History*, Harmondsworth, Penguin, 1991, p 510

48. Wright, *Citizens and Subjects*, 1994; Robertson, *Crimes Against Humanity*, 2000; Krasner, *Sovereignty: Organised Hypocrisy*, 1999

49. G. W. F. Hegel, *Philosophy of Right*, trans. S. W. Dyde, Mineola, Dover, 2005, p 132

50. Underdeveloped in *The Philosophy of Right*, see Marx, 'A contribution to the critique of Hegel's Philosophy of Right' in *Early Writings*, Harmondsworth, Penguin, 1984, p 250-51

51. G. W. F. Hegel, *Logic: Being Part One of the Encyclopaedia of the Philosophical Sciences*, Oxford, University Press, 1975, p 228

52. Colin Wight, 'State agency: social action without human activity?' *Review of International Studies*, 30, 2004, pp 269-280, p 269

53. Jackson, 'Is the State a Person?' *Review of International Studies*, 30, 2004, pp 255-258, p 256

Chapter Two: Demobilising the Nation State

1. Margaret Thatcher, *The Downing Street Years*, London, Harper Collins, 1995, p 742

2. James Heartfield, 'Demobilising the Nation: The Decline of Sovereignty in Western Europe', *International Politics*, November, Volume 46, Issue 6, 2009

3. Paul Ginsborg, *Italy and its Discontents: 1980 - 2001*, London, Allen Lane, 2001, p 159-162

4. Peter Mair and Ingrid van Biezen, 'Party Membership in Twenty European Democracies'. *Party Politics* 7(1), 2001, p 5-21. See also Maria Patricio, 'Orthodoxy and dissent in the Portuguese Communist Party', Journal of Communist

Studies and Transition Politics, Volume 6, Issue 4, 1990, pp 204 – 208, for the decline in the Portuguese Communist Party membership; and Hanley and Millar, *The Lost Revolution: The Story of the Official IRA and the Workers' Party*, Dublin, Penguin, 2009, and Milotte, *Communism in Modern Ireland: The Pursuit of the Workers' Republic Since 1916*, Dublin, Gill and Macmillan, 1984, for the mixed fortunes of the Communist and the Workers Parties of Ireland

5. Niels Christiansen, 'Denmark: End of an Idyll?', in Anderson, Perry and Patrick Camiller, *Mapping the West European Left*, London, Verso, 1994, p 97

6. Peter Mair and Ingrid van Biezen, 'Party Membership in Twenty European Democracies'. *Party Politics* 7(1), 2001, pp 5-21.

    a. Tom Bentley and Paul Miller, 'Party Poopers', *Financial Times* Magazine 24 September 2004

    b. Patrick Seyd and Paul Whiteley, *Labour's Grass Roots*, Oxford, Clarendon, 1992, p 16

    c. Tony Woodley, 'The trade unions now occupy the centre ground', *Guardian*, 20 October 2005

7. Tom Bentley, Ben Jupp and Daniel Stedman Jones *Getting to grips with depoliticisation*, London, Demos, 2000, and see 'Membership down to 31% of workers, notes CSO', *Irish Times*, January 25, 2010, http://www.irishtimes.com/new spaper/opinion/2010/0125/1224263036028.html

8. European Values Survey, *Changing attitudes and beliefs from 85 countries*, Leiden, Brill, 2008, p 40

9. Jonas Pontusson, 'Sweden after the Golden Age', in Perry Anderson and Patrick Camiller *Mapping the West European Left*, London, Verso, 1994, p 23

10. Lionel Fulton, 'Sweden, Worker representation in Europe'. Labour Research Department and ETUI, at http://www. worker-participation.eu/National-Industrial-Relations/ Countries/Sweden/Trade-Union, 2009 and see Claudia

Rodas, 'Sweden's Trade Unions lament sudden loss of members', *The Local – Sweden's News in English*, 22 August 2008, http://www.thelocal.se/13868/20080822/

11. Eric Hobsbawm, 'The forward march of labour halted?', in Martin Jacques and Francis Mulhearn (eds.) *The Forward March Of Labour Halted?*, London, Verso, 1981; André Gorz, *Farewell to the Working Class: an Essay in Post-Industrial Socialism*, London, Pluto Press, 1982

12. Nico Fickinger, 'Unions staying away from picket lines', *Frankfurter Allgemeine Zeitung*, 17 May 2000, English edition, p 3

13. Office for National Statistics. The average days lost through strike action in the 1970s and 1980s were 12.9m and 7.2m per annum respectively

14. Annie Jolivet, 'Grève à la SNCF contre l'ouverture à la concurrence du fret international', March, 2003, http://www.eiro.eurofound.eu.int/2003/04/word/fr0304106ffr.doc

15. See 'Les Français comprennent la colère des ouvriers', *l'Humanité* 31 July 2009

16. Slavoj Žižek, 'Attempts to Escape the Logic of Capitalism', *London Review of Books*, 28 October 1999 , http://www.lrb.co.uk/v21/n21/zize01_.html

17. *Times* 11 October 1994

18. Colin Hay, *Why We Hate Politics*, Cambridge, Polity, 2007, p 21

19. Achille Occhetto, 'Report to the central committee', in *The Italian Communists*, Rome, PCI, Foreign Bulletin of the PCI, No. 4, October – December 1988, p 8

20. Claus Offe, *Contradictions of the Welfare State*, London, Macmillan, 1984

21. In Gordon Brown, *Red Paper on Scotland*, Edinburgh, EUPSB, 1975, p 7

22. Ray Kiely, *The Clash Of Globalisations: Neo-Liberalism, The Third Way And Anti-Globalisation*, Leiden, Brill, 2005, p 283

23. Offe, *Contradictions of the Welfare State*, 1984, p 67, 65; Hay, *Why We Hate Politics*, 2007, p 106

24. Frederick Hayek, *New Studies*, London, Routledge, 1978, p 223

25. Hay, *Why We Hate Politics*, 2007, p 95-7

26. Keith Middlemas, *Orchestrating Europe: The informal politics of the European Union 1973-1995*, London, Fontana, 1995, p 165

27. Keith Middlemas, *Orchestrating Europe*, p 165

28. Niels Christiansen, 'Denmark: End of an Idyll?', in Perry Anderson and Patrick Camiller, *Mapping the West European Left*, London, Verso, 1994, p 98

29. In James Heartfield, 'A Moral Impasse', *Confrontation*, Vol. 2, No. 1, London, Junius, 1996, p 12

30. Paul Whiteley et al, *True Blues: the Politics of Conservative Party Membership*, Oxford, Clarendon Press, 1994, p 231

31. Gopal Balakrishnan , *The Enemy: An intellectual portrait of Carl Schmitt*, London, Verso, 2000, p 264-5

32. Charles S. Maier 'Democracy and its Discontents', *Foreign Affairs*, July/August 1994, pp. 48-64, p 49

33. Whiteley et al, *True Blues*, 1994, p 237

34. In Martin Kettle, 'Europe's left is in crisis'. *Guardian*. 11 June 2009. http://www.guardian.co.uk/commentisfree/2009/jun/11/europe-labour-elections-centre-left

35. World Economic Forum, 'Trust will be the Challenge of 2003', Press Release, 2002, http://www.voice-of-the-people.net/ContentFiles/docs%5CVoP_Trust_Survey.pdf

36. P. Ester et al, *The Individualising Society: Value Change in Europe and North America*, European Value Studies. Tilburg, University Press, 1993

37. *Social Trends*, Office of National Statistics, London, HMSO, 1994

38. Dutch News, 'Single person households set to soar', 20 July 2009   http://www.dutchnews.nl/news/archives/2009/07/

single_person_households_set_t.php; Jim Bennett and Mike Dixon, *Single Person Households And Social Policy: Looking Forwards* London, Joseph Rowntree Foundation/IPPR, 2006

39. Keith Middlemas, *Orchestrating Europe*, 1995, p, 165
40. M. Levi, and D. Nelken (eds), *The corruption of politics and the politics of corruption*, Oxford, Blackwell Publishers, 1996
41. David Leigh and Ed Vulliamy, *Sleaze: The Corruption of Parliament*, London, 4th Estate, 1997, p 39
42. Justin O'Brien, *The Modern Prince: Charles J. Haughey and the Quest for Power*, Dublin, Merlin, 2002, p 164
43. Antonio Negri, *Negri on Negri*, London, Routledge, 2004, p 16-17
44. Anthony Giddens, *Beyond Left and Right: The Future of Radical Politics*, Cambridge, Polity Press, 1994, p 78
45. Andrew Knapp and Vincent Wright, *Government and Politics of France*, London, Routledge, 2006, p 106
46. Tony Blair, *The Third Way: New Politics for a New Century*, London, Fabian Society, 1998, introduction
47. at the *Guardian/New Statesman* conference, 'What's Left?', June 1994
48. Norman Fairclough, *New Labour, New Language?*, London, Routledge, 2000, p 24
49. Fairclough, *New Labour, New Language?*, p 10
50. Lars Mjøset et al, 'Norway: The Changing Model' in Perry Anderson and Patrick Camiller, *Mapping the Left*, London, Verso, 1994, p 68
51. Niels Christiansen, 'Denmark: End of an Idyll?', in Perry Anderson and Patrick Camiller, *Mapping the West European Left*, London, Verso, 1994, p 97
52. Gerhard Schröder, 'Modernise or Die', London *Guardian*, 8 July 2003
53. Quoted in Oskar Lafontaine, *The Heart Beats on the Left*, Cambridge, Polity, 2000, p 102
54. John Lichfield, 'A listening Royal awaits the result of her

political experiment', London *Independent*, 3 February 2007, http://www.independent.co.uk/news/world/europe/a-listening-royal-awaits-the-result-of-her-political-experiment-434815.html; Julian Barnes, 'The clash of the odd couple', London, *Sunday Times*, Review, p. 8, 22 April 2007

55. Martin Kettle, Europe's left is in crisis'. *Guardian*. 11 June 2009. http://www.guardian.co.uk/commentisfree/2009/jun/11/europe-labour-elections-centre-left

56. James Heartfield, 'Capitalism and anti-capitalism', *interventions*, Volume 5, Issue 2, 2003, pp 271-289.

57. Claus Offe, 'Challenging the Boundaries of Institutional Politics', in C. Maier (ed) *Changing the Boundaries of the Political*, Cambridge, University Press, 1987, p 70-71

58. *London Review of Books*, 4 April 2002

59. Max Weber, *The Theory of Social and Economic Organisation*, London, William Hodge and Co 1947, p 329

60. S. Ross, 'Is this what democracy looks like?', *Socialist Register*, 2003, pp 281–304, p 294

61. Alberto Melucci, 'Social Movements and the Democratization of Everyday Life', in John Keane (ed) *Civil Society and the State: New European Perspectives*, London, Verso, 1988, p 249

62. Claus Offe, 'Challenging the Boundaries of Institutional Politics', in C. Maier (ed) *Changing the Boundaries of the Political*, Cambridge, University Press, 1987, p 77

63. Paul Hockenos, *Joschka Fischer and the Making of the Berlin Republic*, Oxford, University Press, 2008, p 239

64. Roger Jowell et al. *British Social Attitudes: The 14th Report: The End of Conservative Values?*, Aldershot, Ashgate, 1997, p 132

65. Rio 2012, Monbiot, *Guardian*, 18 June 2012, http://www.guardian.co.uk/commentisfree/2012/jun/18/rio-2012-earth-summit-protect-elites

66. Colin Hay, *Why We Hate Politics*, Cambridge, Polity, 2007, p

91

67. European Policy Forum, *Making Decisions in Britain*, London, European Policy Forum, 2000, p 11
68. European Policy Forum, Memorandum to the House of Lords Select Committee on Constitution, 2003, available at http://www.publications.parliament.uk/pa/ld200304/ldselec t/ldconst/68/68we25.htm
69. Falconer, "DCA: Justice, Rights and Democracy", Speech to the Institute for Public Policy Research, London, 3 December 2003, http://collection.europarchive.org/tna/20070205203513 /http://www.dca.gov.uk/speeches/2003/lc031203.htm
70. Simon Jenkins, *Accountable to None*, London, Hamish Hamilton, 1995
71. John Carvel, 'North left in the cold as Londoners pack quangos', London *Guardian*, 14 February 2008
72. Mike Power, 'Evaluating the Audit Explosion', Law & Policy, Volume 25 Issue 3, Pages 185 – 202, Dec 2003, p 188; and see also Power, The Auditing Explosion, London, Demos, 1994/6, http://www.demos.co.uk/files/theauditexplosion.pdf
73. Stanton Burnett and Luca Mantovani (1998) *The Italian Guillotine: operation Clean Hands and the overthrow of Italy's first republic*, Lanham, Rowman and Littlefield
74. Burnett and Mantovani 1998, p 122
75. Burnett and Mantovani, 1998, p 78 p 115
76. Morlino et al, *Democracy Report for Italy*, Stockholm, International Institute for Democracy and Electoral Assistance, 2000, p 16
77. M. Levi and D. Nelken, *The corruption of politics and the politics of corruption.* Oxford, Blackwell Publishers, 1996, p 3
78. in David Marsh, *The Bundesbank: The Bank that rule the World*, London, William Heinemann, 1992, p 49
79. Matt Marshall, *The Bank: The Birth of Europe's Central Bank and the Rebirth of Europe's power.* London, Random House, 1999, p 89

80. Andrew Moravcsik, 'Is there a democratic deficit in world politics', *Government and Opposition* 39:2, April 2004, pp 336-363, p 362

81. Andrew Moravcsik, 'Marxist Populism', *Prospect* magazine, London, Issue 141, 22 December 2007, http://www.prospect-magazine.co.uk/article_details.php?id=98912007

82. Colin Hay, *Why We Hate Politics*, Cambridge, Polity, 2007, p 101-6

Chapter Three: The Decline of Nationalism and the Rise of the European Union

1. Bastiaan von Appeldoorn, *Transnational Capital and the Struggle over European Integration*, London, Routledge, 2002, p 67

2. Richard Baldwin and Charles Wyplosz, *The Economics of European Integration*, London, McGraw Hill, 2004, p 17

3. Keith Middlemas, *Orchestrating Europe: The informal politics of the European Union 1973-1995*, London, Fontana, 1995, p 81

4. Martin Marcussen et al in Thomas Christiansen, Knud Erik Jørgensen and Antje Wiener, *The Social Construction of Europe*, London, Sage, 2001, p 106

5. Alistair Horne, *The Savage War of Peace*, London, Macmillan, 1987, p 366

6. Jean Monnet, *Memoirs: The architect and master builder of the European Economic Community*, Garden City, Doubleday, 1978, p 483-4

7. In Paul Lashmar and James Oliver, *Britain's Secret Propaganda War: 1948-1977*, Phoenix Mill, Sutton, 1998, p 150

8. Tony Benn, *Diaries: New Single Volume Edition*, London, Arrow, 1996, p 292, 318

9. Iain Duncan Smith, 'The Big Picture with Jonathan Freedland' Radio Four 16 October 2007

10. Lashmar and Oliver, *Britain's Secret Propaganda War*, pp 145-

51

11. Simone Veil, *A Life*, London, Haus, 2009, p 161-2
12. Iain Duncan Smith, 'The Big Picture with Jonathan Freedland' Radio Four 16 October 2007
13. Pia Wood, 'French Party Political Opposition to European Integration', in Carfruny and Lankowski (eds) *Europe's Ambiguous Unity*, Boulder, Lynne Rienner, 1997, p 133
14. George Ross and Jane Jensen, 'France: Triumph and Tragedy', in Anderson and Camiller (eds) *Mapping the European Left*, London, Verso, 1994, p 172
15. Michalis Spourdalakis, 'The Greek Experience', *Socialist Register* 1985/6, London, Merlin, 1986, p 257
16. Colin Jones, *France: An Illustrated History* Cambridge: University Press, 1994, p 312
17. Spourdalakis, 'The Greek Experience', *Socialist Register* 1985/6, p 252
18. Will Hutton, *The World We're In*. London, Little, Brown, 2002, p 296
19. Mark Kesselman, 'Whither French Socialism', *Socialist Register* 1985/6, London, Merlin, 1986, p 236
20. in Kesselman, 'Whither French Socialism', p 236
21. Charles Grant, *Delors: inside the house that Jacques Built*, London, Nicholas Brealey, 1994, p 55
22. Niels Christiansen, 'Denmark: End of an Idyll?', in Anderson and Camiller, *Mapping the West European Left*, London, Verso, 1994, p 98
23. Timothy Garton Ash, *In Europe's Name*, New York, Vintage, 1994, p 390
24. John Ardagh, *France in the new century*, London, Penguin, 2000, p 687-8
25. European Commission, 'European Governance, A White Paper', Brussels, European Commission, 25.7.2001 COM428, p 7
26. Andrew Moravcsik, *The Choice for Europe: Social Purpose and*

State Power from Messina to Maastricht, London: Routledge, 1998, p 74 – and see discussion in chapter seven

27. Quoted in the *Economist*, 'A special report on the European Union', insert, London, 17 March 2007, p 8

28. quoted in Paul Ginsborg, *Italy and its Discontents: 1980 - 2001*, London, Allen Lane, 2001, p 243; and see Moravcsik, *The Choice for Europe*, 1998, p 74-5; and Lucia Quaglia and Ivo Maes, 'France and Italy's Policies on European Monetary Integration: A Comparison of 'Strong' and 'Weak' States', Comparative *European Politics*, 2, 2004 (51–72)

29. Volker Schneider reports in Maria Cowles et al, *Transforming Europe: Europeanisation and domestic change*, Ithaca, Cornell University Press, 2001, p 70

30. Moravcsik, *The Choice for Europe*, 1998, p 386, 264, 338, 288

31. Nigel Lawson, *The View from No. 11*, London: Corgi, 1993, p 1024, 111

32. Moravcsik, *The Choice for Europe*, 1998, p 290

33. Brittan, *A Diet of Brussels: the changing face of Europe*. London, Little, Brown, 2000, p 35

34. *Guardian*, 9 December 2005

35. *Telegraph*, 9 May 2012 http://blogs.telegraph.co.uk/finance/andrewlilico/100016998/the-paradox-of-the-eu-and-democracy/

36. John Major, *Autobiography*, London, Harper Collins, 1999, p 175; Timothy Garton Ash, 'The Chequers Affair', *New York Review of Books*, Volume 37, Number 14, 27 September 1990; Jaruzelski encounter: *Guardian*, 4 May 2005; Margaret Thatcher, *The Downing Street Years*, London, Harper Collins, 1995, p 769

37. Calleo, *The German Problem Reconsidered*, Cambridge, University Press, 1980, p 1

38. E. H. Carr, *Twenty Years Crisis*, London, Macmillan, 1946, p 83

39. E. H. Carr, *Conditions of the Peace*, London, Macmillan, 1942,

p 216

40. Paul Hockenos, *Joschka Fischer and the Making of the Berlin Republic,* Oxford, University Press, 2008, p 40, quoting Ruud Koopmans

41. Lisa Conant in Cowles et al, *Transforming Europe: Europeanisation and domestic change,* Ithaca, Cornell University Press, 2001, p 103

42. Peter Pulzer, *German Politics 1945-1995,* Oxford, Oxford University Press, 1995, p 52

43. in Peter Katzenstein, *Tamed Power: Germany in Europe,* Ithaca: Cornell University Press1997: 85

44. Middlemas, *Orchestrating Europe,* 1995, p 118,119

45. Hans-Dietrich Genscher, *Rebuilding a House Divided,* New York, Broadway, 1998, p 475; Hockenos, *Joschka Fischer,* 2008, p 261

46. Ian Buruma, *The Wages of Guilt,* London, Jonathan Cape, 1994, p 24-5

47. Thatcher, *The Downing Street Years,* 1995, p 771

48. Buruma, *The Wages of Guilt,* 1994, p 25

49. Genscher, *Rebuilding a House Divided,* 1998, p 443

50. *Guardian,* 15 October 2003

51. Peter Katzenstein, *Tamed Power: Germany in Europe,* Ithaca, Cornell University Press, 1997, p 2, my emphasis

52. John Major, *Autobiography,* London, Harper Collins, 1999, p 297

53. Boutros Boutros-Ghali, *Unvanquished, A US-UN Saga,* London, I.B. Tauris, 1999, p 219

54. Boutros-Ghali, *Unvanquished,* 1999, p 42

55. Michael Ignatieff, *The Warrior's Honour,* New York, Henry Holt, 1998, p 95

56. Nicholas Bayne and Stephen Woolcock, *The new economic diplomacy,* Aldershot, Ashgate, 2007, p 340; *Economist,* 'A babble of summitry', 27 February 1988, U.S. edition

57. Katherine Viner, 'It's a strange life, really', an interview with

Gordon Brown, London, *Guardian* Weekend, 20 June 2009

58. Michael Franklin, *Britain's Future in Europe*, London, Pinter, 1990, p 9-10

59. Alexander Chancellor, 'You can tell how much trouble Berlusconi is in' London *Guardian*, 29 May 2009

Chapter Four: The Domestic Allies of European Integration

1. Tony Judt, 'Dreams of Empire', *New York Review of Books*, 4 November 2004

2. Daniele Ganser, *NATO's Secret Armies: Operation Gladio and Terrorism in Western Europe*, London, Frank Cass, 2005; and see 'Terrorists "helped by CIA" to stop the rise of the left in Italy' *Guardian* 26 March 2001, p 14

3. Joan Urban, *Moscow and the Italian Communist Party*, London, I.B. Tauris, 1986, p 289

4. Copied in *The Italian Communists* Foreign Bulletin of the PCI, No. 4, 1984, p 126

5. Alessandro Natta, *The Italian Communists*, No, 3, 1984, p 18

6. Urban, *Moscow and the Italian Communist Party*, 1986, p 295

7. Alessandro Natta, 'The PCI's European Choice', *The Italian Communists*, No 1, 1986, p 6

8. Alessandro Natta, 'The PCI's European Choice', *The Italian Communists*, No 1, 1986, p 9-10

9. *The Italian Communists*, No 4., 1987, p 35

10. Ginsborg, *Italy and its Discontents*, 2001, p 158

11. Ginsborg, *Italy and its Discontents*, 2001, p 209

12. *The Italian Communists*, No 1, 1988, p 4

13. *The Italian Communists*, No 1., 1988, p 12

14. Ginsborg, *Italy and its Discontents*, 2001, p 160

15. Achille Occhetto *The Italian Communists*, No 3., 1988, p 71

16. *The Italian Communists*, No 4., 1987, p 51

17. Achille Occhetto *The Italian Communists*, No 3., 1988, p 19

18. See Burnett and Mantovani, *The Italian Guillotine: operation Clean Hands and the overthrow of Italy's first republic*, Lanham,

Rowman and Littlefield, 1988

19. Ginsborg, *Italy and its Discontents*, 2001, p 306

20. BBC Online, Scots 'want an independence vote', 30 June 2009. http://news.bbc.co.uk/1/hi/scotland/8125041.stm

21. Tom Nairn, *The Break-up of Britain*, London, New Left Books, 1977, p 145

22. H. J. Hanham, *Scottish Nationalism*, London, Faber, 1969, p 91-118, 146-62, 163

23. Michael Lynch, *Scotland: A New History*, London, Pimlico, 1999, p 443

24. John Foster, 'Scottish National Party Switch on Europe', London, *Morning Star*, 10 October 2007. http://www.morningstaronline.co.uk/index.php/features/snp_switch_on_europe

25. Michael Keating, 'Territorial protest and the European Union: the case of Scotland' in Cafruny and Lankowski (eds) *Europe's Ambiguous Unity*, London, Lynne Rienner, 1997, p 198, 199

26. Nairn, *The Break-up of Britain*, 1977, p 195

27. 'What is Scottish Independence and Independence in Europe?', Scottish National Party website, http://www.snp.org/node/242

28. David Torrance, 'Eamon Gallagher' Glasgow, *The Herald*, 7 July 2009

29. Keating, 'Territorial protest and the European Union: the case of Scotland', 1997, p 206

30. Paul Hockenos, *Joschka Fischer*, 2008, p 151

31. Peter Pulzer, *German Politics 1945-1995*, Oxford, Oxford University Press, 1995, p 140

32. Carl Lankwoski, 'Poetry on Palimpsest: Germany the Greens, and European Integration' in Cafruny and Lankowski (eds) *Europe's Ambiguous Unity*, London, Lynne Rienner, 1997, p 158

33. Lankowski, 'Poetry on Palimpsest: Germany the Greens,

and European Integration', 1997, p 158; Kelly, 1989: 24

34. In Lankowski, 'Poetry on Palimpsest: Germany the Greens, and European Integration', 1997, p 163

35. Paul Hockenos, *Joschka Fischer*, 2008, p 246

36. Petra Kelly, Interview, Living *Marxism*, (4) February 1989, London, Junius, p 27, 26

37. Lankowski, 'Poetry on Palimpsest: Germany the Greens, and European Integration', 1997, p 163

38. Keith Middlemas, *Orchestrating Europe*, 1995, p 202

39. Lankowski, 'Poetry on Palimpsest: Germany the Greens, and European Integration', 1997, p 170

40. Quoted in Paul Hockenos, *Joschka Fischer*, 2008, p 246

41. Hans-Dietrich Genscher, *Rebuilding a House Divided*, New York, Broadway, 1998, p 139

42. Keith Middlemas, *Orchestrating Europe*, 1995, p 75

43. Labour Party, *The New Hope for Britain: Labour's Manifesto*, London, 1983, p 33

44. Quoted in Peter Dorey, *British Politics Since 1945*, London, John Wiley, 1995, p 195

45. John McIlroy, *Trade Unions Today*, Manchester, Manchester University Press, 1995, p 319; Thatcher, *The Downing Street Years*, London, Harper Collins, 1995, p 742

46. Quoted in McIlroy, *Trade Unions Today*, p 319

47. Thatcher, *The Downing Street Years*, p 745

48. Paul Routledge, *Gordon Brown*, London, Simon and Schuster 1998, p 146

49. Robert Griffiths, 'Forward March', *Morning Star*, London, 4 October 2004. http://www.communist-party.org.uk/index .php?option=com_content&view=article&id=3:forward-march&catid=37:2004&Itemid=2

50. Belen Balanyá et al, *Europe Inc*, London, Pluto Press, 2000, p xii

51. Bastiaan van Apeldoorn , *Transnational Capital and the Struggle over European Integration*, London, Routledge, 2002,

p 9; chapter three

52. Balanyá et al, *Europe Inc.*, 2000, p 21

53. Costas Lapavitsas et al, Crisis in the Eurozone, London, Verso, 2012, xv

54. See David Craig and Richard Brooks, Plundering the Public Sector: how New Labour are letting consultants run off with £70 billion of our money, Constable, 2006; Heartfield, 'State Capitalism in Britain', *Mute*, London, 24 June 2009, http://www.metamute.org/en/content/state_capitalism_in_b ritain

55. Maria Green Cowles, 'Setting the Agenda for a New Europe: The ERT and EC 1992,' *Journal of Common Market Studies*, 33, 4, December 1995, p 522

56. Cowles, 'German Big Business and Brussels' Seminar Paper 15, American Institute for Contemporary German Studies, John Hopkins University, November 1995

57. Keith Middlemas, *Orchestrating Europe*, 1995, p 137

58. *Independent*, 11 August 1991

59. H. M. Scobie, *The Spanish Economy in the 1990s*, London, Routledge, 1998, p 126, 129

60. George Monbiot, 'The corporate begging bowl' *Guardian* 13 December 2005

61. David Walker, 'Public Sector Spending Under the Microscope' *Public Eye*, May 2004

62. David Smith and Claire Newell, 'Britain's northern 'soviets' swell on Brown handouts', *Sunday Times*, 28 May 2006

63. For more on this, see James Heartfield, 'The limits of European economic unification', *Critique*, Volume 35, Issue 1, 01 April 2007, Pages 37 – 65

64. Costas Lapavitsas et al, *Crisis in the Eurozone*, London, Verso, 2012, xv

Chapter Five: the developing institutions of the European Union

1. Vivien Schmidt, *Democracy in Europe: The EU and National Polities*, Oxford, Oxford University Press, 2006, p 5

2. David Craig and Matthew Elliott, *The Great European Rip-Off*, London, Random House, 2009, p 36

3. Anand Menon, 'Send the most stupid'. *London Review of Books*, 9 December 1999

4. Paul-Henri Spaak, *The Continuing Battle: Memoirs of a European, 1936-1966*, London, Weidenfeld and Nicolson, 1971, p 197

5. Alan Milward, *The European Rescue of the Nation State* 2nd Edition, London, Routledge, 2000

6. Andrew Moravcsik, 'The Myth of a European Leadership Crisis' 9 April, Euractiv.com at http://www.euractiv.com /en/future-eu/myth-european-ldquoleadership-crisis-rdquo/article-1170502004b

7. Ian Black, 'Battle Erupts as Prodi tries to axe Britain's rebate'. London, *Guardian*, 15 July 2004

8. Angelina Topan, 'The resignation of the Santer-Commission: the impact of 'trust' and 'reputation'. European Integration online Papers (EIoP) Vol. 6 (2002) N° 14. http://eiop.or.at/eiop/texte/2002-014.htm 2002

9. Pascal Lamy, 'The globalisation process and its implications for Egypt', Cairo, Council for Foreign Relations at the Diplomatic Club, 25 March 2001; Edward Heath, *The Course of My Life*, London, Hodder and Stoughton, 1998, p 229

10. Thomas Christiansen and Christine Reh, *Constitutionalizing the European Union*, Houndsmills, Palgrave Macmillan, 2009, p162

11. List from Thomas Christiansen et al *The Social Construction of Europe*, London, Sage, 2001, p15

12. Gregory Millman, *Around the world on a trillion dollars a day*, London, Bantam, 1995, p 819

13. Stephen Tindale, 'A People's Europe', in *What Needs to Change*, edited by Giles Radice, London, Harper Collins,1996, p 231

14. Valerio Lintner, 'The European Community - 1958 to the 1990s' in *Western Europe: Economic and Social Change since 1945*, edited by Max-Stephan Schulze. London, Longman, 1999, p 153, my emphasis

15. Leon Brittan, *A Diet of Brussels: the changing face of Europe*. London, Little, Brown, 2000, p 65

16. Greg Palast, Robert Mundell, evil genius of the Euro, The Guardian, 26 June 2012, http://www.guardian.co.uk /commentisfree/2012/jun/26/robert-mundell-evil-genius-euro

17. see Thomas Diez, in Christiansen et al, *The Social Construction of Europe*, London, Sage, 2001 p 95; Chris Bickerton, 'The Member-State Paradigm', in *European Integration: From Nation-States to Member States*, Oxford University Press, 2012, pp51-71

18. Mark Leonard, *Why Europe will Run the 21st Century*, London: Fourth Estate, 2005, p 24

19. Perry Anderson, 'Depicting Europe', *London Review of Books*, 20 September 2007, available at http://www.lrb.co.uk/v29 /n18/ande01_.html 2007

20. Anderson, 'Depicting Europe', 2007

21. Christiansen et al, *The Social Construction of Europe*, 2001

22. Andrew Moravcsik, 'Marxist Populism', *Prospect* magazine, London, Issue 141, 22 December, http://www.prospect-magazine.co.uk/article_details.php?id=98912007 – though actually Moravcsik rather snatches the point back by adding in the parenthesis: 'or, more properly, the limited, pragmatic, essentially nation state-based multilateralism that prevails in Europe' after 'the transcendence of the nation state'

23. Louis Althusser, *For Marx*, Harmondsworth, Penguin, 1966,

p 112

24. Althusser, *For Marx*, 1966, p 121

25. Keith Middlemas, *The Orchestration of Europe*, 1995, p 669

26. Michael Hardt and Antonio Negri, *Empire*. Harvard, University Press, 2000, p 91, x ii

27. Quoted in Bastiaan van Apeldoorn, *Transnational Capital and the Struggle over European Integration*, London, Routledge, 2002, p 176

28. European Council Presidency, 'Lisbon European Council 23 and 24 March Conclusions', http://www.europarl.euro pa.eu/summits/lis1_en.htm , 2000, paragraph 37

29. Robin Cook, Speech, 16 June 2000. Reproduced at http://www.guardian.co.uk/business/2000/jun/16/emu.thee uro12000

30. European Council Presidency, 'Lisbon European Council 23 and 24 March Conclusions', 2000, paragraph 38

31. See Heartfield, State Capitalism in Britain', 24 June, London, Mute, http://www.metamute.org/en/content/state_ capitalism_in_britain 2009a

32. Paul van Buitenen, *Blowing the Whistle: One man's fight against fraud in the European Commission*. London, Politicos, 2000, p 40

33. Ben Hall, 'European governance and the future of the Commission' Centre for European Reform, Working Paper 13. Available at www.cer.org.uk/pdf/cerwp5.pdf 2000: 13

34. van Buitenen, *Blowing the Whistle*, 2000, p 11– actually 44 547, see above

35. van Buitenen, *Blowing the Whistle*, p12

36. Craig and Elliott, *The Great European Rip-Off*, 2009, p 37

37. Middlemas, *Orchestrating Europe*, 1995, p 237

38. in Jeffrey Checkel and Peter Katzenstein, *European Identity*, Cambridge, Cambridge University Press, 2009, p 90

39. Romano Prodi and Neil Kinnock, *The Commission And Non-Governmental Organisations: Building A Stronger Partnership*,

European Commission 2000, p 4

40. Jan van Deth, 'The "Good European Citizen": congruence and consequences of different points of view', *European Political Science,* Volume 8, Number 2, June 2009, p 178

41. Craig and Elliott, *The Great European Rip-Off,* 2009, p 66

42. Prodi and Kinnock, *The Commission And Non-Governmental Organisations: Building A Stronger Partnership,* p 11

43. Peeters, 'The Principle Of Participatory Democracy In The New Europe: A Critical Analysis', paper given at American Enterprise Institute 11 June 2003 conference on Nongovernmental organizations: the growing power of an unelected few, p 10

44. European Commission, 'Debate Europe — building on the experience of Plan D for Democracy, Dialogue and Debate' COM(2008) 158/4, Brussels, European Commission 2008, p 3

45. Tony Blair, 'On the impact of the modern world on leadership', a speech to the News Corps, in Pebble Beach, California, 30 July 2006

46. Hubert Vedrine, *History Strikes Back: How States, Nations, and Conflicts are Shaping the 21st Century,* Brookings Institution, 2009, p 21

47. Vedrine, *History Strikes Back,* p 20-21

48. Heartfield, 'Conceptualising the anti-capitalism movement in global civil society', in Baker, Gideon and David Chandler, *Global Civil Society,* London, Routledge, 2005

49. *Guardian,* 16 June 2001

50. Middlemas, *Orchestrating Europe,* 1995, p 243

51. Jos de Beus and Jeanette Mak, 'European Integration without Europeanization', *Acta Politica* (40), 2005, p 454

52. Checkel and Katzenstein, *European Identity,* 2009, p 2

53. Bruno Waterfield and Chris Bickerton, *No Means No,* London, Manifesto Club 2008, p 15; John Henley, 'Gallic genius will save France says Villepin', London, *Guardian,* 9 June 2005, p 14

54. Vedrine, *History Strikes Back*, 2009, 64
55. *Le Canard enchaîné*, 21 January 2005
56. Waterfield and Bickerton, *No Means No*, 2008, p 9; Martin Schulz 18 June 2008 Strasbourg
57. Andrew Marr Show BBC1 16 September 2012
58. James Heartfield, 'the EU will thrive on Greece's troubles', Spiked, 25 May 2010, http://www.spiked-online.com/site /article/8915/

Chapter Six: European Identity

1. Kalypso Nicolaïdes, 'We the peoples of Europe', *Foreign Affairs*, November/December 2004, p 101
2. Oskar Lafontaine, *The Heart Beats on the Left*, Cambridge, Polity, 2000, p 200
3. Paul-Henri Spaak, *The Continuing Battle: Memoirs of a European, 1936-1966*, London, Weidenfeld and Nicolson, 1971, p 222
4. Suke Wolton, *The Loss of White Prestige: Lord Hailey, The Colonial Office and the Politics of Race and Empire in the Second World War*, London, Macmillan, 2000
5. Francis Webber, 'European Conventions on Immigration' in Tony Bunyan (ed) *Statewatching the New Europe*, London, Statewatch 1993, p 147
6. In Tony Bunyan, *The Shape of Things to Come: The EU Future Group*, Nottingham, Spokesman 2009, p 13
7. Hastings Ismay quote in Michael Lind, *The American Way of Strategy: U.S. Foreign Policy and the American Way of Life*, Oxford, University Press, 2006, p 134
8. Jean Monnet, *Memoirs: The architect and master builder of the European Economic Community*, Garden City, Doubleday, 1978, p 467;
9. Ernest Mandel, *Europe versus America? Contradictions of Imperialism*, London, New Left Books, 1970, p 134; Mary Kaldor, *The Disintegrating West*, London, Allen Lane, 1978, p

61

10. Christopher Booker and Richard North, *The Great Deception: The Secret History of the European Union*, London, Continuum 2005, p 122

11. Andre Gunder Frank, *The European Challenge*, Nottingham, Spokesman, 1983, p 19; Karl Kaiser et al, *Western Security: What Has Changed? What Should Be Done?* New York, Council on Foreign Relations 1981, p12

12. Tom Nairn, 'The left against Europe?', *New Left Review* 75, September 1972, p 60

13. Kaiser et al, *Western Security: What Has Changed? What Should Be Done?* 1981, p 18

14. Stephen Szabo, *Parting Ways: The crisis in German-American relations*, Washington: Brookings Institute 2004, p 7; Hans-Dietrich Genscher, *Rebuilding a House Divided*, New York, Broadway 1998, p 251

15. Genscher, *Rebuilding a House Divided*, p 300, 322

16. Szabo, *Parting Ways*, 2004, p 1, 77

17. *Times Atlas of European History*, London, News International, 1994, p 118 and *Sunday Telegraph* 22 September 1991, both quoted in Adam Burgess, *Divided Europe*, London, Pluto, 1997, p 24

18. Katinka Barysch, 'EU enlargement: one year on', London, Economist Intelligence, 2005

19. Perry Anderson, *The New Old World*, London Verso, 2009, pp 53-4

20. Renata Uitz, 'Hungary's High Hopes Revisited' in Leonardo Morline and Wojciech Sadorski, *Democratisation and the European Union*, London, Routledge, 2010, p 45; Frank Furedi, 'The EU vs Hungary: the clash of the censors', Spiked-online, 11 January 2011, http://www.spiked-online.com/index.php/site/article/10066/

21 David Chandler, 'Setting the Poles Apart', Spiked-online, 13 November 2006, http://www.spiked-online.com/index

.php?/site/article/2084/; European Stability Initiative quoted in Chandler, *Empire in Denial*, London, Pluto, p 115; Bickerton, *European Integration: From Nation-States to Member States*, Oxford University Press, 2012

22. Richard Body, *Europe of Many Circles: Constructing a Wider Europe*, London, New European Publications, 1990, p 21; Paul-Henri Spaak, *The Continuing Battle: Memoirs of a European, 1936-1966*, London, Weidenfeld and Nicolson, 1971, p 205

23. Jan Zielonka, *Europe as Empire: The nature of the enlarged European Union*, Oxford, Oxford University Press 2007, p 63, 83; Alain Beuve Mery and Serge Marti 'Pourquoi l'Europe de l'Est vote George W Bush' *Le Monde*, 4 March 2003

24. Stephen Twigg, 'We must not turn our back on our best Muslim ally', London *Observer*, 2 October 2005, Lamy in Ian Black, 'Franco-German show of strength puts America and friends in their place', London, Guardian, 14 December 2002

25. *Economist*, 26 December 1993

26. in Middlemas, *Orchestrating Europe*, 1995, p 182

27. Jeremy Rifkin, *The European Dream: How Europe's Vision of the Future is Slowly Eclipsing the American Dream*, Cambridge, Polity, 2004, p 3; Zygmunt Bauman, *Europe: An unfinished adventure*, Cambridge, Polity Press, 2004, p 160; Robert Shapiro, *Futurecast 2020: A global vision of tomorrow*, London, Profile Books, 2008, p 62-3, 251

28. Frank Field, *Making Welfare Work: Reconstructing Welfare for the Millennium*, Institute of Community Studies, 1995; Timothy Smith, *France in Crisis: Welfare, Inequality and Globalization since 1980*, Cambridge, Cambridge University Press, p 2004

29. Bourdieu in Smith, *France in Crisis*, p 41, 55

30. Delors in Middlemas, *Orchestrating Europe*, 1995, p 161, 181; Mendrano in Checkel and Katzenstein, *European Identity*, Cambridge, Cambridge University Press, 2009, p 82

31. Robert Kagan, *Paradise and Power: American and Europe in the New World Order*, London, Atlantic Books, 2003, p 3

32. Zygmunt Bauman, *Europe: An unfinished adventure*, Cambridge, Polity Press, 2004, p 90

33. Mark Leonard, *Why Europe will Run the 21st Century*, London, Fourth Estate 2005, p 36, p 46; Bauman, *Europe*, 2004, p 89; Timothy Garton Ash, 'First know your donkey' (subtitled: 'Ukraine is the right way to spread freedom, Iraq the wrong way') London, *Guardian*, 27 January 2005 http://www.guardian.co.uk/world/2005/jan/27/iran.ukraine 2005

34. Global Security, 'World Wide Military Deployments', 2009, http://www.globalsecurity.org/military/world/deploy.htm; Leonard, *Why Europe will Run the 21st Century*, 2005, p 62

35. Ulrich Beck, *Cosmopolitan Vision*, Cambridge, Polity Press, 2006, p 171, 71; Jacques Derrida and Jürgen Habermas, 'February 15, or, what binds European together', in Levy, Daniel, Max Pensky and John Torpey (eds.) *Old Europe, New Europe, Core Europe*, London, Verso, 2005, p 12, discussed more fully in chapter eight

36. Paul Hockenos, *Joschka Fischer and the Making of the Berlin Republic*, Oxford, University Press 2008, p 182-3

37. See Robert Moeller, *War Stories: The Search for a Useable Past in the Federal Republic of Germany*, University of California Press, 2001; Weiszäcker in Hockenos, *Joschka Fischer*, 2008, p184; Koehler in *Guardian*, 9 May 2005

38. Peter Novick, *The Holocaust and Collective Memory*, London, Bloomsbury, 2001, p 234, citing Wuthnow's *Meaning and moral order, explorations in cultural analysis*, Berkeley 1987, p130-1; and Novick, p 234, 'Why do they come?', *Boston Globe* 11 September, 1994, p 26; Bryan Cheyette, 'Appropriating Primo Levi', *The Cambridge Companion to Primo Levi*, ed. Robert Gordon, Cambridge University Press, 2007, p 67

39. Carolyn Eisenberg, *Drawing the Line - The American decision*

to divide Germany, Cambridge, University Press, 1996, p 24, and see Heartfield, *Unpatriotic History of the Second World War*, London, Zer0, 2012, chapter 29; Markus Wolf, *Memoirs of a Spymaster*, London, Pimlico, 1998, p 251; Genscher, *Rebuilding a House Divided*, 1998, p 293; Elazar Barkan, *The Guilt of Nations*, New York, WW Norton, 2000, p 8

40. Barkan, *The Guilt of Nations*, 2000, p ix; Hubert Vedrine, *History Strikes Back: How States, Nations, and Conflicts are Shaping the 21st Century*, Brookings Institution, 2009, p 89

41. G. W. F. Hegel, *Phenomenology of Spirit*. Oxford, University Press, 1977, p 282; Sigmund Freud, *The Ego and the Id*, London, The Hogarth Press Ltd, 1949, p 70-84

42. Checkel and Katzenstein, *European Identity*, 2009; Christiansen and Reh, *Constitutionalizing the European Union*, 2009; Paul Ricoeur, 'Universality and the Power of Difference', in *States of Mind: Dialogues With Contemporary Thinkers on the European Mind*, Richard Kearney (ed) Manchester, University Press, 1995, p 33; and see Bauman, *Europe*, 2004, p 7

Chapter seven: positivist approaches to European Integration

1. Ernst Haas, *Beyond the Nation State, functionalism and the international organisation*, Stanford, University Press 1964, p 8

2. Per Hammarlund, *Liberal Internationalism and the Decline of the State*, Houndsmills, Palgrave Macmillan, 2005, 17; 'David Mitrany: Obituary', The *Guardian*, 28 July 1975; Sir Frederick Pedler, 'Mitrany in Unilever', *Millennium - Journal of International Studies* September 1976 (5), p 198

3. David Mitrany, *The Road to Security*, Peace Aims Pamphlet, December, London, National Peace Council, 1944, p 12

4. David Mitrany, *The Functional Theory of Politics*, London, Martin Robertson and Co, 1975, p 20

5. David Mitrany, *The Progress of International Government*,

London, Allen and Unwin, 1933, p 37

6.   Haas, *Beyond the Nation State*, p 5

7.   Hammarlund, *Liberal Internationalism and the Decline of the State*, 2005, p 27

8.   Mitrany, *The Functional Theory of Politics*, p 27

9.   Sir Frederick Pedler, Mitrany in Unilever, *Millennium - Journal of International Studies* September 1976 (5), p 198

10. Mitrany, *The Functional Theory of Politics*, p 17-18

11. Haas, *Beyond the Nation State*, p 11

12. Haas, *Beyond the Nation State*, p 11

13. Mitrany, *The Functional Theory of Politics*, p 123-4; Sir Frederick Pedler, Mitrany in Unilever, *Millennium - Journal of International Studies* September 1976 (5), p 199

14. Quoted in Mitrany, *The Functional Theory of Politics*, p 28

15. Harold Macmillan, *Diaries: The Cabinet Years 1950-57*, London, Macmillan, 2003, p 352

16. Paul-Henri Spaak, *The Continuing Battle: Memoirs of a European, 1936-1966*, London, Weidenfeld and Nicolson, 1971, p 212

17. Mitrany, *The Road to Security*, p 12, my emphasis

18. Christopher Booker and Richard North, *The Great Deception: The Secret History of the European Union*, London, Continuum, 2005, p 9

19. Mitrany, *The Road to Security*, p 12; Mitrany, *The Functional Theory of Politics*, p 121, 46

20. Mitrany, *The Road to Security*, p 12

21. Haas, *Beyond the Nation State*, p 13

22. Haas, *Beyond the Nation State*, p 11

23. 'By its very nature...' quoted in Haas, *Beyond the Nation State*, p 7, my emphasis; Mitrany, The International NGOs: Experiment in Representation , *The Guardian*, 10 April 1954

24. Haas, *Beyond the Nation State*, p 7

25. Deutsch and Edinger, *Germany Rejoins the Powers* Stanford, University Press, 1958, p 28

26. David Mitrany, *The Functional Theory of Politics*, p 43-4;'Protecting the citizen 1: The Swedish System', *Manchester Guardian* 6 August 1957 and 'Protecting the citizen 2: A Warden of Rights', *Manchester Guardian* 7 August 1957

27. Mitrany, *The Functional Theory of Politics*, p 46

28. Haas, *Beyond the Nation State*, p 9; Mitrany, *The Functional Theory of Politics*, p 113, 17, 65

29. Mitrany, The International NGOs: Experiment in Representation , *The Guardian*, 10 April 1954

30. Mitrany, *The Functional Theory of Politics*, p 65

31. Mitrany, *The Functional Theory of Politics*, p 18

32. Mitrany, *The Functional Theory of Politics*, p 118

33. Sir Frederick Pedler, Mitrany in Unilever, *Millennium - Journal of International Studies* September 1976 (5), p 196

34. Ernst Haas, 'Science and progress in international relations', interview with Harry Kreisler, Institute of International Studies, U. C. Berkeley, 2000, at http://globetrotter.berkeley.edu/people/Haas/haas-con3.html

35. Haas, 'Science and progress in international relations'

36. Ernst Haas, *The Uniting of Europe*, London, Stevens and Sons, 1958, p 3

37. Haas, *The Uniting of Europe*, p 12

38. Haas, *The Uniting of Europe*, p 15, 14

39. Haas, *The Uniting of Europe*, p 15

40. Haas, *The Uniting of Europe*, p 5, 6; Craig Raine, *A Martian Sends a Postcard Home*, Oxford, University Press, 1979

41. Haas, *The Uniting of Europe*, p 19

42. Haas, *The Uniting of Europe*, p 51

43. Haas, *The Uniting of Europe*, p 26

44. Haas, *The Uniting of Europe*, p 16-17

45. Haas, *The Uniting of Europe*, p 17

46. Haas, *The Uniting of Europe*, p 153

47. Haas, *The Uniting of Europe*, p 154

48. Haas, *The Uniting of Europe*, p 154

49. Haas, *The Uniting of Europe*, p 154

50. Samuel Beer et al, Memorial Minute Adopted by The Faculty of Arts and Sciences, Harvard University 'Karl W. Deutsch: International Political Scientist' at http://www.harvard-squarelibrary.org/unitarians/deutsch.html, no date

51. Karl Deutsch et al, *Political Community in the North Atlantic Area*, New Jersey, Princeton University Press 1968, p 3

52. Arend Lijphart, 'Karl W Deutsch and the New Paradigm in International Relations', in R Merrit and B Russet (eds) *From National Development to Global Community - Essays in honour of Karl W Deutsch*, London, Allen and Unwin , 1981

53. Lijphart, 'Karl W Deutsch...', 1981, p 237-8; Deutsch et al, 1968, p 82

54. Deutsch et al, *Political Community in the North Atlantic Area*, 1968, p 126, 133, 154; Karl Deutsch and L. Edinger, *Germany Rejoins the Powers* Stanford, University Press 1958, p 157

55. Lijphart, 'Karl Deutsch...' 1981, p 240, 242

56. Donald J. Puchala, 'Integration Studies and the Study of International Relations', in R Merrit and B Russet (eds) *From National Development to Global Community - Essays in honour of Karl W Deutsch*, London, Allen and Unwin, 1981, p 151, 148, 150, 161

57. Puchala, 'Integration Studies...' 1981, p 145-6

58. Andrei Markovits and Warren Oliver , 'The political sociology of integration and social development' in R Merrit and B Russet (eds) *From National Development to Global Community - Essays in honour of Karl W Deutsch*, London, Allen and Unwin, 1981, p 176

59. Markovits and Oliver , 'From National Development...', 1981, p 177

60. Robert Pfaltzgraff, 'Karl Deutsch and the Study of Political Science', *Political Science Reviewer*, Vol 2 Fall 1972, p 105-6

61. Deutsch et al, *Political Community in the North Atlantic Area*, 1968, p 3

62. Dean Acheson, *Present at the Creation*, New York, Doubleday, 1969

63. In Jonathan Steele, 'Patten admits EU "boring and secretive" poses problem', London, *Guardian*, 25 February 2002

64. Brunello Vigezzi, *The British Committee on the Theory of International Politics (1954-1985): The rediscovery of history*, Milan, Edizioni Unicopli, 2005, p 356

65. Martin Wight, 'Why is there no international theory', a paper prepared for the first meeting of The British Committee on the Theory of International Politics, 9 January, 1959 reproduced in Vigezzi, *The British Committee...*, 357, 360-61, 364, 365; and see E. H. Carr, *Twenty Years Crisis*, London, Macmillan, 1946

66. Martin Wight, *Power Politics*, revised edition, Harmondsworth, Penguin, 1979, p 106, 29, 28, 50, 61, 108-9, 168-185, 125; and see G. W. F. Hegel, *Philosophy of Right*, trans. S. W. Dyde, Mineola, Dover 2005, p 197

67. Vigezzi, *The British Committee ...*; Tim Dunne, *Inventing International Society: A history of the English School*, Houndsmills, Macmillan, 1998

68. Martin Wight, *Systems of States*, Leicester, Leicester University Press, 1977, p 23; and see Vigezzi, *The British Committee...*, p 51

69. in Vigezzi, *The British Committee...*, 2005, p 63

70. Wight, *Systems of States*, p 125

71. Wight, *Power Politics*, p 92-4

72. Hedley Bull, *The Anarchical Society: A study in the order of world politics*, London, Macmillan, p 258

73. Bull, *The Anarchical Society*, p 276, 277, 281

74. Bull, *The Anarchical Society*, p 147

75. Bull, *The Anarchical Society*, p 146

76. Bull, *The Anarchical Society*, p 177, 264, 177

77. Bull, *The Anarchical Society*, p 265

78. Bull, *The Anarchical Society*, p 265
79. Robert Kagan, *Paradise and Power: American and Europe in the New World Order*, London, Atlantic Books, 2003, p 5
80. Bull, *The Anarchical Society*, p 204
81. Bull, *The Anarchical Society*, p 267
82. Bull, *The Anarchical Society*, p 255; Jan Zielonka, *Europe as Empire: The nature of the enlarged European Union*, Oxford, Oxford University Press, 2007, p 119
83. Bull, *The Anarchical Society*, p 85, 86
84. Bull, *The Anarchical Society*, p 87
85. Alan Milward, *The European Rescue of the Nation State* 2nd Edition, London, Routledge, 2000, p 18
86. Alan Milward, *The Frontier of National Sovereignty: History and theory 1945-1992*, London, Routledge 1993, p 26
87. Milward, *The Frontier of National Sovereignty*, p 24
88. Milward, *The European Rescue of the Nation State*, p 428
89. Milward, *The European Rescue of the Nation State*, p 431
90. Milward, *The European Rescue of the Nation State*, p 435
91. Vigezzi, *The British Committee...*, 2005, p 35
92. Wight, *Power Politics*, p 28-9
93. Tim Dunne, *Inventing International Society: A history of the English School*, Houndsmills, Macmillan, 1998
94. Stanley Hoffmann, *The European Sisyphus: Essays on Europe 1964-1995*, Boulder, Westview Press, 1995, p 32
95. Hoffmann, *The European Sisyphus*, p 32-4
96. Hoffmann, *The European Sisyphus*, p 32, 34
97. Hoffmann, *The European Sisyphus*, p 56, 50
98. Hoffmann, *The European Sisyphus*, p 55-6
99. Hoffmann, *The European Sisyphus*, p 20-21, 55
100. Hoffmann, *The European Sisyphus*, p 60, 67
101. David Barsamian, 'Telling the Truth about Imperialism'. Noam Chomsky interviewed, *International Socialist Review*, November-December, 2003. At http://www.chomsky.info /interviews/200311—.htm

102. Hoffmann, The European Sisyphus, p 3

103. Andrew Moravcsik, *The Choice for Europe: Social Purpose and State Power from Messina to Maastricht*, London, Routledge, 1998a, 18, 4, 5

104. Moravcsik, *The Choice for Europe*, p 22, 23, 27

105. Moravcsik, *The Choice for Europe*, p 30

106. Moravcsik, *The Choice for Europe*, p 36

107. Moravcsik, *The Choice for Europe*, p 272, 273

108. Moravcsik, *The Choice for Europe*, p 405, 265, 273, 406, 333

109. Moravcsik, *The Choice for Europe*, p 275; and see Margaret Thatcher, 'The European elections', Speech, Nottingham, 12 June 1989, reproduced at http://www.margaretthatcher.org/speeches/displaydocument.asp?docid=107698

110. Moravcsik, *The Choice for Europe*, p 213, 200; 'The Reich food estate', in Alfred Sohn-Rethel, *Economic and Class Structure of German Fascism*, London, CSE books, 1978; Robin Page, 'Restoring the countryside', in Anthony Barnett and Roger Scruton (eds) *Town and Country*, London Jonathan Cape, 1998, p 100; Milward, *The European Rescue of the Nation State*, pp 225-237; Heartfield, 'Town and country in perspective', in Ian Abley and James Heartfield (eds) *Sustaining Architecture in the Anti-Machine Age*, London, John Wiley Academic, 2001, p 144

111. Moravcsik, *The Choice for Europe*, p 356-8

112. Maria Green Cowles, 'Setting the Agenda for a New Europe: The ERT and EC 1992,' *Journal of Common Market Studies*, 33, 4, December 1995, p 522

113. Moravcsik, *The Choice for Europe*, p 386

114. Moravcsik, *The Choice for Europe*, p 263, 266, 283

115. Moravcsik, *The Choice for Europe*, p 290

116. Moravcsik, *The Choice for Europe*, p 74, 268, 273

117. Andrew Moravcsik, *Centralization of Fragmentation: Europe Facing the Challenges of Deepening, Diversity and Democracy*, New York, Council on Foreign Relations, p 42

118. Basil Davidson, *Special Operations Europe: Scenes from the Anti-Nazi War,* Newton Abbott, Readers Union, 1981, p 132

119. Robert S. Litwak, *Detente and the Nixon Doctrine: American Foreign Policy and the pursuit of stability,* 1969-1976, Cambridge, University Press, 1986, p 153

120. Ben Rosamond, *Theories of European Integration,* Houndmills, Palgrave Macmillan 2000, p 151

121. Paxton, *Vichy France: Old Guard and New Order 1940-1944,* New York, Columbia University Press, 1982, p 136

122. in Checkel and Katzenstein, *European Identity,* Cambridge, Cambridge University Press 2009, p 81

Chapter eight: post-positivist theories of European integration

1. Edmund Husserl, *The Crisis of European Sciences and Transcendental Phenomenology,* Evanston, Northwestern University Press, 1970, p 168; Max Scheler, *Problems of A Sociology of Knowledge,* London, Routledge and Kegan Paul 1980, p 33

2. Frankfurt Institute, *Aspects of Sociology,* London, Heinemann Educational Books, 1973, p 23

3. Peter Winch, *Idea of a Social Science and its Relation to Philosophy,* Routledge, London, 2nd Edition, 1990, p. 100

4. Winch, *Idea of a Social Science,* p 107; Peter Berger and Thomas Luckmann, *The Social Construction of Reality: A treatise in the sociology of knowledge,* Harmondsworth, Penguin, 1991 (orig. 1966), p 198

5. Georg Lukacs, *Marxism and Human Liberation,* edited by E San Juan Jr., Dell Publishing, New York, 1973, p 246-7

6. Lyotard, *The Post Modern Condition: A Report on Knowledge,* Manchester, University Press, 1989 (orig. 1979), p xxiii, xxiv; Jacques Derrida, *Edmund Husserl's Origin of Geometry,* Lincoln, University of Nebraska Press, 1989, p 149

7. Ernest Gellner, *Thought and Change,* London, Weidenfield and Nicholson ,1964, p 169; Eric Hobsbawm, *Nations and*

Nationalism since 1780: Programme, Myth and Reality, Cambridge, University Press, 1991, p 10

8. Marshall Sahlins, *Waiting for Foucault and other aphorisms,* Charlottesville, Prickly Pear, 1999, p 8

9. Benedict Anderson, Imagined Communities, London, Verso, 1991 (orig. 1983), p 6; Edward Said, *Orientalism: Western Conceptions of the Orient,* Harmondsworth, Penguin, 1991 (orig. 1978), p 3

10. John Gerard Ruggie, *Constructing the World Polity: Essays on International Institutionalization,* London, Routledge, 1998, p 13, 139

11. Ruggie, *Constructing the World Polity,* p 143-4

12. Ruggie, *Constructing the World Polity,* p 174

13. Ruggie, *Constructing the World Polity,* p 171, 140

14. Ruggie, *Constructing the World Polity,* p 143, 172

15. Ruggie, *Constructing the World Polity,* p 142

16. Barry Buzan and Richard Little, *International Systems in World History,* Oxford, University Press, 2000, p 23, 359

17. David Held, *Models of Democracy,* Cambridge, Polity, p 295, 297, 29 ; and see Paul Hirst and Graham Thompson, *Globalisation in Question,* 2nd Edition Cambridge, Polity Press, 199918 Held, *Models of Democracy,* p 298

19. Held, *Models of Democracy,* p 299

20. Held, *Models of Democracy,* p 304

21. David Held, *Global Covenant: The Social Democratic Alternative to the Washington Consensus,* Cambridge, Polity, p 2004, p 140

22. Held, *Models of Democracy,* p 305

23. Held, *Models of Democracy,* p 305

24. Held, *Models of Democracy,* p 311

25. David Held, *Introduction to Critical Theory: Horkheimer to Habermas,* London, Hutchinson, 1983, p 161, 169, 174

26. Saif Al-Islam Alqadhafi, 'The Role of Civil Society in the Democratisation of Global Governance Institutions: From

'Soft Power' to Collective Decision-Making?' A thesis submitted to the Department of Philosophy of the London School of Economics for the degree of Doctor of Philosophy, London, September 2007, p 148; Gaddafi's son in civil war warning, 21 February 2011; ,Gaddafi's son in civil war warning', Al Jazeera http://www.aljazeera.com/news/africa/2011/02/2011220232725966251.html; Amelia Hill, 'Gaddafi's son 'will be in turmoil' says LSE professor who acted as adviser', 21 February 2011, http://www.guardian.co.uk/world/2011/feb/21/saif-al-islam-gaddafi-turmoil

27. Ulrich Beck, *The Reinvention of Politics: Rethinking Modernity in the Global Social Order*, Cambridge, Polity Press 1997 (originally 1993), p 23, 100; *Risk Society: Towards a New Modernity*, London, Sage, 1994 (originally 1986), p 48, 49; *Ecological Politics in an Age of Risk*, Cambridge, Polity Press, 1995, p 102

28. Ulrich Beck, *Cosmopolitan Vision*, Cambridge, Polity Press, 2006, p 5, 24, 9; *The Reinvention of Politics*, p 75

29. Beck, *Cosmopolitan Vision*, p 19, 27 20-21, 23

30. Beck *Cosmopolitan Vision*, 19, 173

31. Beck, *Cosmopolitan Vision*, p 19

32. Beck, *Cosmopolitan Vision*, p 173, 172, 100

33. Ulrich Beck, *Power in the Global Age*. Cambridge, Polity Press 2005, p 95; Beck and Giddens, 'Nationalism has now become the enemy of Europe's nations', London: *Guardian* newspaper, 4 October 2005, http://www.guardian.co.uk/politics/2005/oct/04/eu.world

34. Beck, *Cosmopolitan Vision*, p 166, 164

35. Beck, *The Reinvention of Politics*, p 44

36. Ulrich Beck, This economic crisis cries out to be transformed into the founding of a new Europe', London, *Guardian*, 13 April 2009

37. Peter Mandelson and Roger Liddle (1996) *The Blair Revolution*, London, Faber

38. Anthony Giddens, *The Third Way: The Renewal of Social Democracy*, Cambridge, Polity Press, 1998, p 137

39. Giddens, *The Third Way*, p 140, 129, 137

40. Giddens, *The Third Way*, p 142

41. Quoted in Axel Honneth, *The Critique of Power: Reflective Stages in a Critical Theory*, Cambridge, Mass., MIT Press, 1993, p 242

42. Jürgen Habermas, *The Postnational Constellation: political essays*, Cambridge, Polity Press, 2007, p 4; Habermas, *Between Facts and Norms*, Cambridge, Polity Press 1997, p 490, Axel Honneth, *The Critique of Power*, p 284

43. Martin Heidegger, *Being and Time*, Oxford, Basil Blackwell, 1990, p 166; Jürgen Habermas, *Autonomy and Solidarity: Interviews with Jürgen Habermas*, Peter Dews (ed.), London, Verso, 1992, p 81

44. Jürgen Habermas, *The Divided West*, Cambridge, Polity 2006, p 19, 35

45. Jürgen Habermas, *The Postnational Constellation: political essays*, Cambridge, Polity Press, 2007, p 46; Pulzer, *German Politics 1945-1995*, 1995, p 45-50; and see Istvan Meszaros, *The Power of Ideology*, London, Merlin, 1990 for a discussion of the relation between critical theory and post-war reconstruction

46. Habermas, *The Postnational Constellation*, p 69, 79, 81, 51, 87

47. Habermas, *The Postnational Constellation*, p 81, 71, 88

48. Habermas, *The Postnational Constellation*, p 88, 90, 96

49. Habermas, *The Postnational Constellation*, p 99

50. Habermas, *The Postnational Constellation*, p 100,101, Shlomo Avineri, *Hegel's Theory of the Modern State*, Cambridge, Cambridge University Press, 1974, p 192, 196

51. Jacques Derrida and Jürgen Habermas, 'February 15, or, what binds European together', in Levy, Daniel, Max Pensky and John Torpey (eds.) *Old Europe, New Europe, Core Europe*, London, Verso, 2005, p 6

52. Jacques Derrida, *The Other Heading: Reflections on Today's Europe*, Nebraska, Indiana University Press 1992, p 26; Derrida and Habermas, 'February 15, or, what binds European together', p 12

53. Alexander Wendt, *Social Theory of International Politics*, Cambridge University Press, 1999,p 110, 172; John Searle, *The Construction of Social Reality*, London, Allen Lane, 1995

54. Wendt, *Social Theory of International Politics*, p 14

55. Wendt, *Social Theory of International Politics*, p 11

56. Wendt, *Social Theory of International Politics*, p 280

57. Wendt, *Social Theory of International Politics*, p 280, 177 and see 182; Martin Wight, *Power Politics*, revised edition, Harmondsworth, Penguin, 1979, p 45-6

58. Wendt, *Social Theory of International Politics*, p 13, 21

59. Wendt, *Social Theory of International Politics*, p 18, 255, 295

60. Wendt, *Social Theory of International Politics*, p 364, 242-3

61. Thomas Christiansen, Knud Erik Jørgensen and Antje Weiner Christiansen et al, *The Social Construction of Europe*, London, Sage, 2001, p 5, 9, 12, 85

62. *The Social Construction of Europe*, p 73, 82, 77-8, 72, 71

63. *The Social Construction of Europe*, p 95, 93

64. In *The Social Construction of Europe*, p 101-120, quote 102

65. 4 September 1992; *The Social Construction of Europe*, p 107

66. *The Social Construction of Europe*, p 140-57, 153, Nuttall – 152

67. *The Social Construction of Europe*, p 148

68. *The Social Construction of Europe*, p 155

69. *The Social Construction of Europe*, p 186

70. Thomas Christiansen and Christine Reh, *Constitutionalizing the European Union*, Houndsmills, Palgrave Macmillan, 2009, p 4, 13 (my emphasis)

71. Christiansen and Reh, *Constitutionalizing the European Union*, p 5, quoting M. Andenas

72. Christiansen, 'Towards Statehood? The EU's move towards Constitutionalisation and Territorialisation', Arena Working

Paper No. 21, August 2005, p 11

73. Christiansen and Reh, *Constitutionalizing the European Union*, p 5; Ulrich Beck, *Cosmopolitan Vision*, Cambridge, Polity Press , 2006, p 172 ; Criticisms of Britain's lack of a constitution: Conor Foley, *Human Rights, Human Wrongs: The Alternative Report to the United Nations Human Rights Committee*, London, Rivers Oram, in association with Liberty, 1995, p 65; Charter 88, Charter 88, http://www.unlockdemocracy.org.uk/?page_id=551, 1988; on Dicey see Tony Wright, *Citizens and Subjects*, London, Routledge, 1994

74. Christiansen and Reh, *Constitutionalizing the European Union*, p 62

75. Christiansen et al, *The Social Construction of Europe*, 2001, p 38

76. Wendt, *Social Theory of International Politics*, p 76

77. Mark Lilla, 'The Politics of Jacques Derrida', *New York Review of Books*, 25 June 1998, p 36-41; reproduced at http://jya.com/lilla-derrida.htm; Jason Powell, *Jacques Derrida – A Biography*, London, Continuum, 2006, p 79; Cusset, 2008, p 29; Richard Popkin, 'Comments on Professor Derrida's Paper', Philosophy and Phenomenological Research, Vol. 30, No. 1, (Sep., 1969), p 64; Luc Ferry and Alain Renaut, *Heidegger and Modernity*, Chicago, University of Chicago Press, 1991; François Cusset, *French Theory: How Foucault, Derrida, Deleuze, and Co. Transformed the Intellectual Life of the United States*, University of Minnesota Press, 2008

78. Jacques Derrida, *The Other Heading: Reflections on Today's Europe*, Nebraska, Indiana University Press, 1992, p 63

79. Quoted in Tony Judt, *A Grand Illusion: An Essay on Europe.* New York, Hill and Wang 1996, p 14

80. Derrida, *The Other Heading*, p 48

81. Derrida, *The Other Heading*, p 50-51

82. Derrida, *The Other Heading*, p 54

83. Derrida, *The Other Heading*, p 39
84. Derrida, *The Other Heading*, p 29, 9
85. Derrida, *The Other Heading*, p 13
86. Derrida, *The Other Heading*, p 32
87. Derrida, *The Other Heading*, p 33
88. Derrida, *The Other Heading*, p 56 57
89. Jan Zielonka, *Europe as Empire: The nature of the enlarged European Union*, Oxford, Oxford University Press 2007, p 1, 4, 2
90. Zielonka, *Europe as Empire*, p 5
91. Zielonka, *Europe as Empire*, p 68
92. Zielonka, *Europe as Empire*, p 72
93. Zielonka, *Europe as Empire*, p 67
94. Zielonka, *Europe as Empire*, p 126
95. Zielonka, *Europe as Empire*, p 119
96. Zielonka, *Europe as Empire*, p 126
97. Zielonka, *Europe as Empire*, p 127
98. Robert Cooper, 'The new liberal imperialism' London *Observer*, London 7 April 2002
99. Robert Cooper, *The Post Modern State and the World Order*, London, Demos, available at http://www.demos.co.uk/files/postmodernstate.pdf?12409394252000, p 20
100. Robert Cooper, Working hard for Europe,' *Café Babel*, 12 November 2005, http://www.cafebabel.com/eng/article/15 26/robert-cooper-working-hard-for-the-eu.html
101. Robert Cooper, *The Breaking of Nations: Order and Chaos in the Twenty-First Century*, New York, Atlantic Monthly Press, 2004, p 168
102. Cooper, *The Breaking of Nations*, p 71-72
103. *Sunday Times*, 15 July 2007
104. Robert Cooper 'Mapping Out Europe's Strategy', *Globalist*, 13 April 2005 http://www.theglobalist.com/StoryId.aspx?StoryId=3852
105. European Values Survey, *Changing attitudes and beliefs from*

85 countries, Leiden, Brill, 2008; World Economic Forum, 'Trust will be the Challenge of 2003', Press Release, http://www.voice-of-the-people.net/ContentFiles/docs%5CVoP_Trust_Survey.pdf, 2002

106. Mark Leonard, *Why Europe will Run the 21st Century,* London, Fourth Estate 2005, p 24-5. In his next book Leonard's interest moves on to What Does China Think?, where he writes that 'China has joined the United States and Europe as a shaper of world order', London, 4th Estate, 2008, p 5-6

107. Slavoj Žižek, *The Ticklish Subject: The Absent Centre of Political Ontology,* London, Verso 1999, p 1

108. Louis Althusser, 'Ideological State Apparatuses', in Slavoj Zizek (ed), *Mapping Ideology,* London, Verso, 1994, p 218; Althusser, *The Future Lasts a Long Time,* London, Vintage, p 129, 218

109. Michel Foucault, *The Order of Things: The Archeology of the Human Sciences,* London, Tavistock, 1986, p 387

110. Julia Kristeva, *Crisis of the European Subject* New York, Other Press, 2000, p 114-8, 126-8, and see Reimut Reiche, *Sexuality and Class Struggle,* London, New Left Books, 1970

111. James Heartfield, *The 'Death of the Subject' Explained,* Sheffield, Sheffield Hallam University Press, 2002

112. Maria Green Cowles, James Caporaso and Thomas Risse, *Transforming Europe: Europeanisation and domestic change,* Ithaca, Cornell University Press, 2001, p 101

113. In Cowles et al, *Transforming Europe,* p 92

114. Maria Green Cowles, 'Setting the Agenda for a New Europe: The ERT and EC 1992,' *Journal of Common Market Studies,* 33, 4, December 1995; Cowles et al, *Transforming Europe,* p 159-79

115. Andrew Moravcsik, *The Choice for Europe: Social Purpose and State Power from Messina to Maastricht,* London, Routledge; Bastiaan von Apeldoorn, *Transnational Capital and the*

Struggle over European Integration, London, Routledge, 2002, p 62

116. See Anthony Barker, *Ruling by Taskforce*, London, Politico's (in assocation with Democratic Audit) 1999, p 31

117. Cowles et al, *Transforming Europe*, p 63, 64

118. Cowles et al, *Transforming Europe*, p, 12

119. Perry Anderson, *The New Old World*, London Verso, 2009, p ix

Index

Contemporary culture has eliminated both the concept of the public and the figure of the intellectual. Former public spaces – both physical and cultural – are now either derelict or colonized by advertising. A cretinous anti-intellectualism presides, cheerled by expensively educated hacks in the pay of multinational corporations who reassure their bored readers that there is no need to rouse themselves from their interpassive stupor. The informal censorship internalized and propagated by the cultural workers of late capitalism generates a banal conformity that the propaganda chiefs of Stalinism could only ever have dreamt of imposing. Zer0 Books knows that another kind of discourse – intellectual without being academic, popular without being populist – is not only possible: it is already flourishing, in the regions beyond the striplit malls of so-called mass media and the neurotically bureaucratic halls of the academy. Zer0 is committed to the idea of publishing as a making public of the intellectual. It is convinced that in the unthinking, blandly consensual culture in which we live, critical and engaged theoretical reflection is more important than ever before.